I0763094

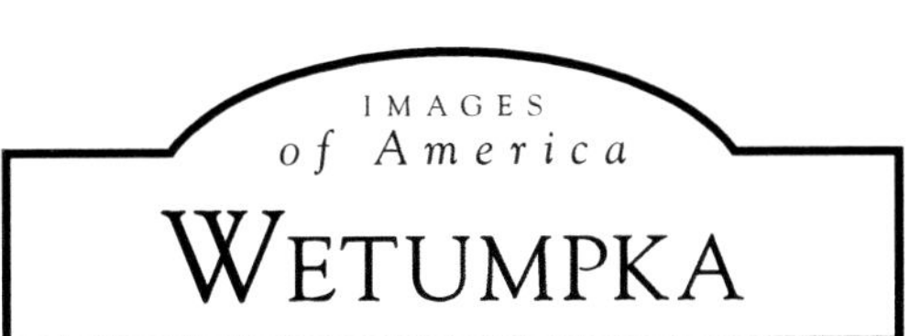
IMAGES
of America
WETUMPKA

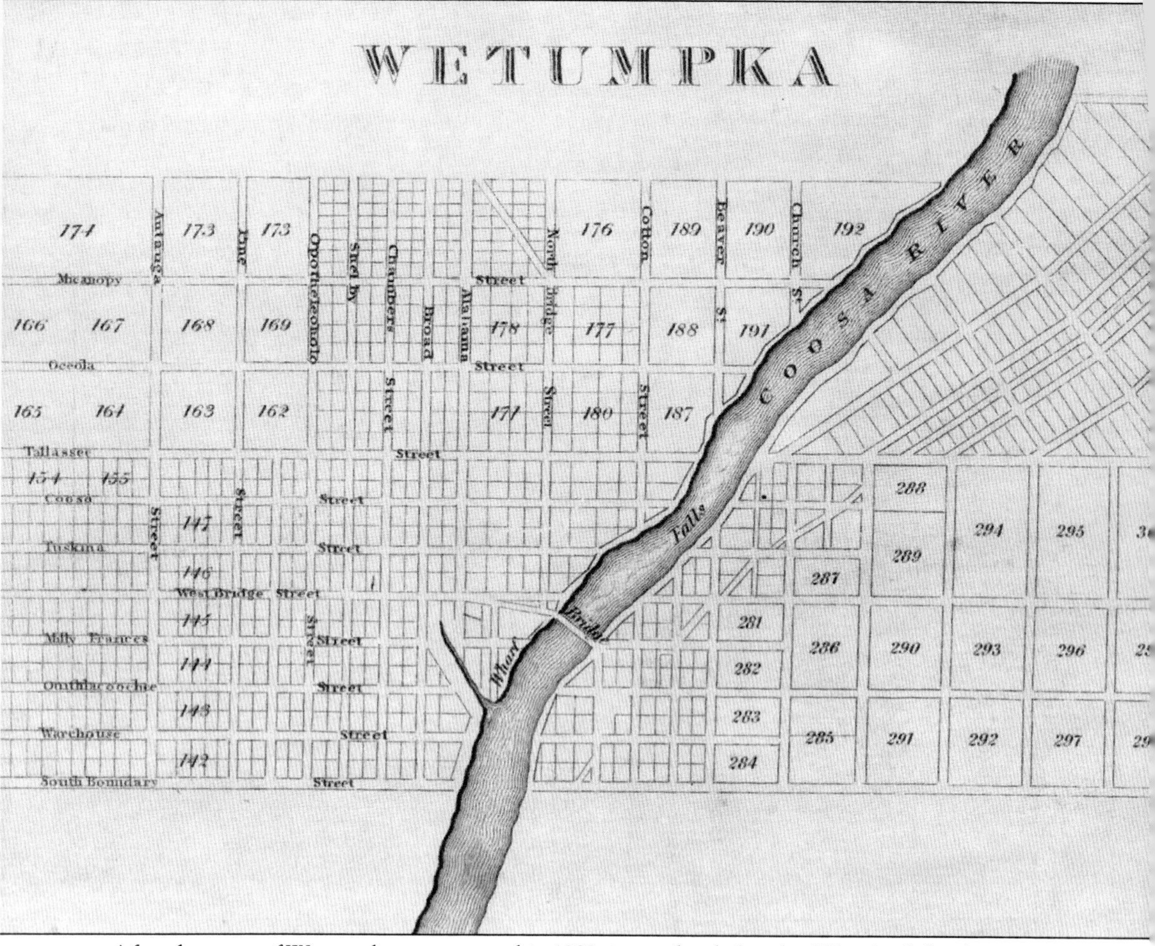


After the town of Wetumpka was mapped in 1832, it was divided and sold by the federal government. Topographical features and early roads gave the district a unique angular grid pattern. (Elmore County Historical Society.)

**On the Cover:** There have been outstanding bands and directors throughout Wetumpka's history. Professor Crosby's School of Music Band started in the late 1930s. (Elmore County Historical Society.)

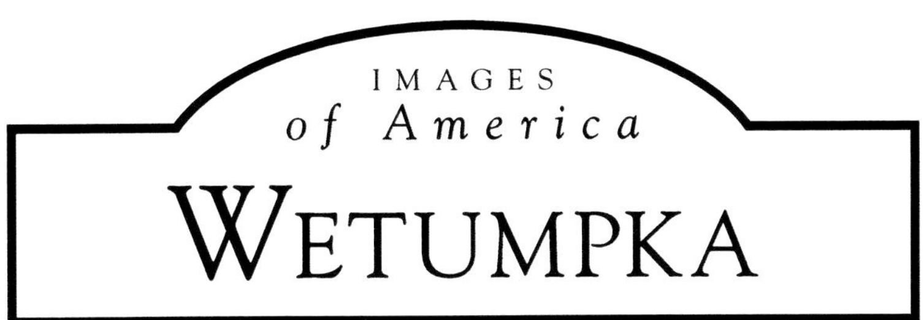


Jan Wood and Joe Allen Turner

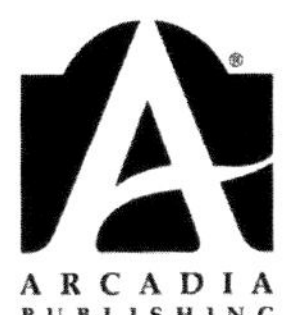

ISBN 978-1-4671-1124-9

Published by Arcadia Publishing
Charleston, South Carolina

Printed in the United States of America

Library of Congress Control Number: 2013941812

For all general information, please contact Arcadia Publishing:
Telephone 843-853-2070
Fax 843-853-0044
E-mail sales@arcadiapublishing.com
For customer service and orders:
Toll-Free 1-888-313-2665
Visit us on the Internet at www.arcadiapublishing.com

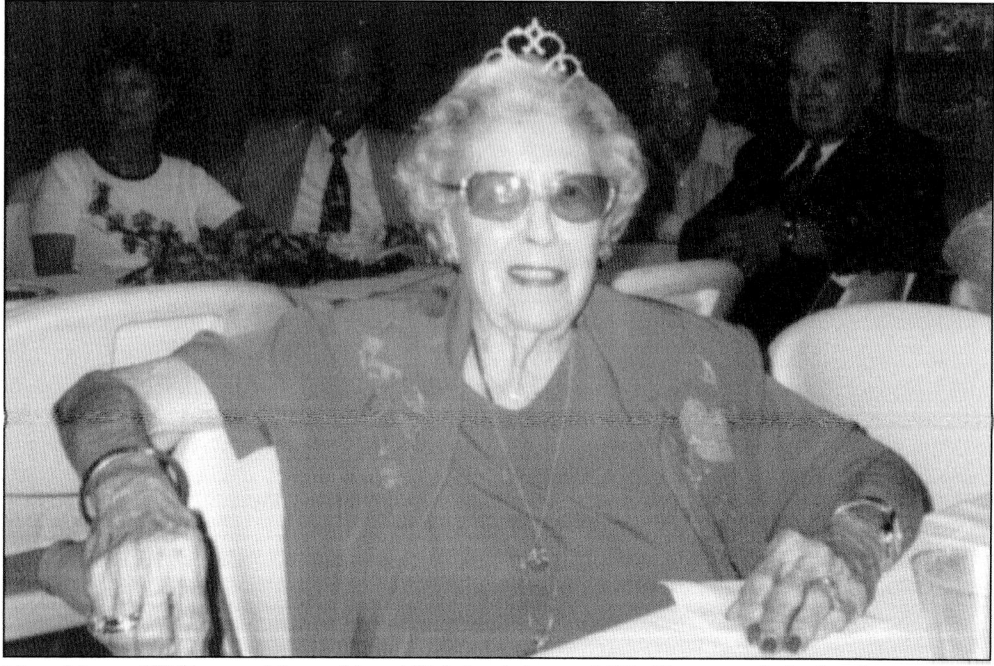

Mary Hogan Williams celebrated her 108th birthday in 2013. She attended school at Speigner and State Secondary Agricultural School and later taught in the same two-room schoolhouse she attended. She married Emmett O'Neal Hogan. Their son was born in Alabama in 1930. Being a Navy family, they lived in points across the world. Williams worked for the American Red Cross and War Finance Committee during World War II, and Gov. "Big Jim" Folsom during his first term. First United Methodist Church has been her church since 1941. Her Coosa Street residence, which she has described as "the social center of Wetumpka," was home for 50 years before she moved away. "Miss Mary" was a founding member of the Elmore County Historical Society in 1971. Some of her treasured collectables from around the world are on display in the Elmore County Museum. She was crowned ECHS Peach Queen in 2009. (Text partly from an article by Peggy Blackburn, managing editor, the *Wetumpka Herald*; photograph, Peggy Blackburn.)

# Contents

# Acknowledgments

Thanks go to the Elmore County Historical Society (ECHS) for its collective support of this project; to Barry and Patty Chrietzberg, of Chrietzberg Photography, for the scans, photographs, and the images submitted to the "Yesteryears" website and their consistent assistance in working with those images; to Kristin Myers for taking updated pictures of homes, churches, cemeteries, and her series of postcards of historic locations; to Peggy Blackburn for the historical photographs on her "Yesteryears" website and other captions and articles; to Tanner Knight for his total guidance of my neophyte computer skills; to Nancy Smith for her editing and proofreading skills; to the Wetumpka Impact Crater Commission for the use of artist Jerry Armstrong's paintings, as well as photographs from its promotional brochure; to Fort Toulouse–Fort Jackson State Historic Site and Ned Jenkins, archaeologist for Fort Toulouse; to the City of Wetumpka and Janice Whorton for prepared Native American artists' concepts; to the Elmore County Black History Museum and Lewis E. Washington Sr., Elaine Pace, and Gwen Turner for photographs and information; to Martha Dykes, John Enslen, Velma Nix Gober, Joey Brackner, Otis Pearsall, James Hicks, the Clinton Barrett family, G. Truman Welch, Ann Moon Lambert, and Jack and Shirley Ross DeVenney for photographs and information. My special appreciation goes to Jason Humphrey, our acquisitions editor at Arcadia Publishing, for his unwavering guidance through each step of this book process.

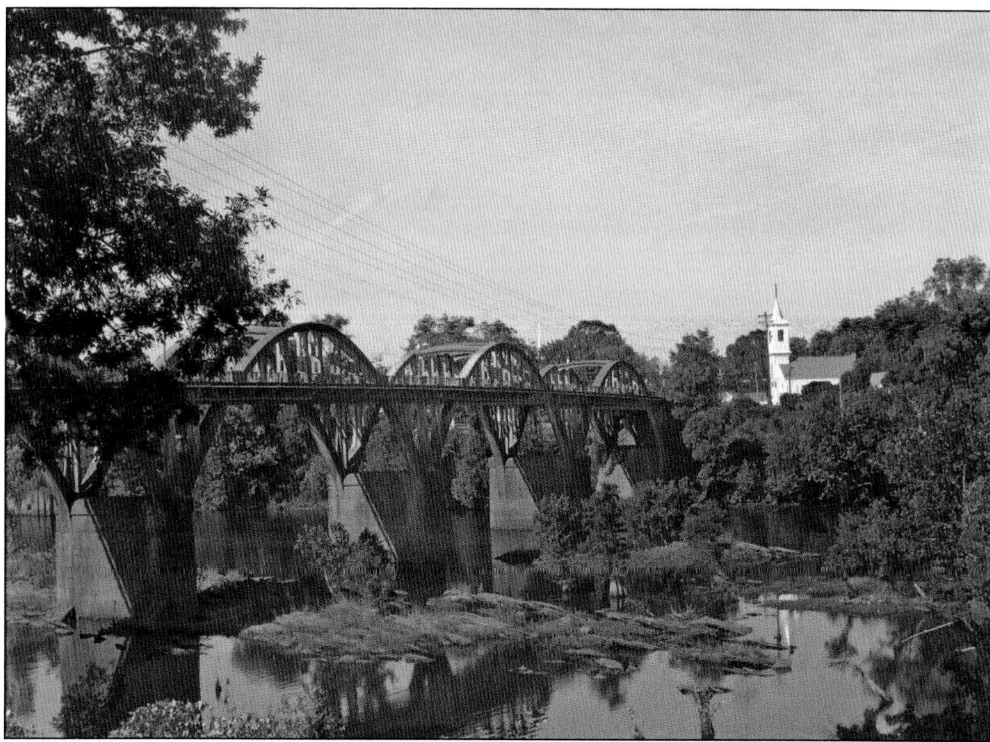

The Bibb Graves Bridge stands as the central landmark for the city of Wetumpka. Completed in 1931, it has been utilized as the connector between East and West Wetumpka and has been used for many local events throughout the history of the city. The bridge has served as a location from which to see some of the vestiges of the impact crater that dates from around 85 million years ago to local celebrations of events central to the lives of the townspeople. (Kristin Myers.)

# INTRODUCTION

The history of Wetumpka begins some 83 to 85 million years ago with the greatest known natural disaster in the prehistory of what is now Alabama. The hills just east of downtown Wetumpka contain the eroded remains of a five-mile-wide meteor crater that was blasted into the bedrock sometime relatively near the end of the age of the dinosaurs. Around the circular pattern of hills, the hard rocks of the Piedmont are bent sharply up and point toward the center of the impact, which suggests an incredible explosion that would have destroyed all life within a radius of about 40 miles. Scientists estimate that the energy released by this impact event was over 175,000 times the energy of the nuclear bomb detonated at Hiroshima, Japan, in 1945.

For more than 6,000 years, Native Americans occupied the territory around Wetumpka, having first settled at the confluence of two great rivers—the present-day Coosa and Tallapoosa—where remnants of early mounds date back to sometime between 1100 and 1600 AD. In the early 18th century, the Creek tribes built forts and, eventually, farmsteads as the French established Fort Toulouse. Fort Jackson, built around 1814, was named for the fort's most famous military figure, Andrew Jackson.

The East Wetumpka Commercial District is significant because it embodies characteristics representative of 19th-and-early-20th-century commercial growth in Alabama, from around 1820 to 1931. The commercial growth of Wetumpka is indicative of economic development in Alabama as affected by pioneer settlement, displacement of Native Americans, transportation methods and routes, agricultural trends, and national and local politics. Wetumpka was incorporated in January 1834—the eastern part on January 17 and the western part on January 18. On January 30, 1839, another portion known as The Fraction was incorporated, and the three portions became one Wetumpka.

In 1836, two years after its founding, Wetumpka was a growing town of 1,200 people. In her book *A History of Wetumpka*, Elizabeth Porter states that "an early eastern newspaper asserted that Wetumpka, Alabama, and Chicago, Illinois, were the two most promising cities of the West."

Before 1875, the town's population was more than 3,000. By 1879, it had suffered a decline due to changing social and economic life. In 1899, Wetumpka contained 619 people; in 1906, population was up to 851; and in 1934, it had grown to 2,000, which allowed it to be properly called a city.

The commercial district retains its historical identity as a turn-of-the-century commercial center and remains Wetumpka's central business district. The district is a cohesive group of primarily two-story brick storefronts that are three to six bays in width and tend to reflect the community's economic evolution, as well as contemporary architectural styles, in their scale and embellishment. As was typical in 19th-century Alabama towns, the former bank buildings of 1905 and the c. 1900 hotel provide a strong presence.

Street patterns in the district were mapped in 1832 when the town was divided into lots and sold by the federal government. Strong topographical features and early roads influenced growth and gave Wetumpka's commercial district a unique angular grid pattern. Within this pattern, all of the buildings are uniformly set back from the street and linked by cement and stone walks, steps, and walls.

A five-point intersection forms the hub of the district. The courthouse defines the southern edge of the district, while the northern tip is commanded by a three-story brick building that was unique for its scale and embellishment as well as its historical associations with the black community. The eastern boundary follows the base of a steep ridge, while the western boundary is formed by the Bibb Graves Bridge over the Coosa River.

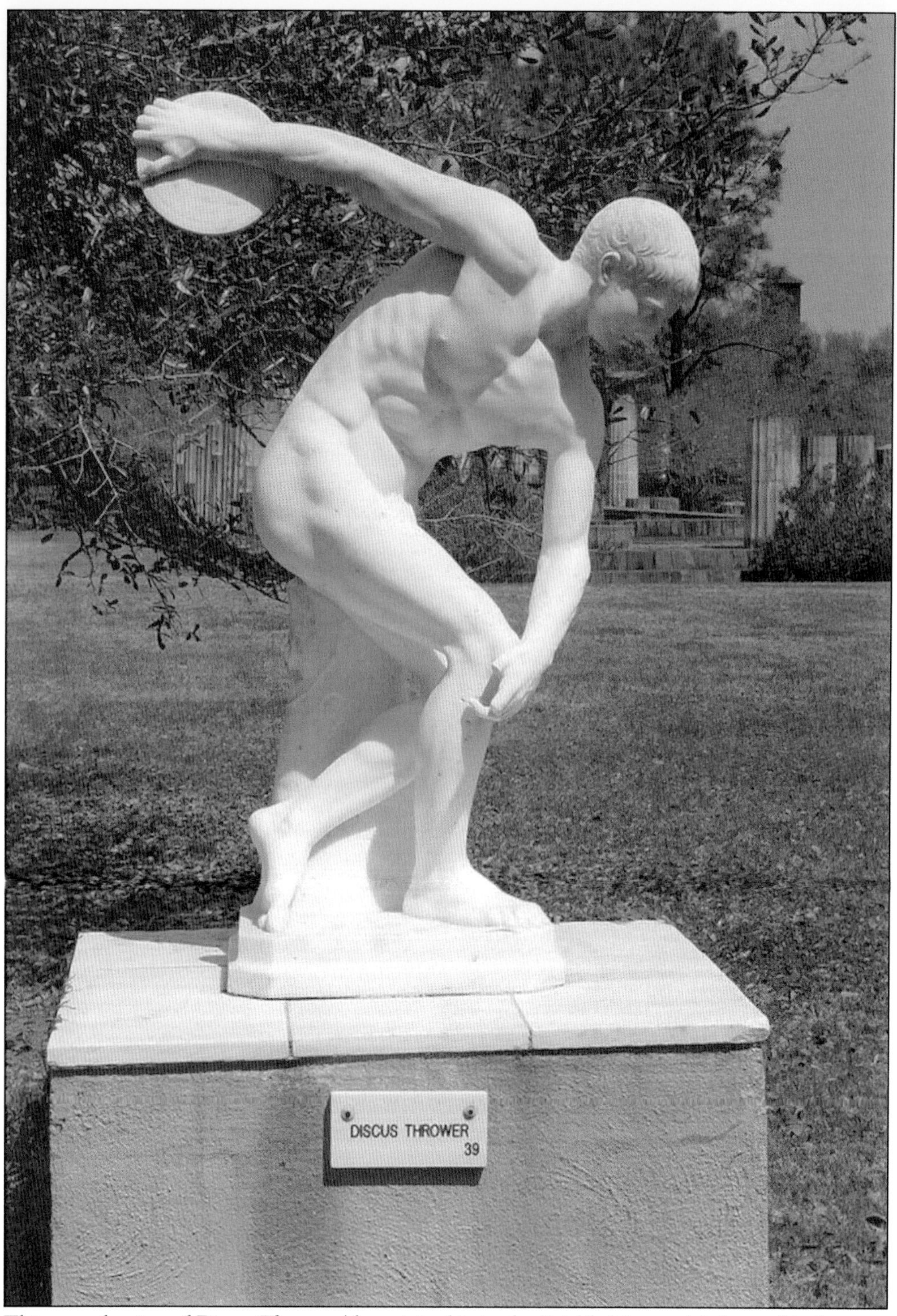


This reproduction of *Discus Thrower* (the original is in the British Museum) is located in Jasmine Hill Gardens and Outdoor Museum. (Peggy Blackburn.)

# *One*

# Prehistoric Happenings and Native Culture

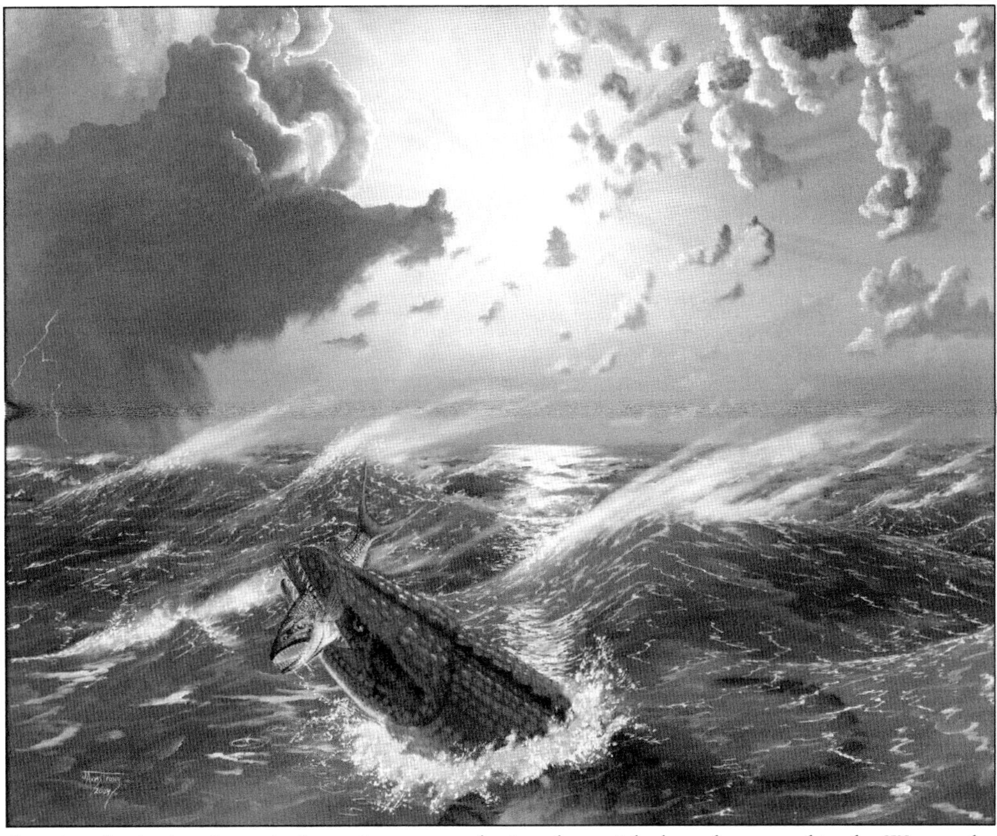

A series of paintings by artist Jerry Armstrong depict what might have happened in the Wetumpka area around 85 million years ago. Here, a marine reptile bites a fish in the shallow seawater that covered Wetumpka and Central Alabama at the time the Wetumpka asteroid streaked through the sky, hurtling through space at a speed of 10 to 20 miles per second. (Wetumpka Impact Crater Commission.)

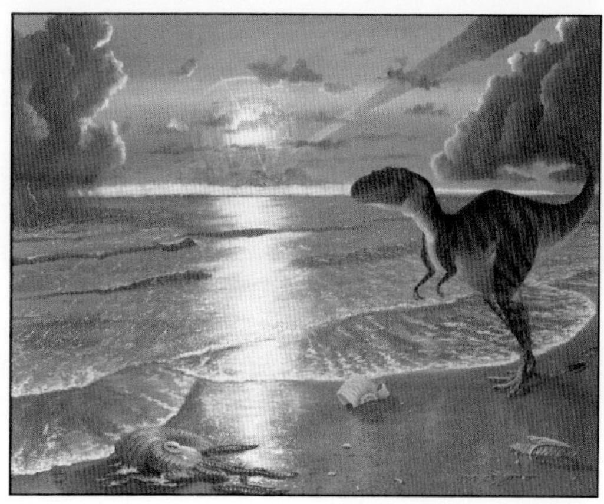

A small tyrannosaurid is depicted on the shoreline just north of Wetumpka when it witnesses the asteroid or comet impact 15 miles offshore. The mighty blast occurred relatively late in the dinosaur age. The impact created a crater approximately five miles wide, a horseshoe-shaped ridge of hills just southeast of downtown Wetumpka. Around the semicircular pattern of hills that make up the remaining rim of the crater, the hard rocks of the Piedmont are sharply bent and point away from the center of the impact. (Wetumpka Impact Crater Commission.)

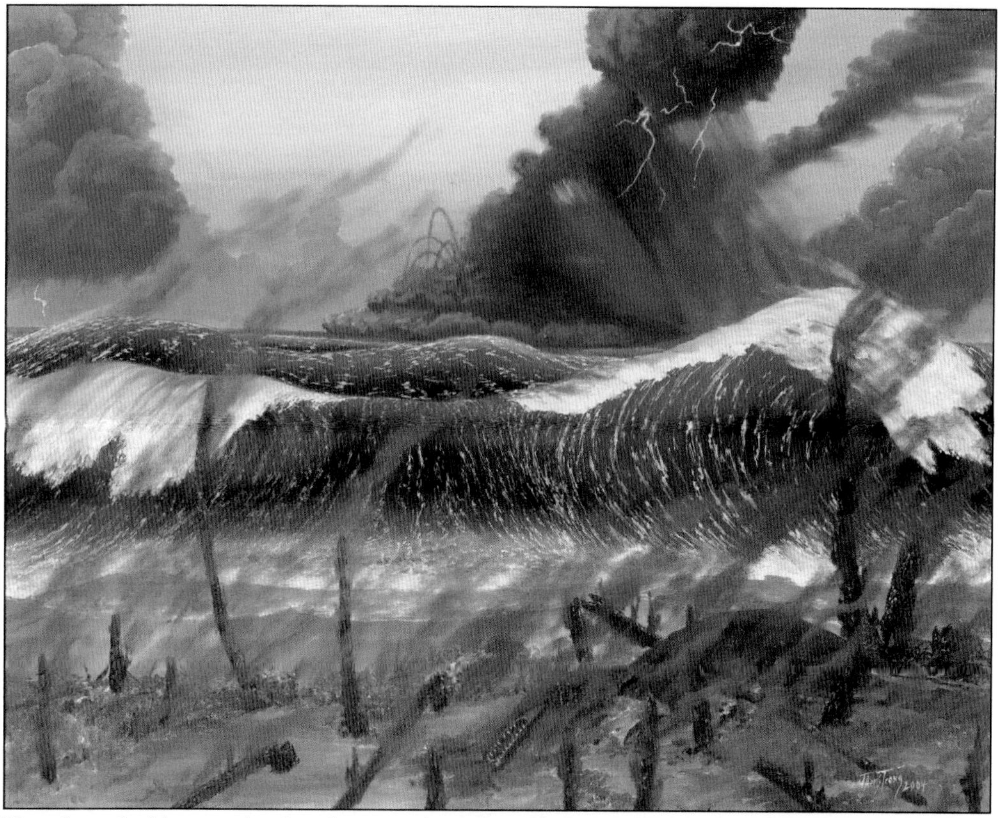

Heat from the blast set the shoreline woods on fire. The normally horizontal layers of more recent surface rocks are mixed in and around the crater, suggesting an incredible explosion that would have destroyed all life within a 40-mile radius. In fact, a meteor of this gigantic size would have vaporized most meteoric matter and hurled debris skyward for hours. A chain reaction of events would have created a massive earthquake measuring up to 9.0 on the Richter scale. (Wetumpka Impact Crater Commission.)

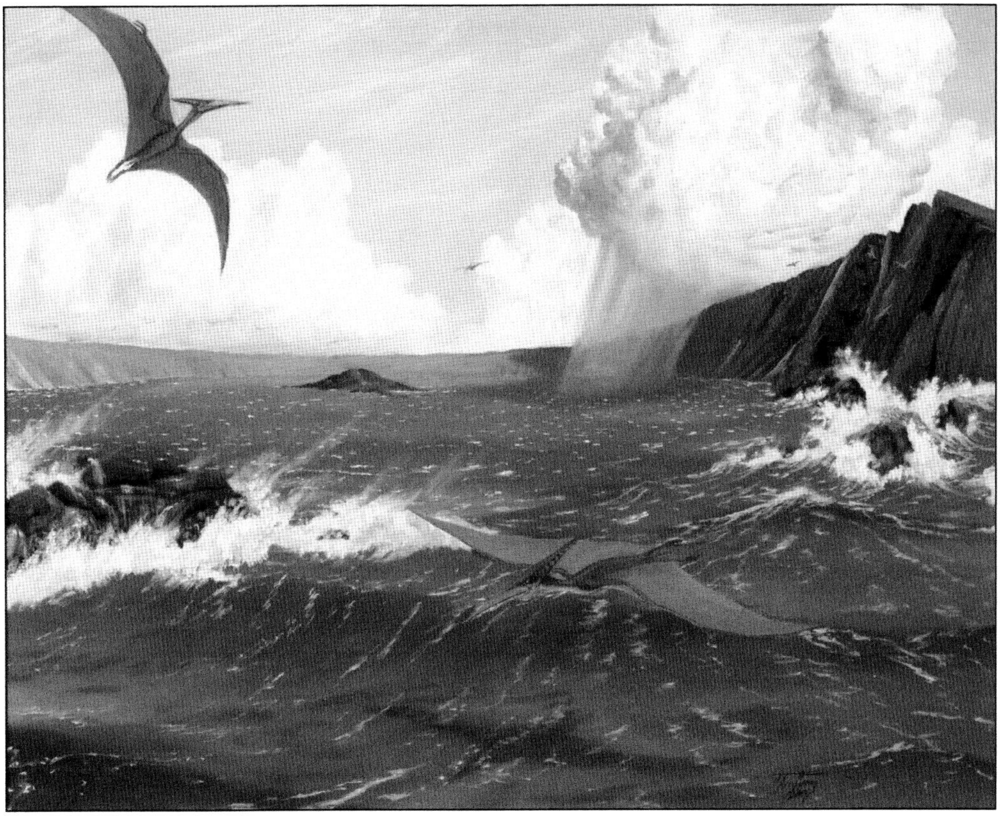

It is thought that present-day Wetumpka was under a shallow sea some 200 feet deep. Scientists estimate that the energy released by the Wetumpka impact event was over 175,000 times the energy of the nuclear bomb detonated at Hiroshima, Japan, in 1945. It is estimated that all life would have been destroyed in present-day Alabama and western Georgia. (Wetumpka Impact Crater Commission.)

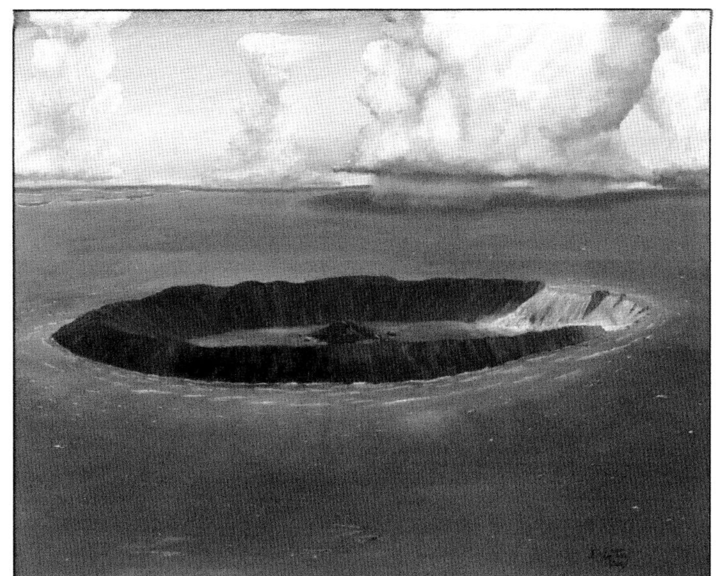

After impact, the weaker southwestern rim collapsed, causing a catastrophic flood across the interior. One can clearly see vestiges of the disaster along the rock formations which face the US Highway 231 bypass. Crater spectators can also view it from the Bibb Graves Bridge looking north at the upturned rock formations that are clearly visible in the Coosa River. (Wetumpka Impact Crater Commission.)

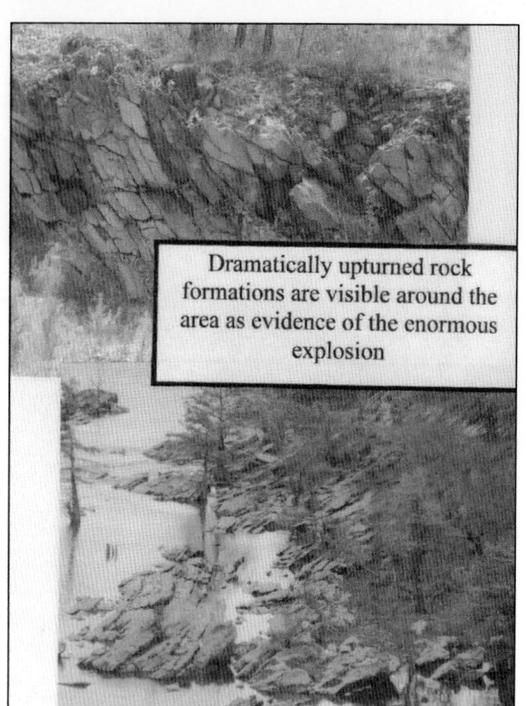


Outcroppings of dramatically upturned rock formations are visible in the Coosa River and along US Highway 231. In the center, rock and soil layers are chaotically intermixed. The vivid formations of upturned rock in the hills surrounding Wetumpka and in the Coosa River offer evidence of the enormous explosion caused by the impact of this meteor, which is estimated to have been between 1,000 and 4,500 feet in diameter. (Wetumpka Impact Crater Commission.)

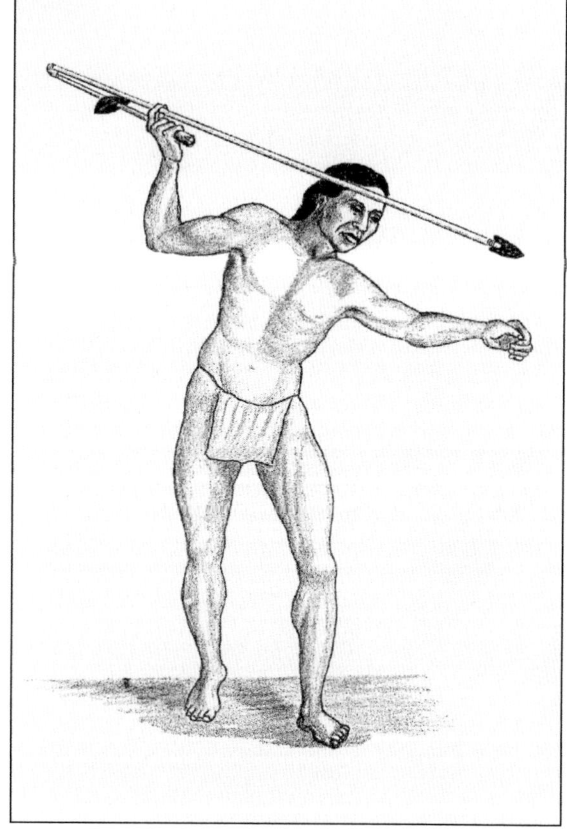

In the absence of photography, this image is an artist's representation of the inhabitants of the local area during the time period termed by archaeologists as the Late Archaic, 4000–1000 BC. Numerous technological and social changes occurred during this period. One of the most important advancements during this era was the increasing reliance on certain plants for food and containers such as bottle gourds. (Ned Jenkins, Fort Toulouse/Jackson and *Tribes That Slumber*, by Thomas M.N. Lewis and Madeline Kneberg; City of Wetumpka.)

Inhabitants in this artist's representation, who lived during the archaeological Woodland period 1000 BC–AD 1000, are characterized by the development of pottery, construction of burial mounds, and expanded reliance on plant cultivation. Extensive trade connections brought about changes in the style and manufacturing techniques of ceramic pots and the development of a complex religious system. Between AD 500–1000, several advancements were made, such as corn being considered an important crop and the development of the bow and arrow. (Ned Jenkins, Fort Toulouse/Jackson and *Tribes That Slumber*, by Thomas M.N. Lewis and Madeline Kneberg; City of Wetumpka.)

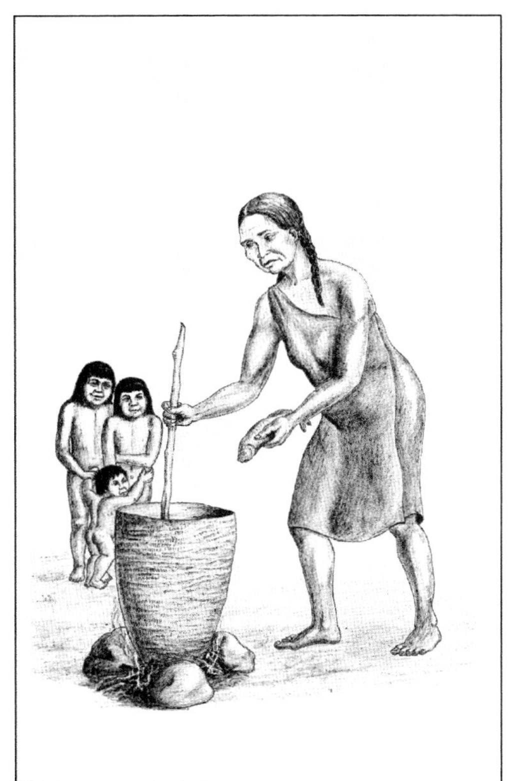

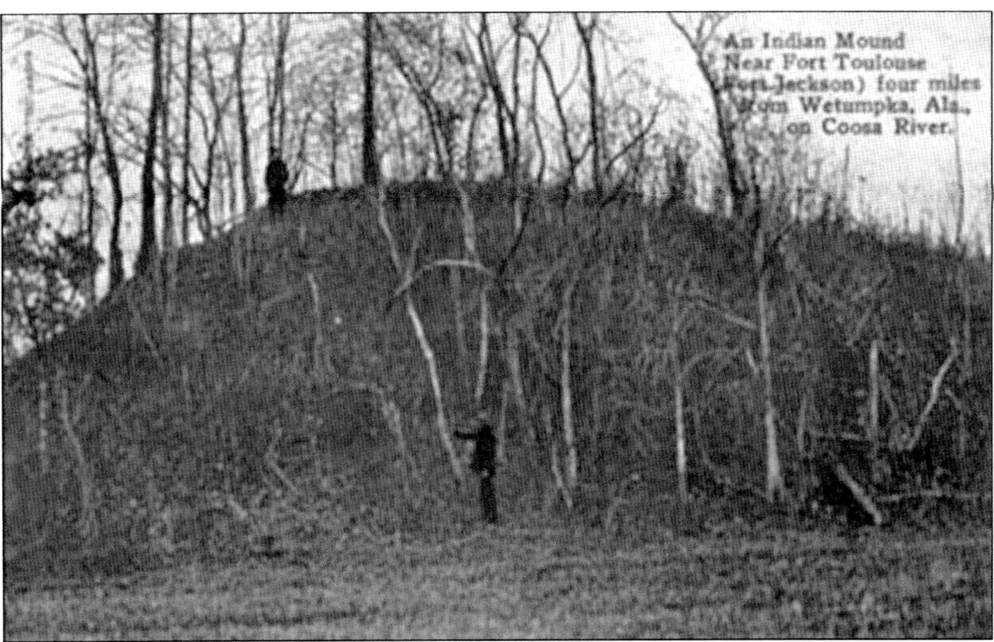


In AD 1100–1600, this Indian mound served as a place of residence for the chief. When a chief died, his house was torn down or burned, adding another layer to the mound and adding to the mound's size. The village beside the mound was lived in from AD 100 until the spring of 1814 when Andrew Jackson's troops arrived after the Battle of Horseshoe Bend. (Peggy Blackburn.)

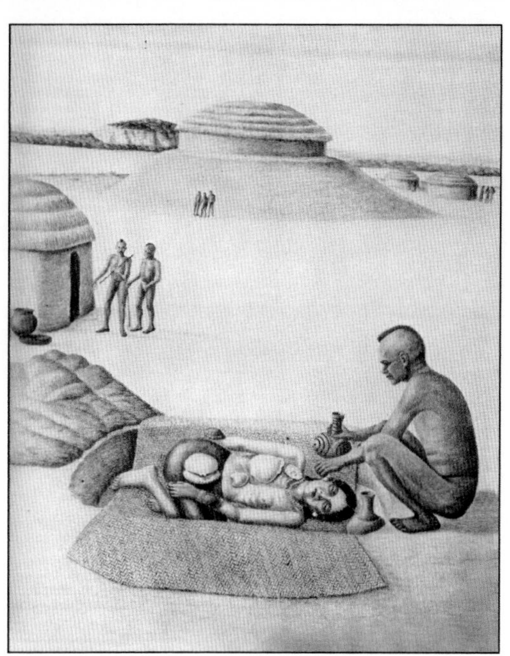

This artist's archaeological representation depicts the last prehistoric stage of inhabitants in the area before the arrival of the Europeans. This was also the most complex and labeled the Mississippi AD 1000–1540 period. Most previous societies were egalitarian, sharing wealth and resources. This system changed with the rise of Mississippian chiefdoms. The elite groups held political, spiritual and economic power, while the community supplied crops and labor. Characteristics are the predominance of shell-tempered pottery, large flat-topped earthen mounds, trade networks, and a highly structured religion. (Ned Jenkins, Fort Toulouse/Jackson and *Tribes That Slumber*, by Thomas M.N. Lewis and Madeline Kneberg; City of Wetumpka.)

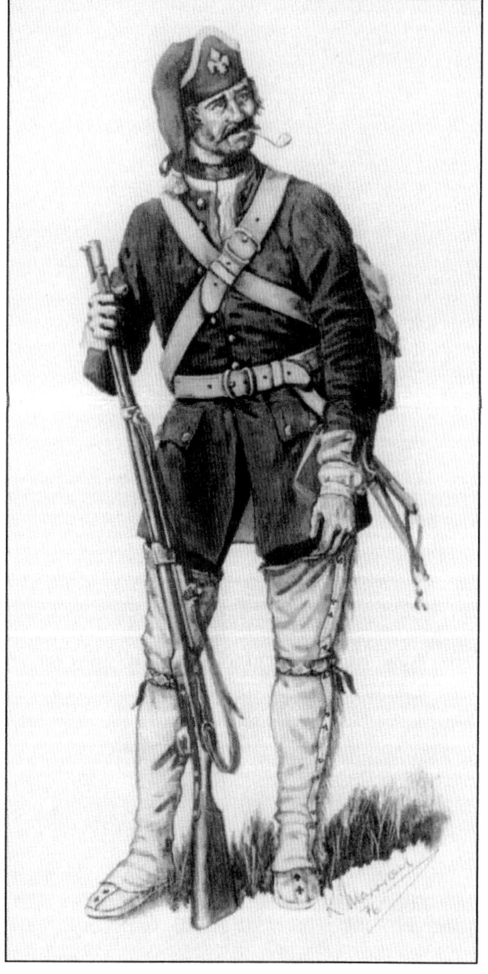

In the historic 1540–1800 period, traders and settlers arrived shortly after European explorers traversed the Southeast. Their early contact with the Indians was limited to trading—deerskins and shells for silver jewelry, glass beads, and iron items. Along with new technologies, the Europeans brought new diseases to which the Indians had no resistance. Local native populations are believed to have greatly decreased during this period. (City of Wetumpka.)

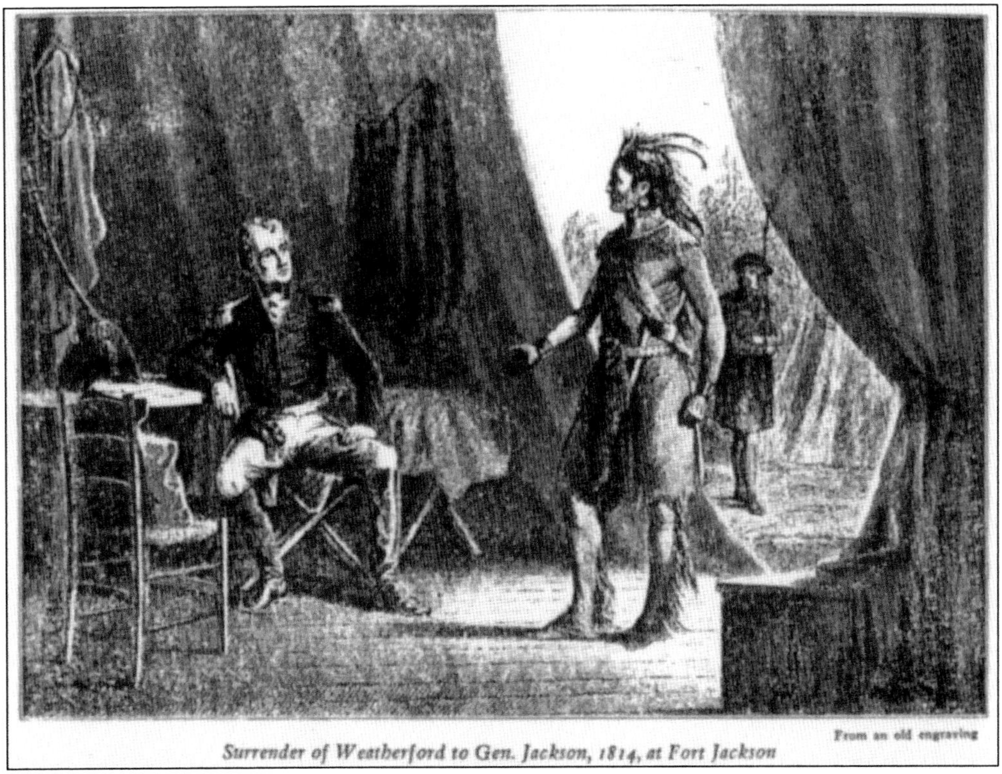

*Surrender of Weatherford to Gen. Jackson, 1814, at Fort Jackson*

From an old engraving

The treaty with the Creek was signed at Fort Jackson, a few miles south of present-day Wetumpka, on August 9, 1814. Sometime before the peace talks, Red Stick leader William Weatherford learned of Gen. Andrew Jackson's order for his arrest and instead turned himself in, surrendering to General Jackson, who chastised the Creek leader for his role in the Fort Mims massacre. Weatherford eloquently renounced further hostilities and sought food and clothing for the many Creek displaced by the war and whose desperate condition was noted by officials at Fort Jackson. (Fort Toulouse/Jackson.)

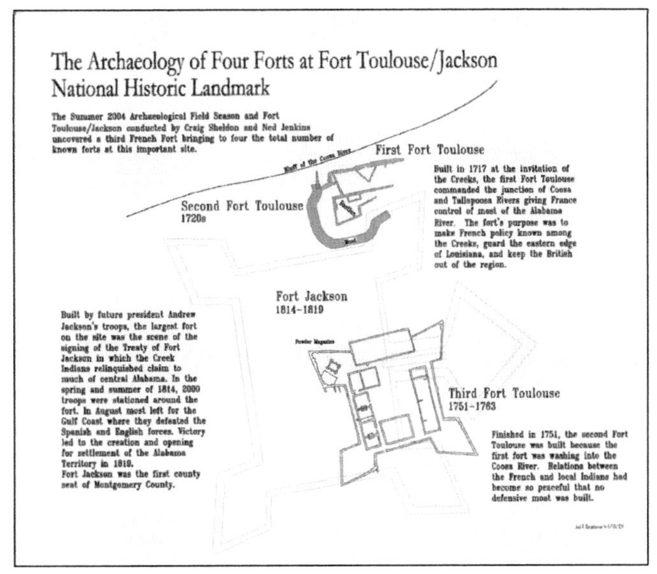


Through many years of extensive archaeological research done by several people dedicated to the development of Fort Toulouse, there have been three different fort locations clearly found and mapped in this view. The earliest of these was built in 1717, and others have been outlined. (Fort Toulouse/Jackson.)

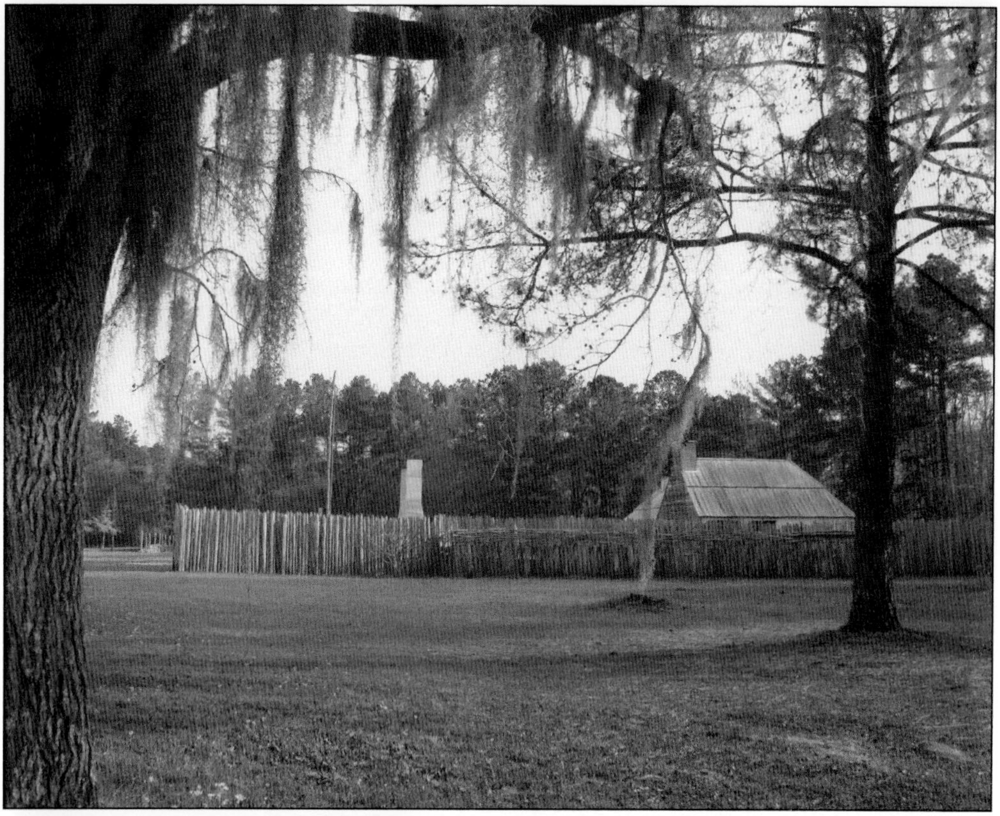

Fort Toulouse was guarded by its palisade between 1717 and 1763. In those same years, three different forts known as Fort Toulouse were constructed adjacently on high ground near the junction of the Coosa and Tallapoosa Rivers. The Creek Indians invited the French to build a fort here so they would have a source for muskets and other European trade items. The primary function of the fort was as a diplomatic post so French policy could be made known among the Indians and to keep the British out of the region. (Fort Toulouse/Jackson.)

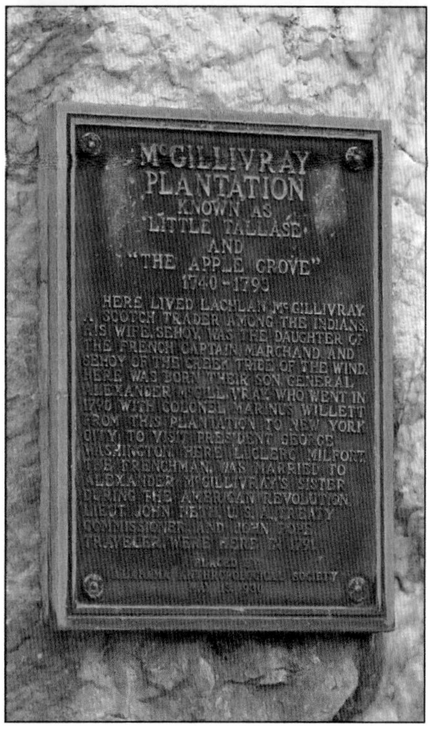


Alexander McGillivray (1759–1793) a Creek leader, had a plantation near Wetumpka during his period of greatest influence. Son of a Scottish trader and his French-Creek wife, McGillivray had a well-rounded education but returned to Creek country after the War for Independence. During this time, he served as a British agent and sent Indian war parties against the United States frontier. He led the Creeks, and in 1784, he negotiated on behalf of the Creeks and Seminoles to begin trading with Spain. This monument is on the site of his plantation. (Fort Toulouse/Jackson.)

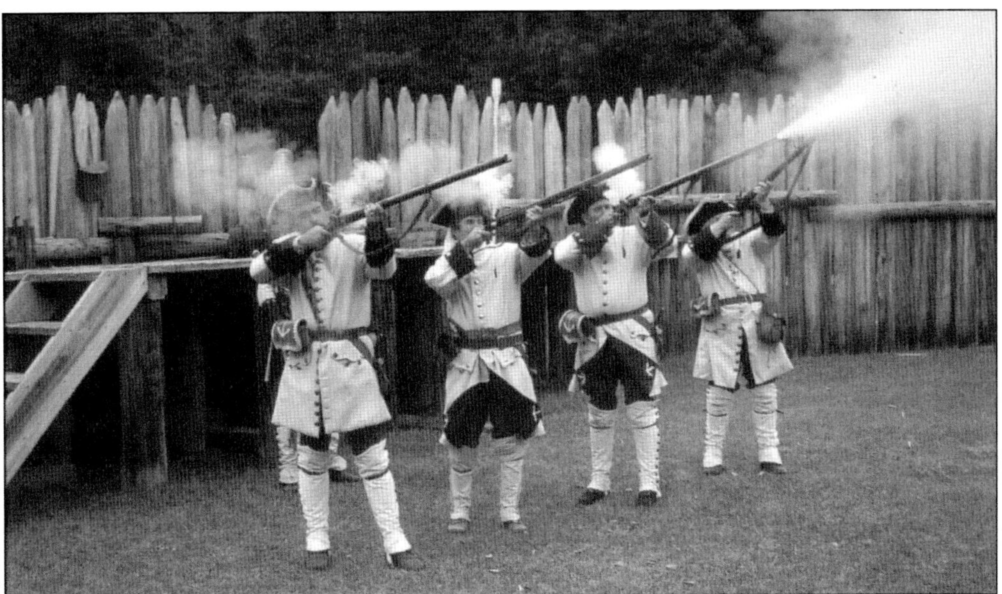

French Colonial Marines were stationed at Fort Toulouse from 1717 until 1763. Many lived with wives and children at small farmsteads located 100 to 200 yards from Fort Toulouse. The privates were peasant-class people from France, while the officers were the second, third, or fourth sons of French nobility from New France (Canada). (Fort Toulouse/Jackson.)

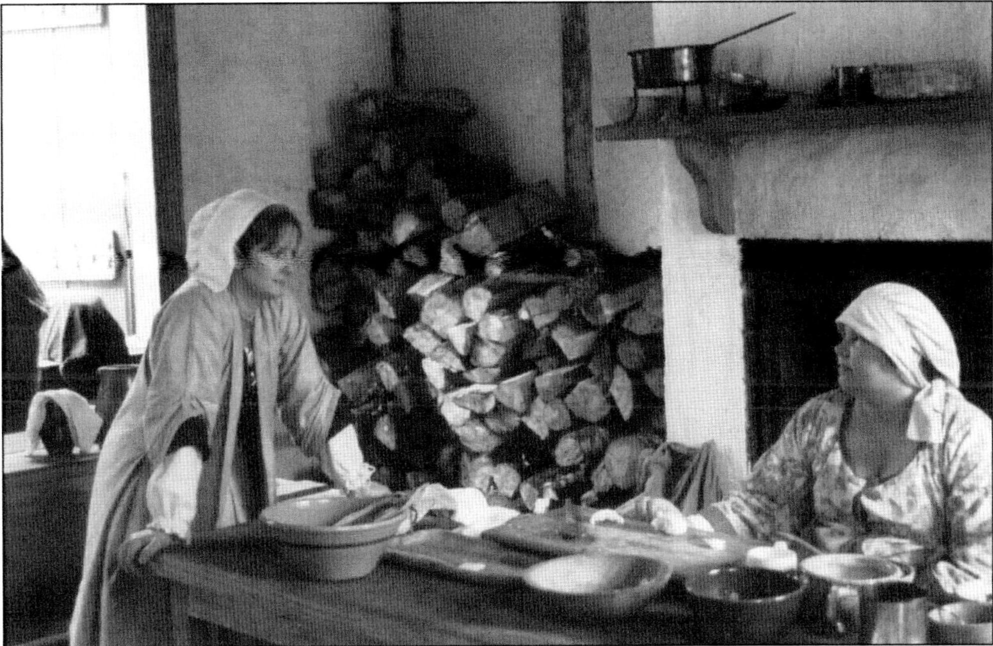

Women arrived at Fort Toulouse as early as 1720, as French Colonial Marines began to build farms, raise families, and grow crops near the fort. French children became numerous at Fort Toulouse, as Marie Fonteneau, wife of Sgt. Jean Louis Fonteneau, raised 12 children here. Most male children grew up to become French Marines and married girls who had grown up here. The fort has a fully restored replica of the kitchen, outdoor oven, officer's barracks, and palisade—which guarded the living quarters of the families. (Fort Toulouse/Jackson.)

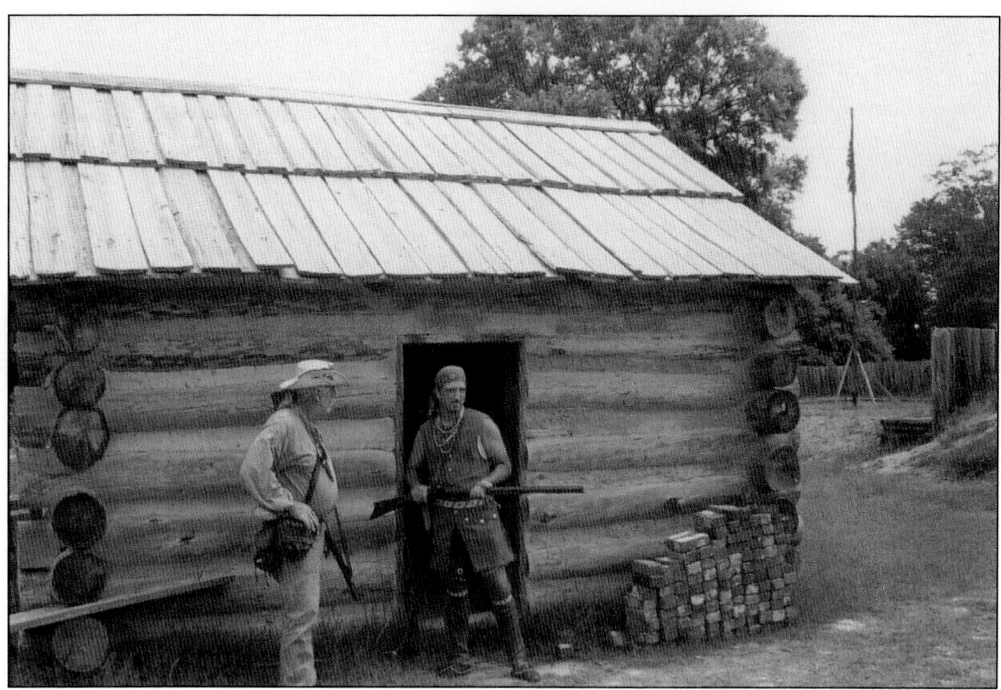

Fort Jackson was an earthen redoubt built by Americans in 1814 after the Battle of Horseshoe Bend. It served as a staging area for Andrew Jackson's assault on the Spanish and British along the gulf. In August 1814, the Treaty of Fort Jackson ceded over 15,000,000 acres of land to the United States government, the settling of which resulted in Alabama becoming a state in 1819. Although Fort Jackson was decommissioned in 1819, that same year it became the hub of Fort Jackson Town and the first county seat for Montgomery County. (Fort Toulouse/Jackson.)

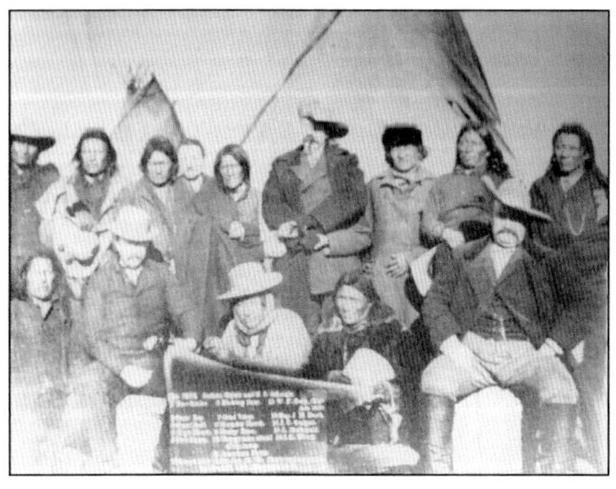

When Wetumpka was becoming a city in 1834, the Native Americans had already abandoned the area. The Creeks surrendered in April 1832 at the signing of the Treaty of Cusseta. Inhabitants of Fort Toulouse were forced to march on the Trail of Tears to desolate western lands. Ned Jenkins, archaeologist at Fort Toulouse, believes that this picture originated from a Buffalo Bill's Wild West Show that probably appeared in the vicinity of Montgomery, Alabama, much later—probably in the 1880s. (Peggy Blackburn.)

# *Two*

# Development of Commerce in Wetumpka

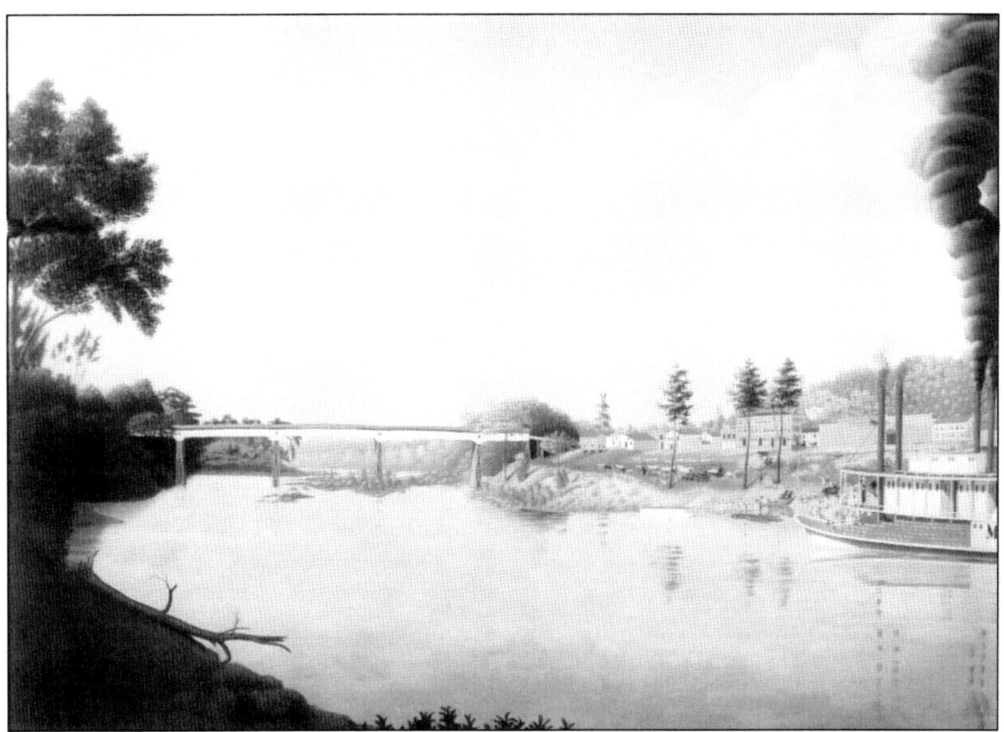

In 1847, Adrian E. Thompson created this oil painting, *Wetumpka Bridge, Alabama*. The original hangs in the Museum of Fine Arts, Boston. (ECHS.)

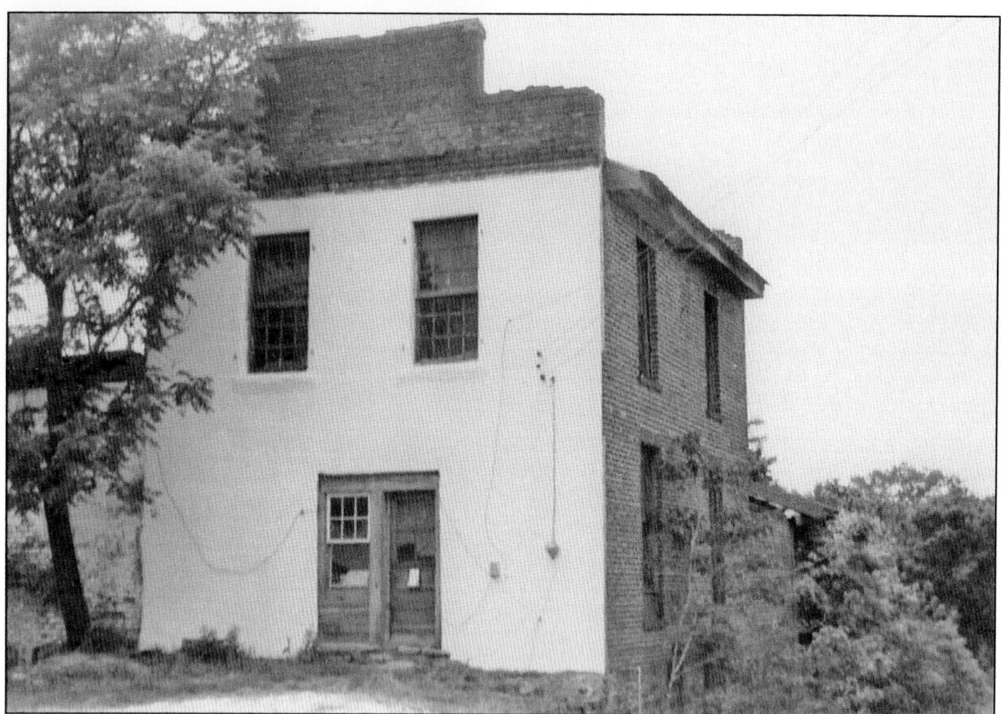
The Alliance Warehouse is believed to have been built by natives in the 1820s for use as a trading post. It is the oldest business establishment in Wetumpka and is located at the southwest corner of Ready and Wharf Streets on the east bank of the Coosa River just south of Bibb Graves Bridge. This structure is two-story masonry and designed with double entrance doors and upper and lower windows in the fashion of a pioneer store or trading post, in which the proprietors' living quarters were usually above the business floor. The brick in this structure was handmade by Indians. (Peggy Blackburn.)

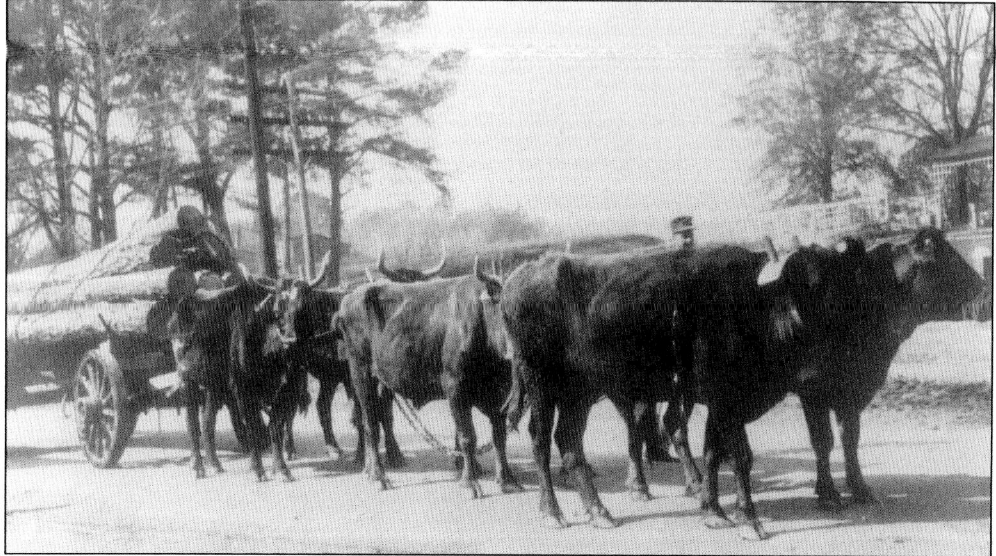
Early commerce included businesses concerned with timber and sawmilling. This oxteam was an integral part of the local lumber industry. (Peggy Blackburn.)

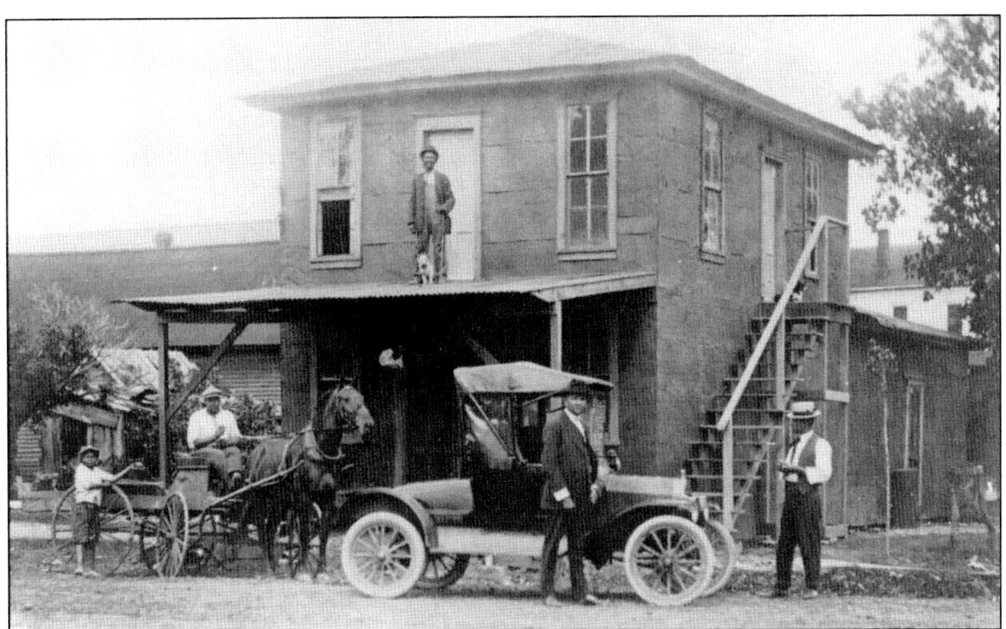

According to John Enslen, this two-story building was situated near the present-day location of the Dairy Queen on South Main Street. Adam Enslen's home is visible at the back. The building probably housed an office for a cotton warehouse downstairs and a residence for workers upstairs. Note the dog on the porch roof. (John Enslen and Peggy Blackburn.)

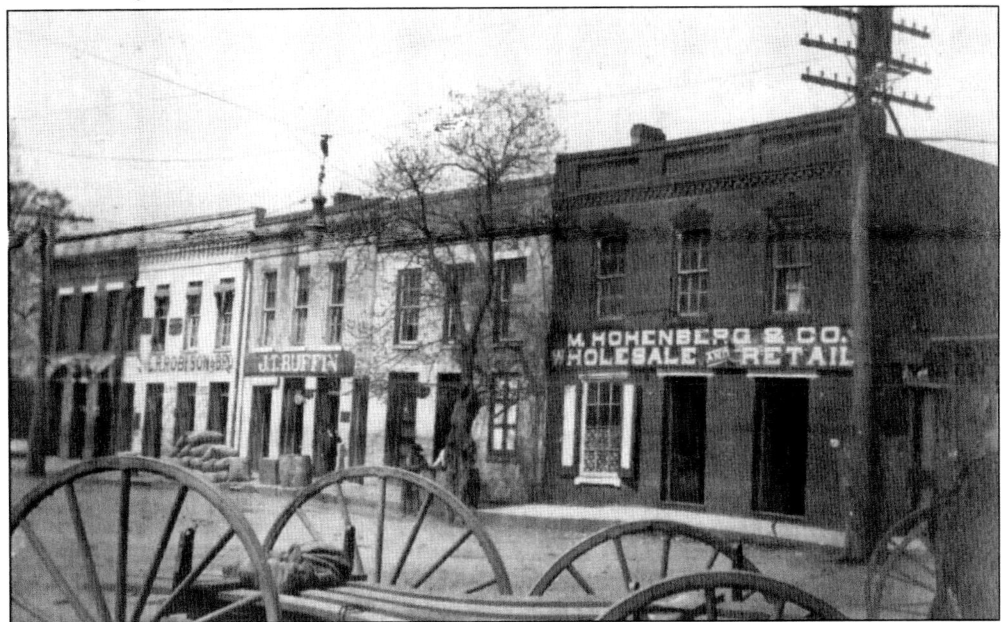


These buildings on the north side of East Bridge Street in downtown Wetumpka were constructed around 1855 after a destructive fire in 1852. This image dates to 1900. The buildings remain today, with updated facades completed around 1925. The one-story brick storefront was altered with a neoclassical entrance. All of the stores rest on tall brick piers. Dr. W.L. Bloxom, dentist, and Dr. E.P. Moon had offices here in the 1920s and early 1930s. King's Barbershop was here in 1938. Demp Thrash's Barber Shop was in this location from the 1940s to the 1960s. (Otis Pearsall.)

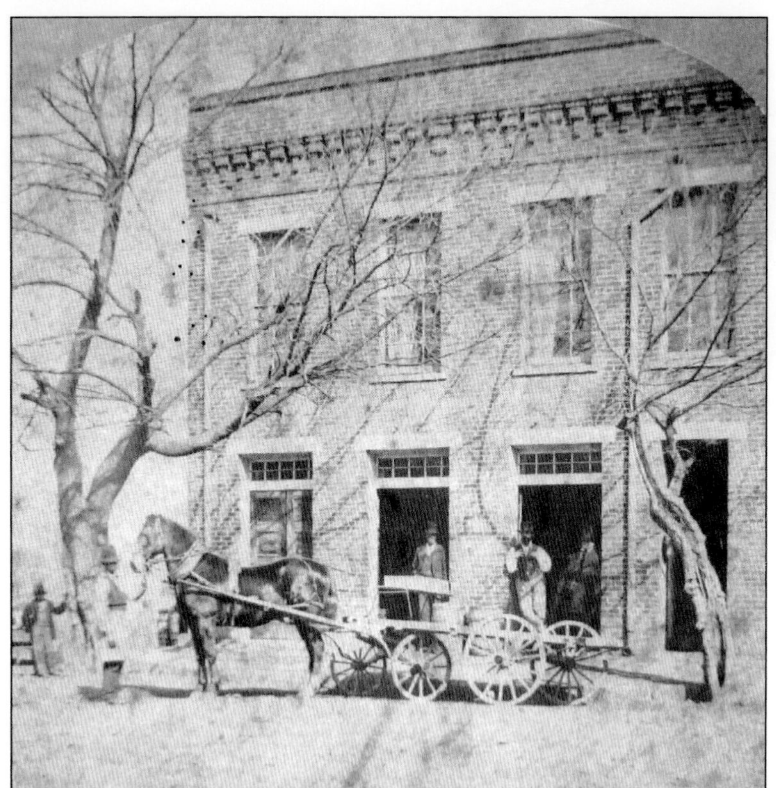

The Cabot Lull mercantile business was located in this building in 1886. Floodwaters reached to the height of 5.5 feet. Lull was nearest the river and his loss was heavy, not less than $800. (ECHS.)

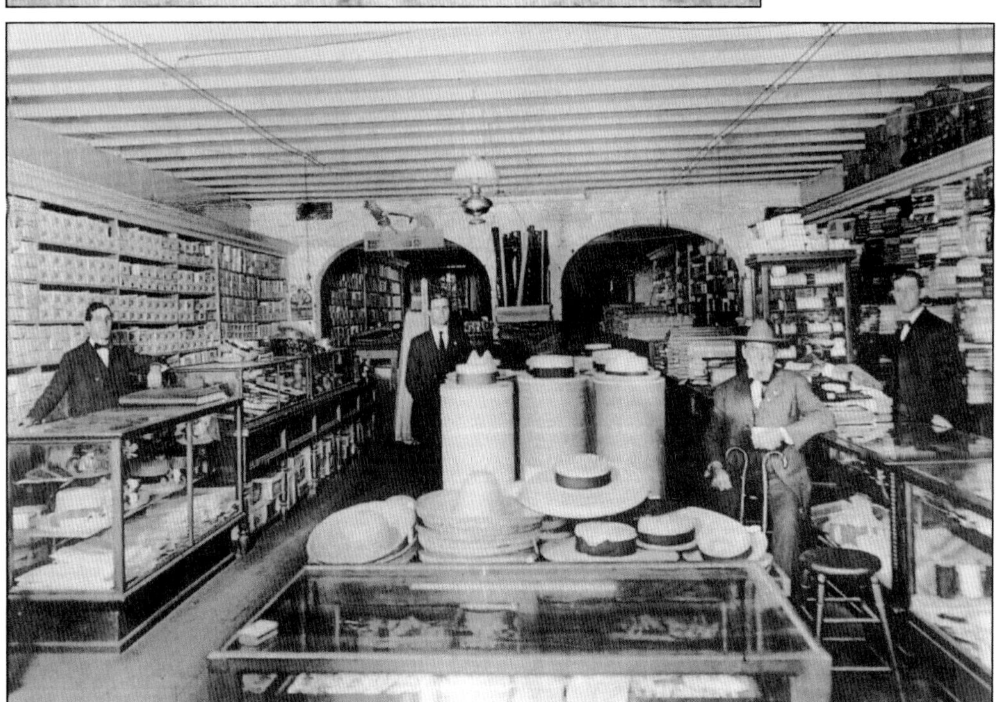

The L.R. Robison and Brother store interior is shown in 1900. Pictured on the extreme left is Horatio A. Robison, and at the extreme right is Leon R. Robison, his brother. (*Alabama Heritage*.)

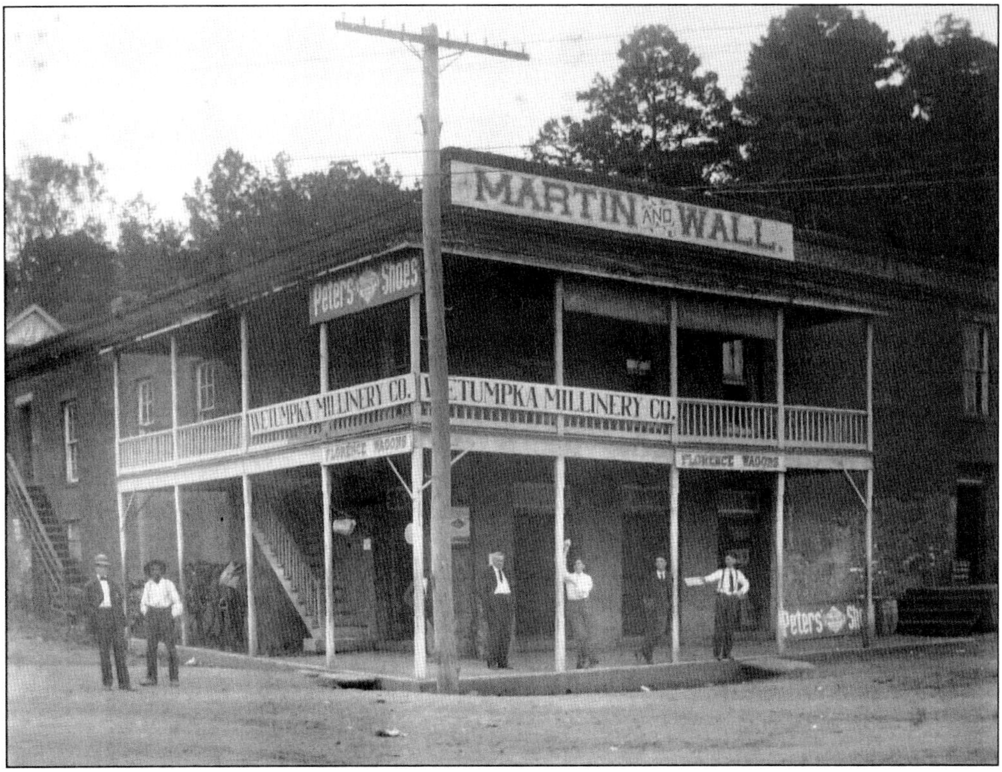

This building was constructed by Lonnie DeKalb Rouse in the center of town and housed his mercantile business. The structure was purchased by James Augustus Wall in the early 1900s and housed the hardware business of Martin and Wall. Berta Wall operated a millinery shop on the second floor. (ECHS.)

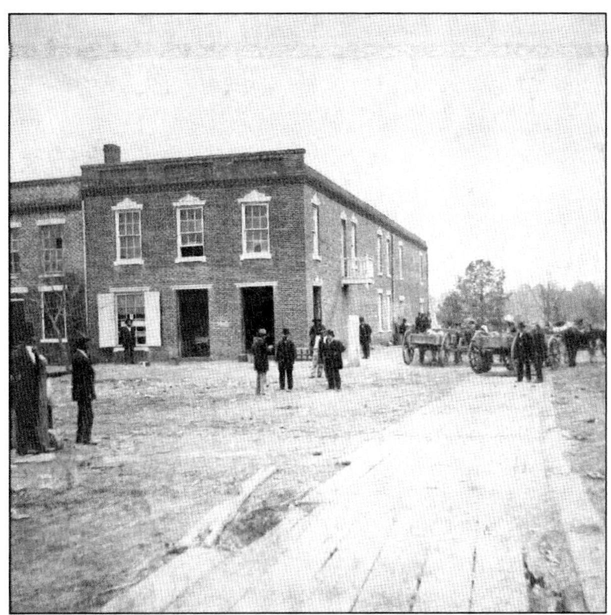

The "Due Corner" survived the great flood of 1886, as well as three fires. Alexander Gordon Due had a Civil War cotton business here, and the space was later occupied by Hohenberg-Lacy-Farrow Mercantile Company. In Horatio Tulane's will, probated in 1897, the building was left to his nieces and nephews, then it was to go to Elmore County for "the care of the poor and destitute." Note the plank road, a section of the central plank road that extended from Montgomery through Wetumpka to Winterboro. After the early 1850s, the feasibility of a plank road was called into question due to maintenance expense. (ECHS.)

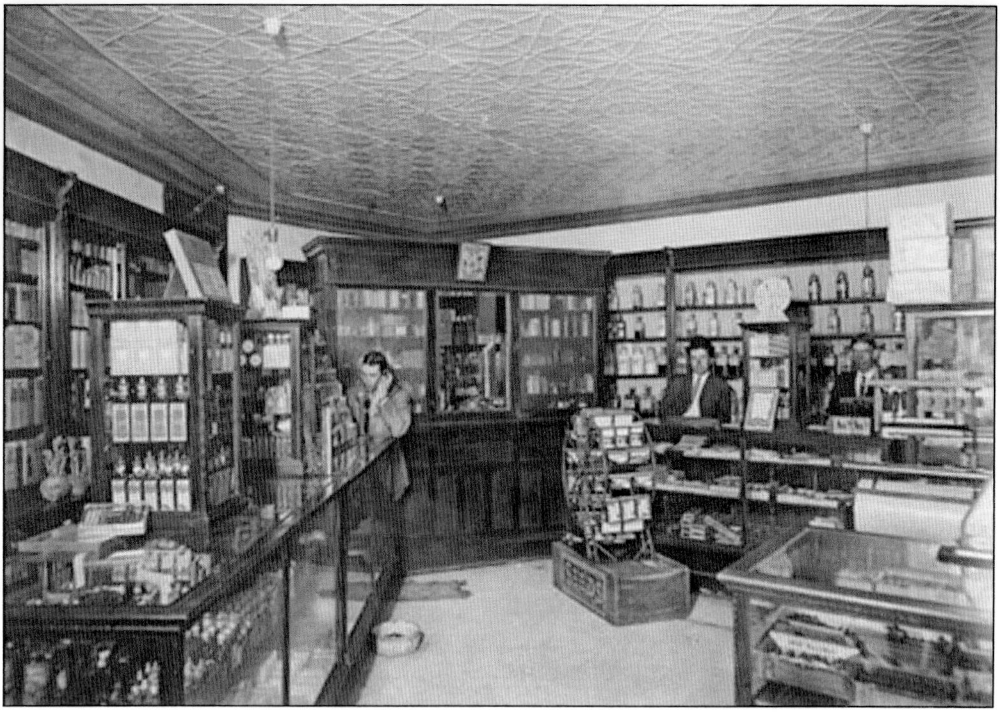

This is the interior of Wetumpka Drug Store on Court Street. (Peggy Blackburn.)

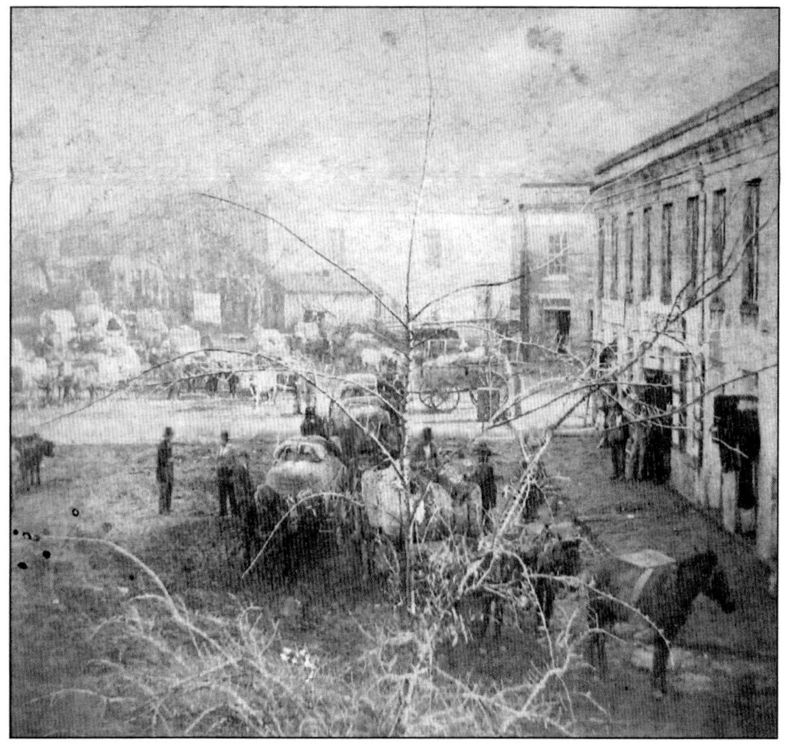

This view of Bridge Street around 1880 is looking toward the center of town. The buildings on the extreme right adjoin the present-day Wetumpka Area Chamber of Commerce. At the top left, East Bridge flows into Company Street. (ECHS.)

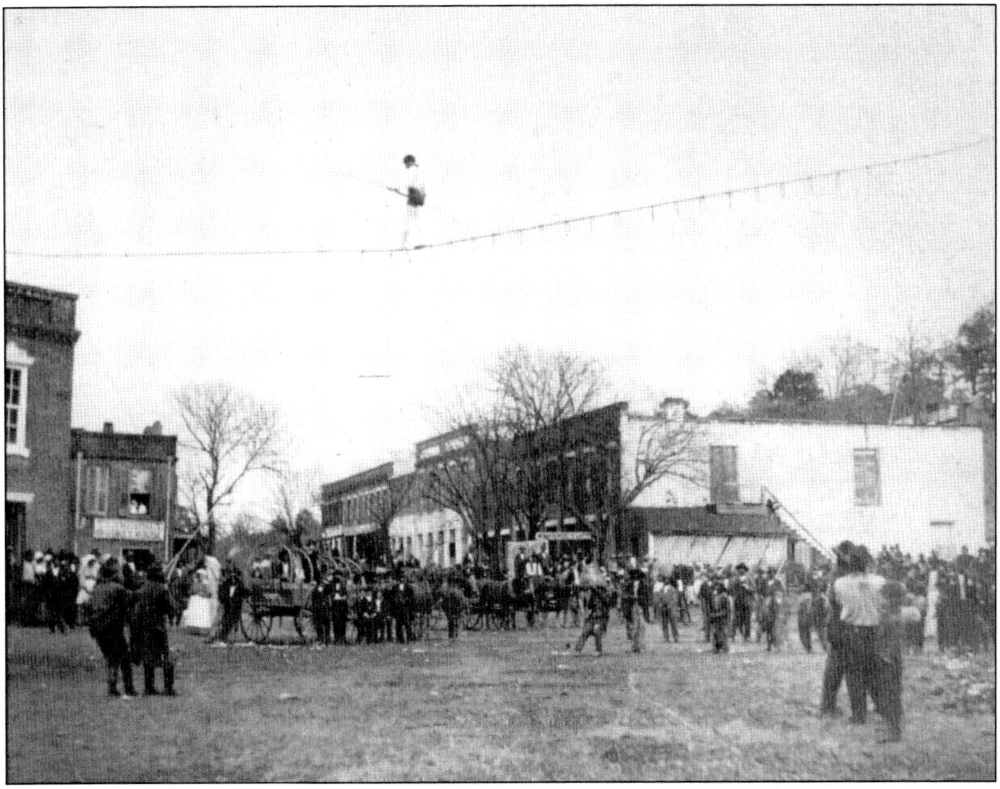

Company Street begins in downtown Wetumpka at the junction of Hill and Bridge Streets. In the mid-1840s, the townspeople gave the name "Chicken Row" to the block. The merchants along this block had chickens in coops out in front of their stores. The merchants did not think that name sounded dignified, so they began calling it "Poultry Avenue." Even today, this block is still called Chicken Row. Company Street attracted many people on the day this photograph was taken, when a tightrope-walker traveled high above the street, delighting citizens. (Joey Brackner.)

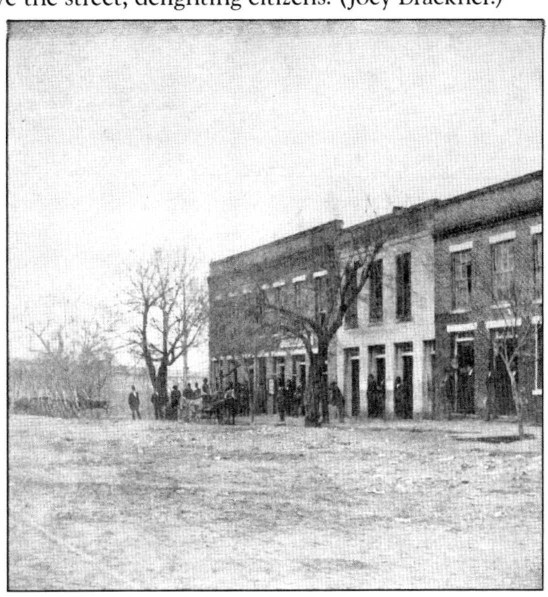

Wetumpka has been ravaged by floods and fires since its early days. Very heavy rain in 1841 washed away the Coosa River Bridge, built in 1834. In 1845, a fire destroyed all business houses on the north side of East Bridge Street. Again in 1852, a fire destroyed 42 business houses. These structures were rebuilt by 1855. In 1902 and again in 1908, two more disastrous fires caused great damage to the downtown area. A great flood in 1886 destroyed the Covered Bridge. Other damaging floods occurred in 1919 and 1938. (ECHS.)

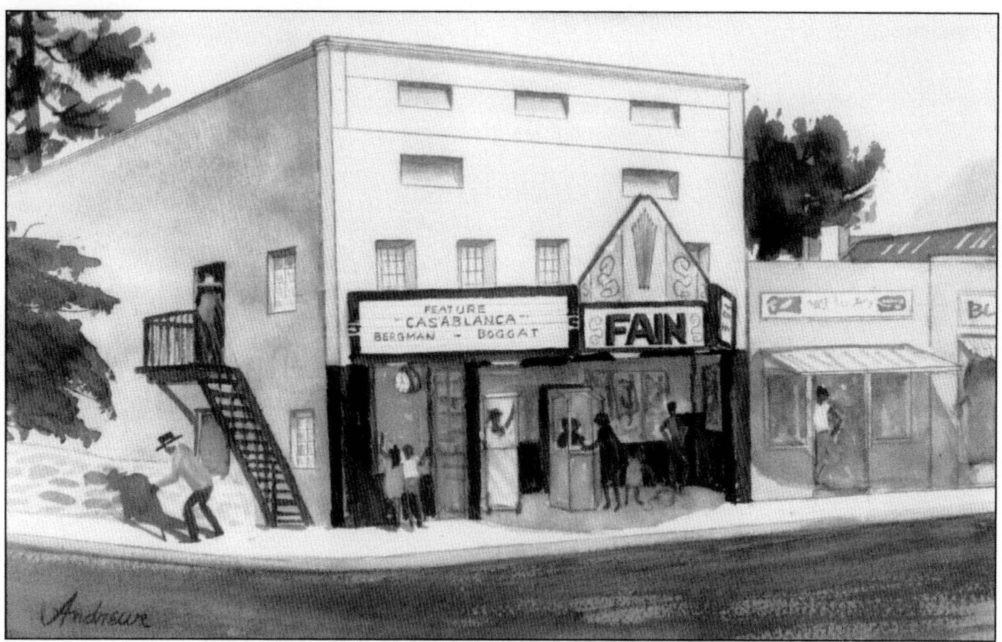


For many years, the Fain Theater was the only picture show in town. Edward C. and Lula D. Murrell Fain opened their theater in 1913. It was first located upstairs in a building at the corner of Hill and Bridge Streets, where cane-bottom chairs were tilted slightly by elevating the front legs on two-by-fours for viewing silent movies. Fain Theater moved to several locations, but its last one was on East Bridge Street, opening in September 1937 with the showing of *A Star is Born*, featuring Janet Gaynor and Frederic March. Mrs. Fain continued to sell tickets until age 89, and her beloved theater closed in 1975. This painting was done by Phillip Andrews. (ECHS.)

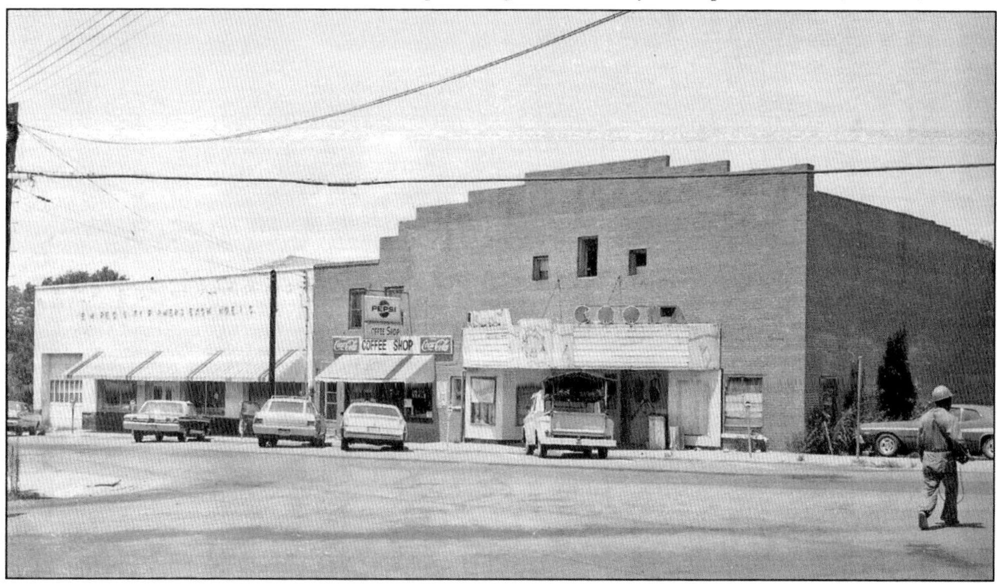


A second movie house, the Coosa Theater, opened in the late 1940s and operated about 10 years. It was located at the opposite end of downtown, off present-day Orline Street near the livery stable. Edward L. Clark operated the theater in partnership with Isabelle Enslen. A double feature was *Bush Pilot* and *Tumbleweed*. In 1948, a traffic light was installed at that corner. (Peggy Blackburn.)

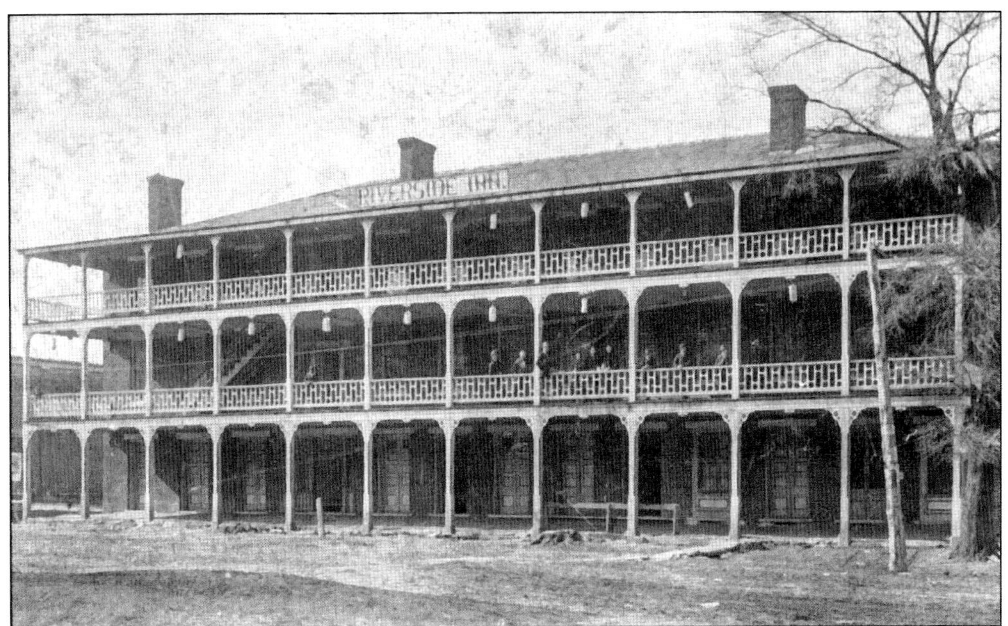


The Coosa River was not navigable beyond Wetumpka; therefore, riverboat travel ended there. Hotels were needed to accommodate travelers. In response, John Horton opened a boardinghouse in 1833 in a two-room log house. The same year, W.C. Bachelor had a hotel at Harrogate Springs resort. In 1835, Hardy Griffin built the three-story Mansion House. Other hotels operating during this time were the American Hotel, the Gallagher Hotel, and the White Halls Hotel. In 1845, Coosa Hall was built near the Coosa River. It remained in business later as Riverside Inn (pictured) until it burned in 1904. The Lancaster in the center of town was constructed after 1902 and operated under various owners until the mid-1940s. (ECHS.)

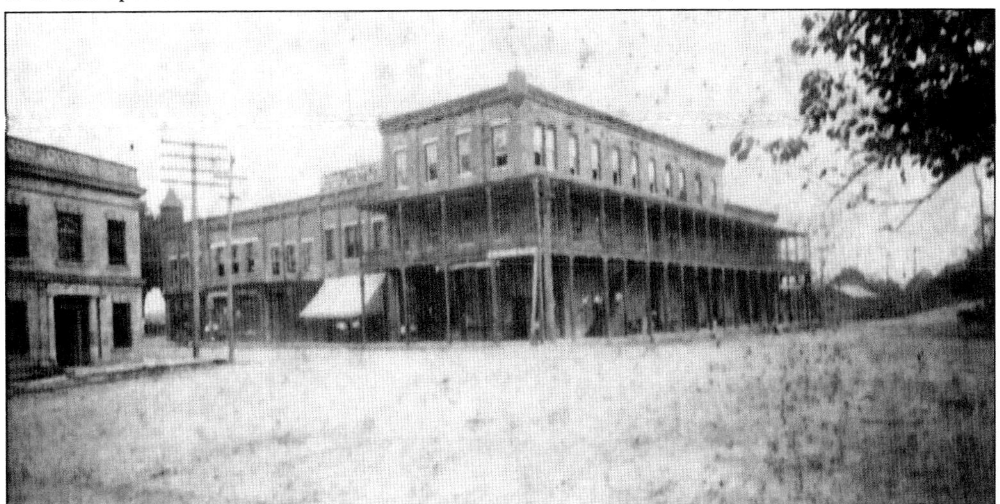

About midnight on a cold January night in 1903, fire broke out in a general mercantile store on the site of this building. The fire destroyed the store and did great damage to the other two-story brick building on the block, with damages totaling over $70,000. The store structure was owned by the John Austin Lancaster estate and was rebuilt, with a third story added, and opened as Hotel Lancaster (pictured here on the right) on the corner of Court and East Bridge Streets. The other buildings in the block were either rebuilt or refurbished. (Peggy Blackburn.)

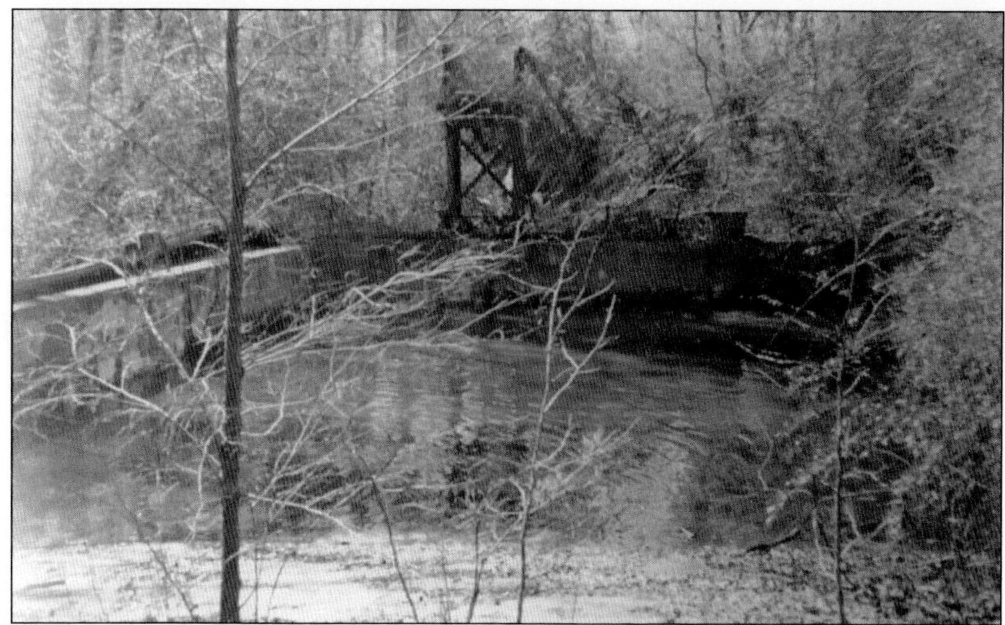

Harrogate Springs came from two small artesian springs about a mile upstream—one iron water and the other sulfur. First, there was a swimming pool (pictured), a dance hall, a barbecue smokehouse, and later two tennis courts. From 1928 to 1930, big bands played in the dance hall. There was a Victrola. The swimming pool was about 80 feet long by 35 to 40 feet wide. Several reservoirs filled with pine straw served to warm up the very cold water and filter out the snakes and trash. This facility closed to the public about 1970. (John Enslen and Peggy Blackburn.)

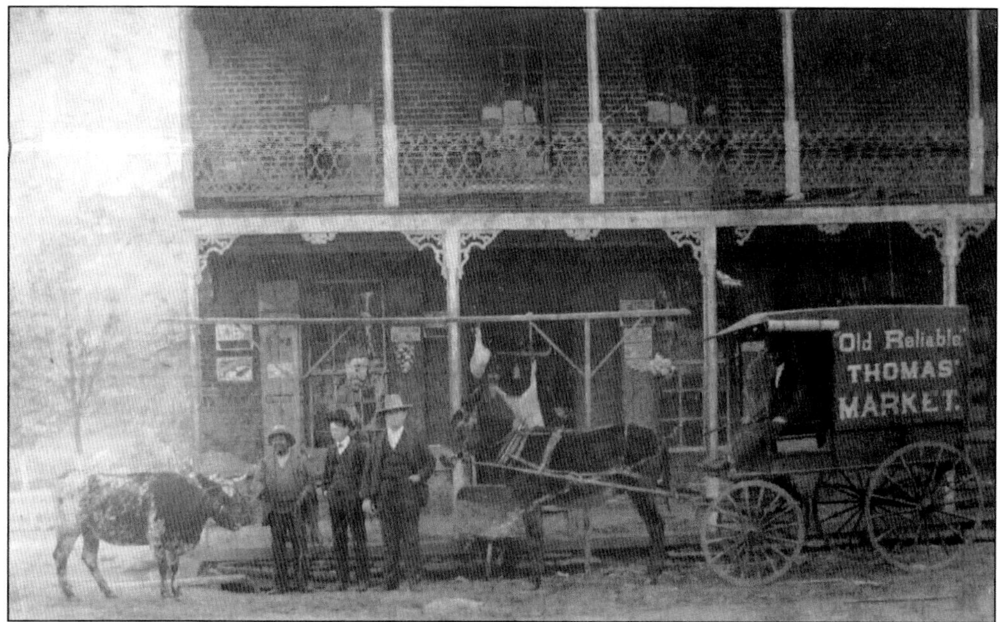


Old Reliable Thomas Market was on the corner of West Commerce Street facing South Main Street. The Old Reliable Market was owned and operated by Walter Thomas. Hale's Grocery was later located there. (ECHS.)

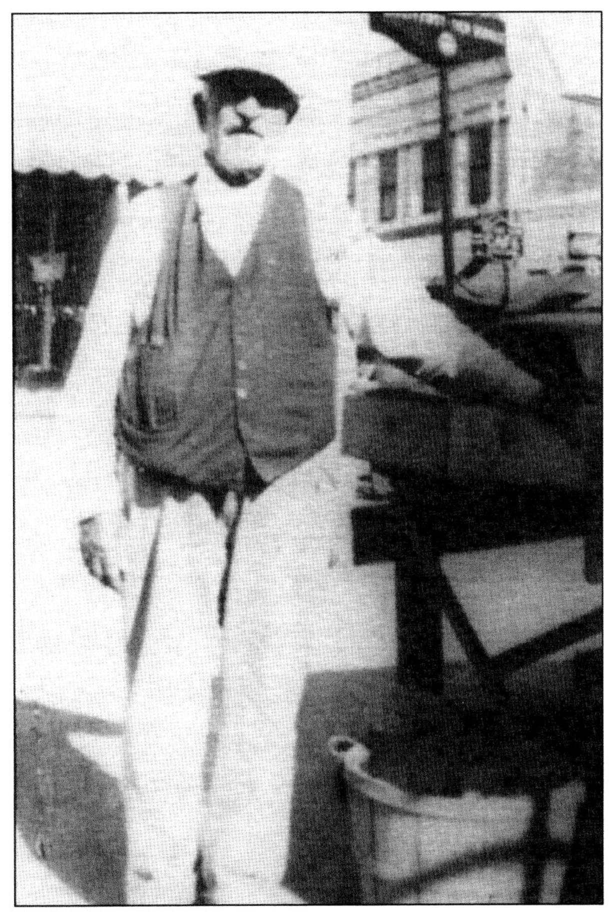

Joel Katz (1863–1949), a native of Austria-Hungary, came to the United States and settled in Montgomery around 1890. He made daily trips to Wetumpka in his horse-drawn wagon to sell fruits and vegetables door to door. After discontinuing his route, he parked his truck at the First National Bank corner and continued his business until the late 1940s. (ECHS.)

As motor vehicles became popular, several filling stations opened downtown. One was located in the northwest corner of the hotel building during the 1920s and 1930s. Another was in the southwest corner of the "Gaddis" building in front of the courthouse. After World War I, Ullmert L. Hughes organized a bus line, the Twin Coach Line, which served towns in central Alabama. Pictured is a Hughes shuttle bus that operated between Wetumpka and Montgomery in 1927. The company failed after the stock market crashed in 1929. (ECHS.)

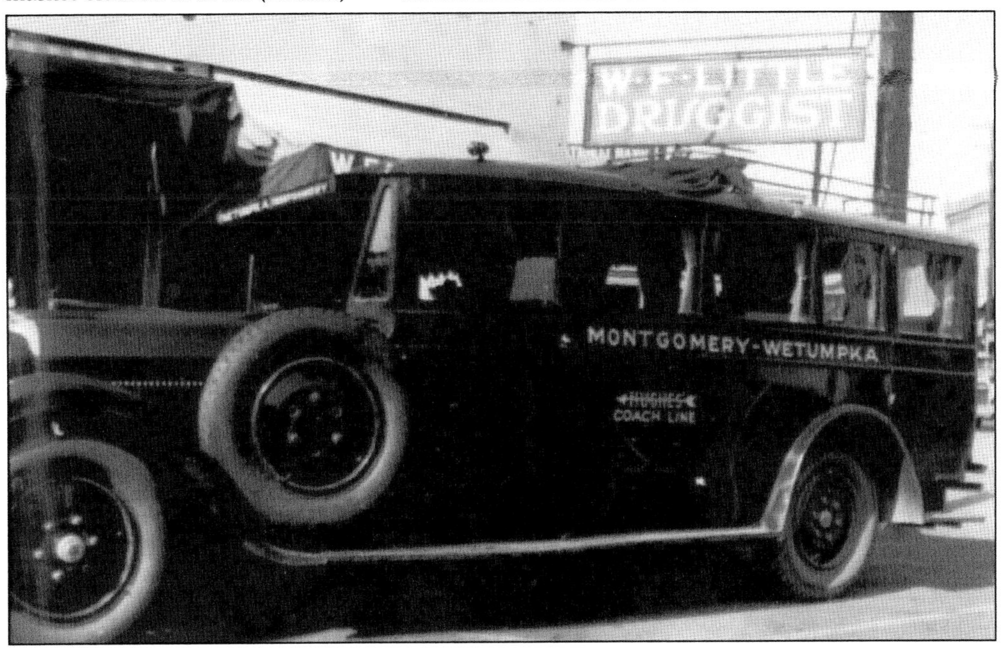

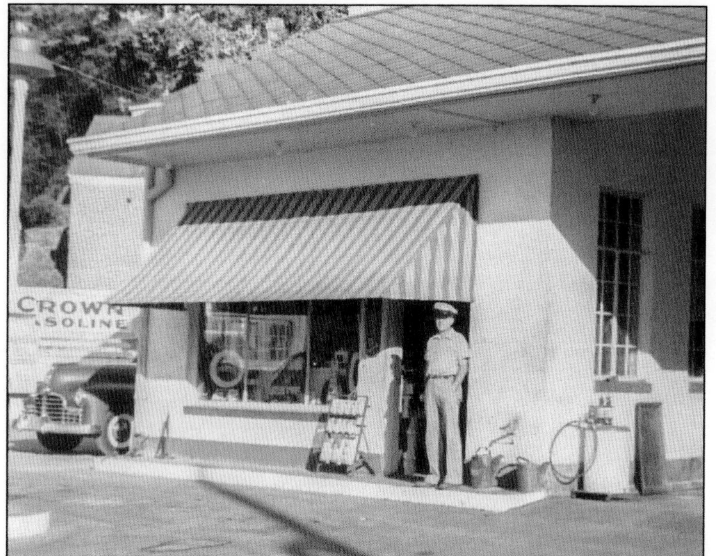


In 1933, Cliff Turner (pictured) opened a Mobil station—later known as Standard Oil—selling gasoline and offering full automobile service. The photograph was made around 1950. (ECHS.)

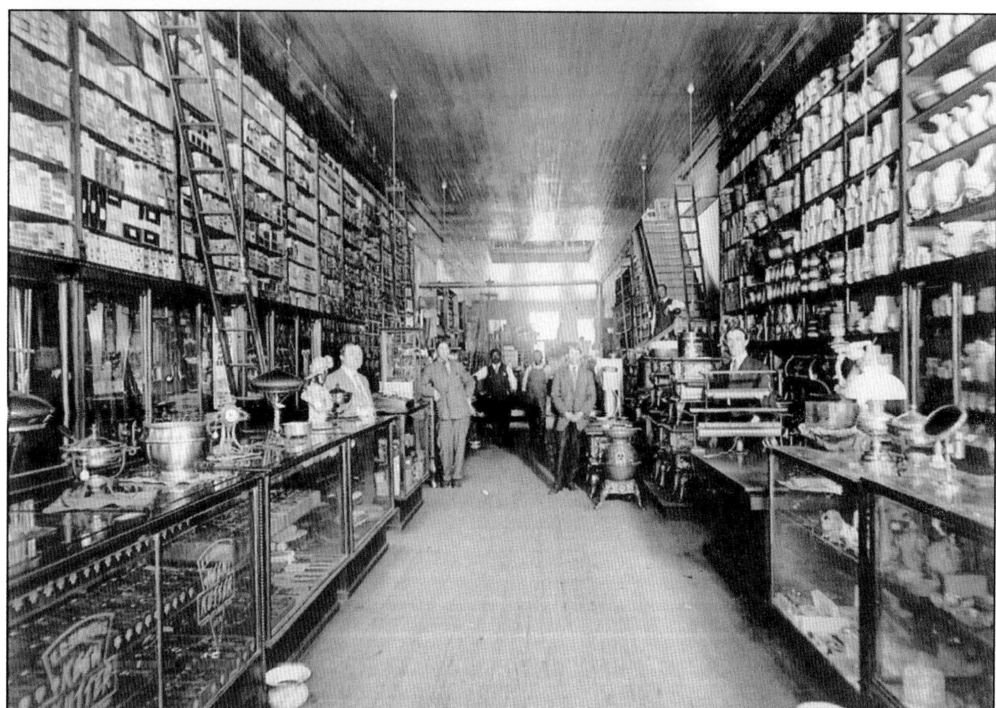

Martin Hardware is pictured. Prior to Martin's ownership, J. Rufus Gamble operated a dry goods and grocery business in this building. Sometime before 1900, the business became Howle, Smith and Gamble Hardware Company, then Smith and Gamble, and then simply Gamble Hardware until 1916. The hardware passed into the Martin family—John D. Martin, Paul H. Martin, and Silas B. Martin, sons of the Rev. Darius S. Martin of Coosa County. It remained Martin Hardware until the 1980s when it closed. In 1907, another hardware in Wetumpka was operated by Walter S. Thornhill in association with W. Watt Jones. Other members of the Thornhill family were associated with the firm after Jones left the business. Thornhill Hardware remained in business until 1971. (ECHS.)

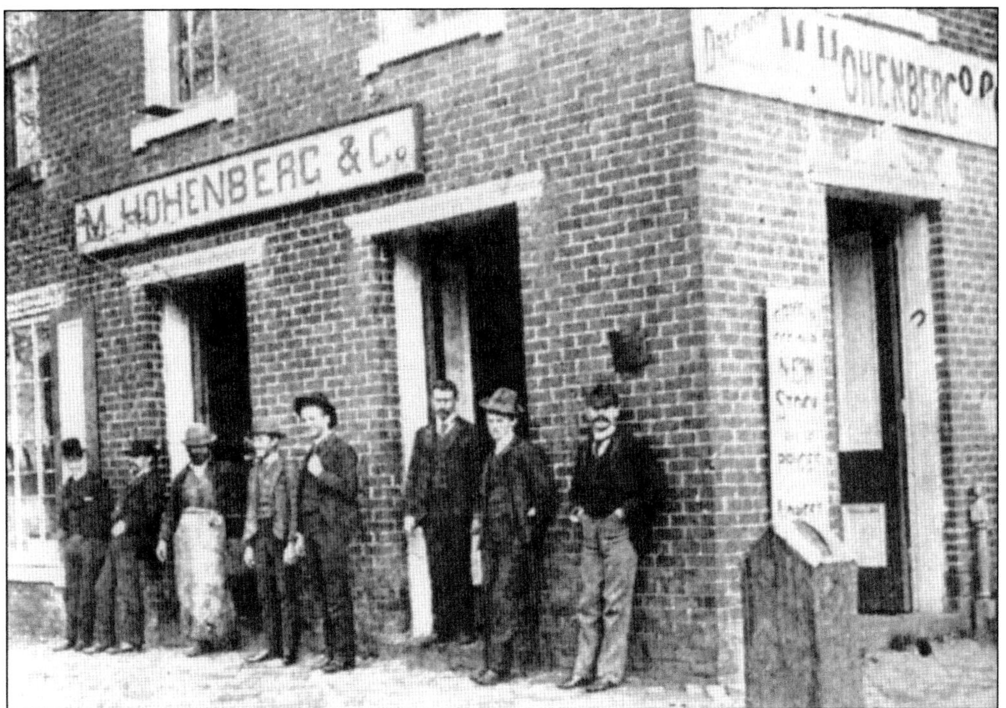


Most dry goods stores began as general merchandise stores; M. Hohenberg and Co. was such a business. Hohenberg-Lacy-Farrow converted to dry goods. Other Wetumpka dry goods retailers included L.R. Robison and Brothers, Bloxom and Poole, Austin and Sanford, Ed Sanford, and T. S. Sanford's. (ECHS.)

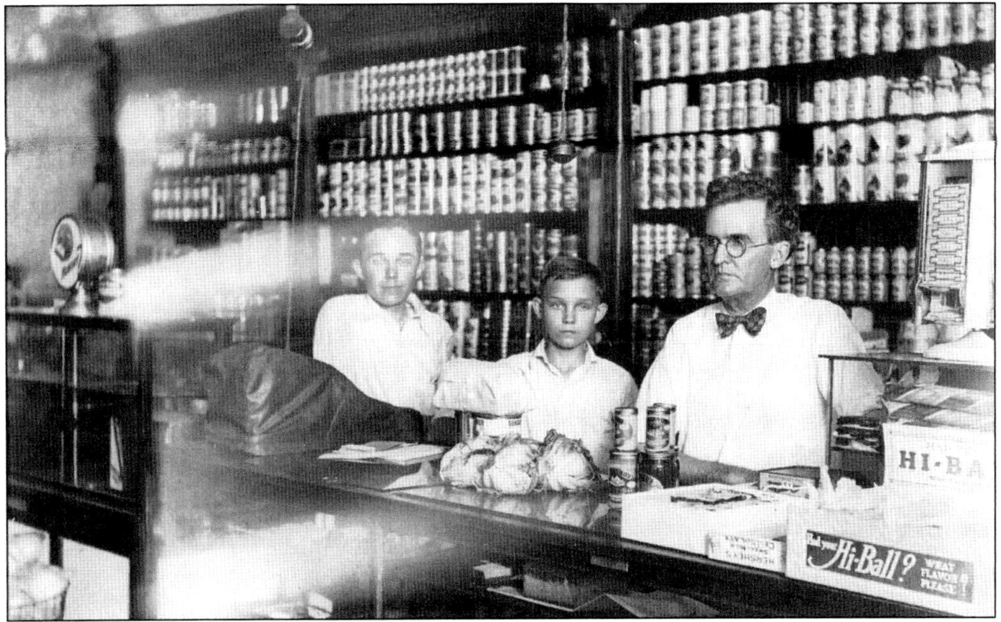


Fruits and other produce were sold from general merchandise stores until merchants began to devote space to one or two types of goods. One such store was the OK Bakery; pictured here are Clifton Turner (left), William Turner (center), and owner Homer H. Parker. (ECHS.)

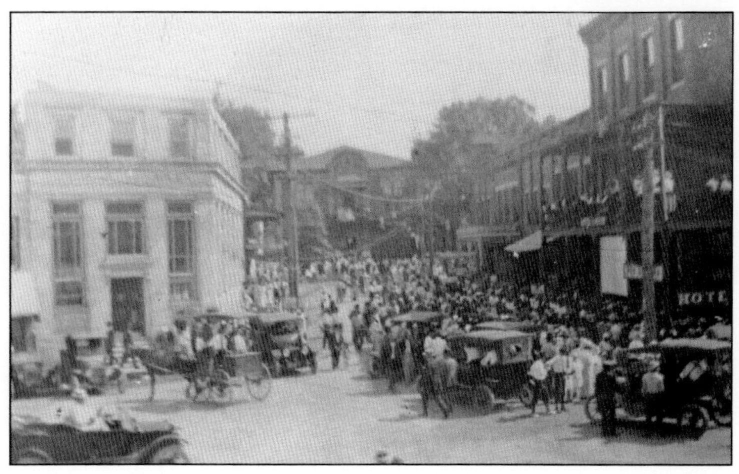

The building pictured was originally constructed as the Bank of Wetumpka in 1901. It was remodeled in 1913. William L. Lancaster was president; J. Michael Jenkins was vice president; Benjamin L. Gaddis was cashier. The bank ceased to function during the Great Depression. (Peggy Blackburn.)

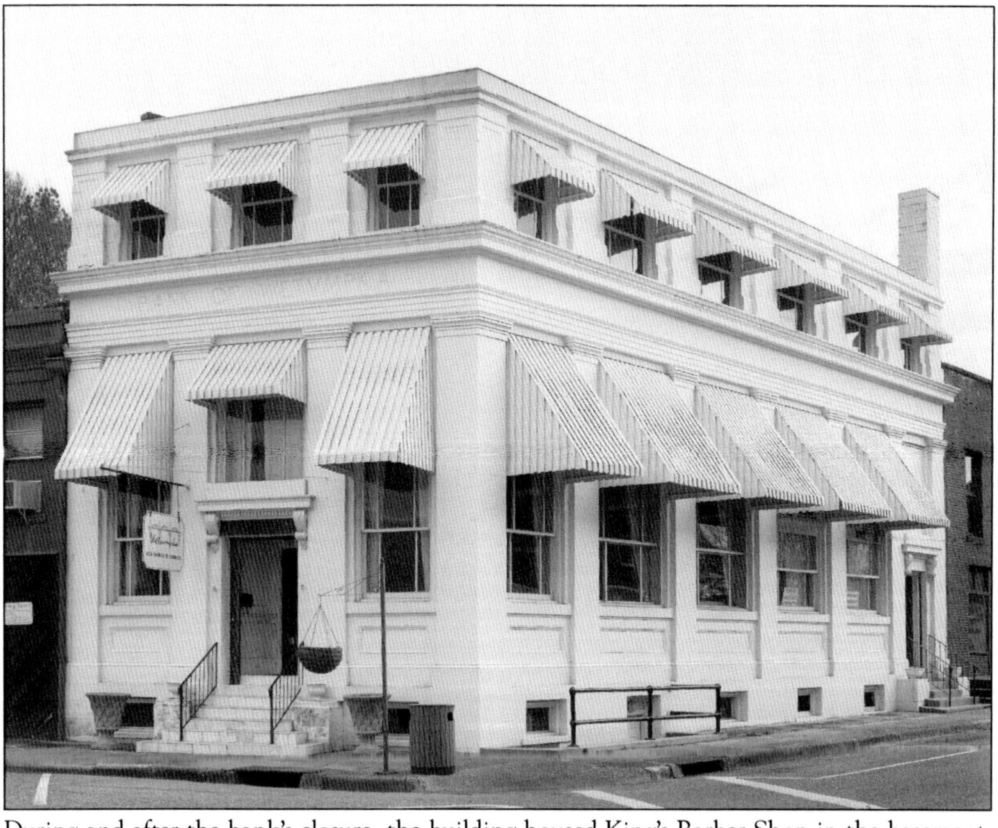

During and after the bank's closure, the building housed King's Barber Shop in the basement, offering 20¢ haircuts in the 1920s. The ground level housed Perkins' Beauty Salon in the late 1930s to the 1940s and J.C. Hayes Jewelry Store in the late 1940s; attorneys-at-law Huddleston, Glover, Macon, Graff, and Jones all maintained offices on the upper floor for several years. The Tasty Grill was in business until the late 1970s. River Bank Restaurant and Alternatives Drug Prevention and Treatment followed from the 1980s until June 1995, when the Wetumpka Area Chamber of Commerce purchased the building. (Barry Chrietzberg.)

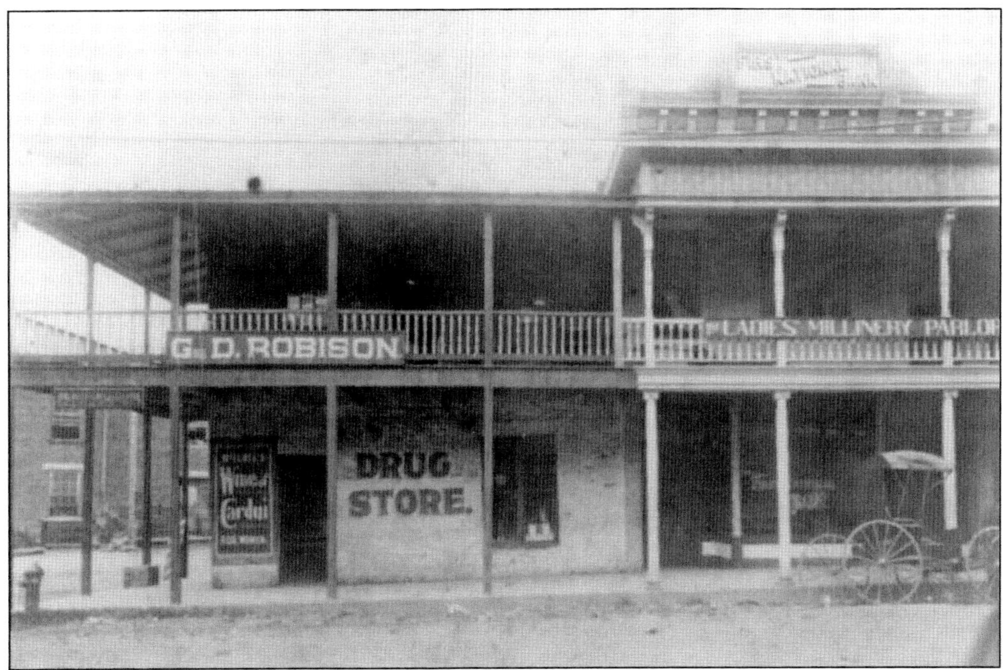


The First National Bank opened its doors on March 21, 1905. The following officers were elected: Morris Hohenberg (president), Adolphe Hohenberg (vice president), Frank W. Lull (vice president), and C.G. McMorris (cashier). The first loan was made to W.Y. Williams on the day the bank opened. In 1908, a disastrous fire occurred. The First National Bank, George D. Robison's Drug Store, Peake's Barber Shop—all on the lower floor of the building—and Miss Mollie Doster's Millinery Parlor and the Central Telephone Station on the second floor were all almost irreparably damaged. Downtown areas of Wetumpka had previously suffered fires in 1845, 1852, and 1902. (Peggy Blackburn.)

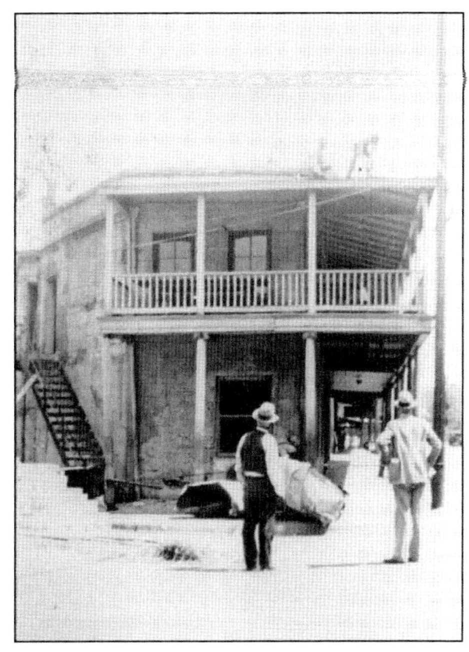

This two-story triangular brick bank and office building was characterized by the First National Bank clock mounted on the corner. It is constructed of tan brick with decorative masonry banding at the cornice line and urn finials on top of the corners, plus metal sash windows. Hohenberg and Company purchased this corner in 1891 and opened the First National Bank here in 1905. The building was either remodeled or rebuilt around 1910. W.L. Stowe is the man standing at left; an unidentified gentleman stands at right. (Peggy Blackburn.)

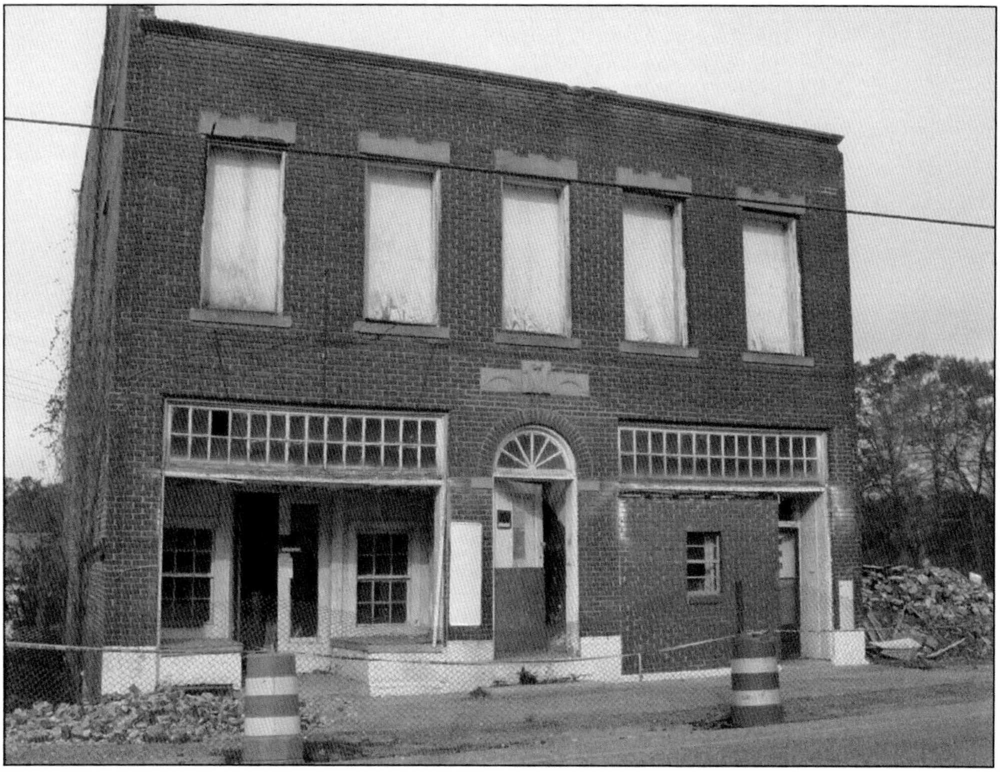

The Love and Do Well Society was a benevolent society in the black community. Isom Rose was the primary force in the organization. He built this three-story structure to house his funeral home business and to serve as a headquarters for the organization. Charles K. McMorris had a funeral parlor as early as 1866 for the white residents. (Peggy Blackburn.)

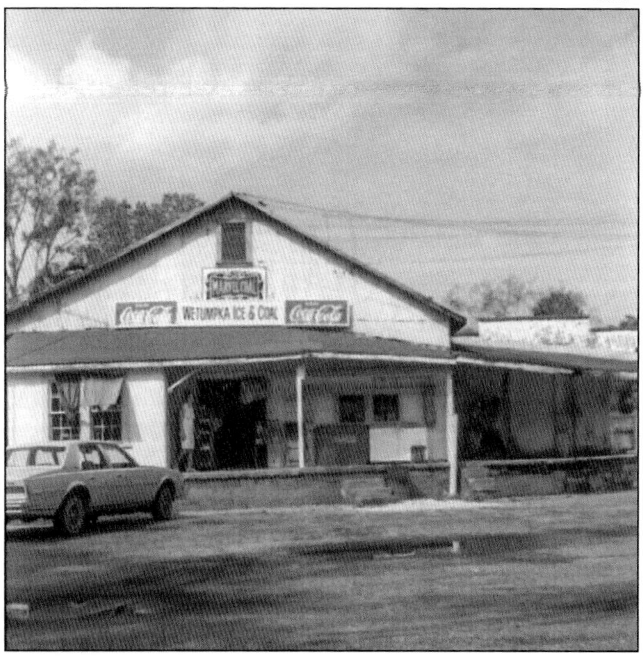


J.Z. Wade of Clanton organized an ice manufacturing company in Wetumpka in 1925. The company made 25 tons of ice every 24 hours. The business was later sold to Clyde J. Moore and became the Wetumpka Ice and Coal Company. (ECHS.)

# *Three*

# The Coosa River

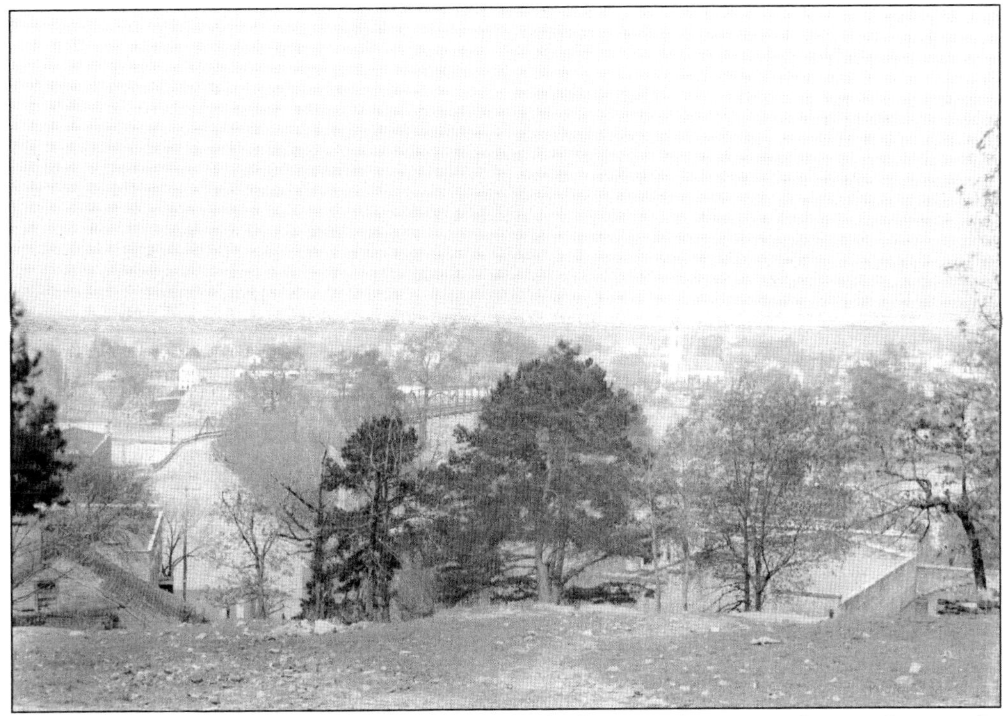

Although referenced in *History of Wetumpka* by Elizabeth Porter, there are no known photographs of bridges built in 1830 and also in 1834. In this view looking from Prospect Hill, there have been at least five bridges across the Coosa River in the same general location. The Wetumpka Toll Bridge Company was formed January 17, 1834, on the same day that East Wetumpka was incorporated as a town. This bridge was much shorter than later bridges because the riverbanks had not receded as much at that time. (Peggy Blackburn.)

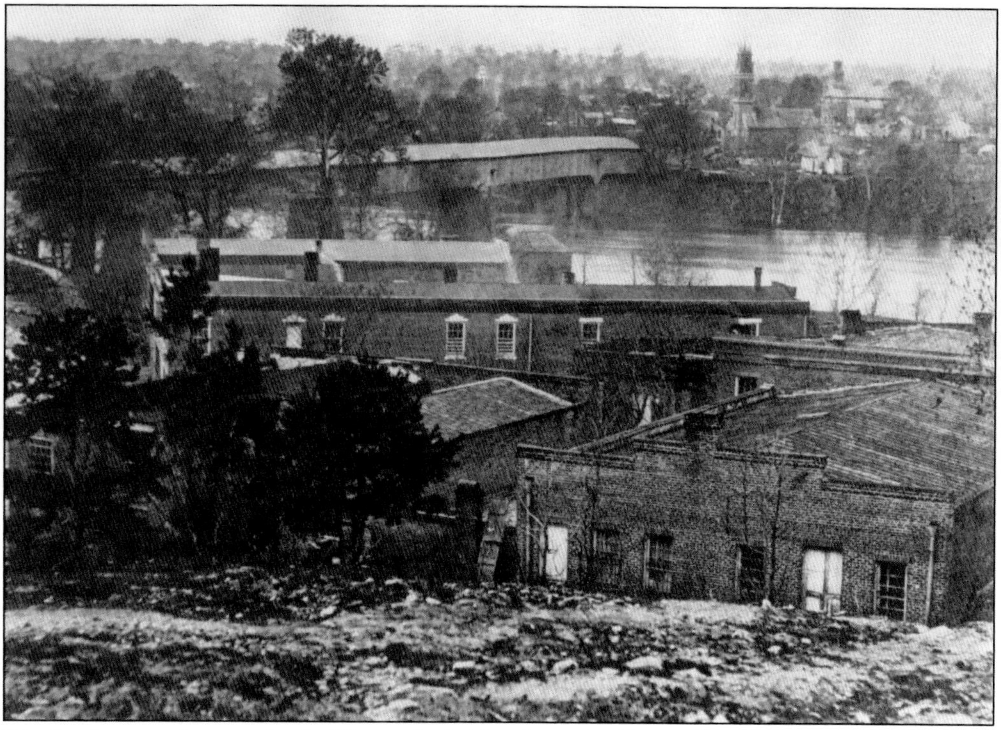

The first known photograph of a Wetumpka bridge shows the Covered Bridge of 1844. The building contract was awarded to John Godwin from Columbus, Georgia, but the actual construction of the bridge was under the direction of Horace King, a slave of Godwin's. King was a builder and engineer of extraordinary skill. Though he was born a slave, his character traits won him the respect of all who knew him. He was emancipated and was in great demand for bridge-building by Confederate forces during the Civil War. The Covered Bridge was carried away by the great flood of March 1886. (Peggy Blackburn.)

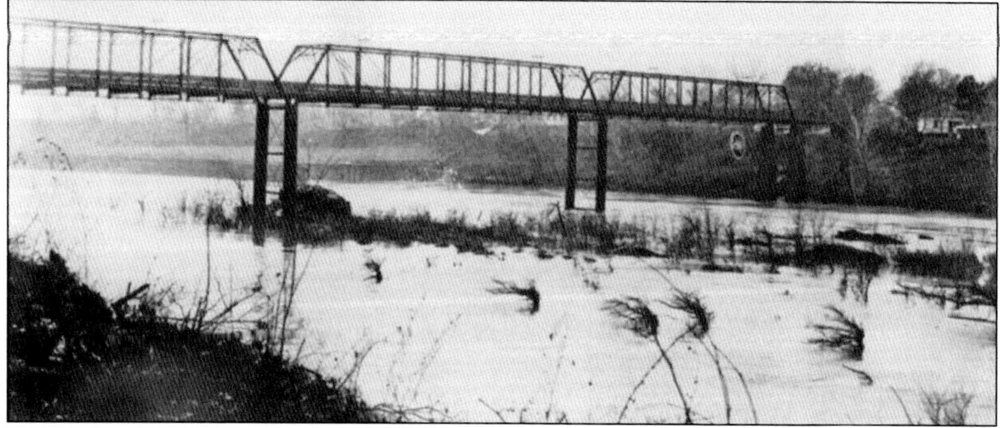

Five bridges have been constructed across the Coosa River in Wetumpka; this one was built in 1887 and was known as the Iron Bridge. There was no bridge from April 1886 until October 1887, so people used a ferry. This Iron Bridge was built by Southern Bridge Company of Birmingham. It was a difficult construction year with several floods that caused collapses of the span. This bridge was completed in late 1887 and connected east and west Wetumpka for 40 years until the building of the Bibb Graves Bridge. (Peggy Blackburn.)

In 1927, research determined it to be more expedient to build a new bridge than to repair the Iron Bridge. The picturesque Bibb Graves Bridge, named after Alabama governor Bibb Graves, was completed in 1931. The bridge, which spans the Coosa River, was designed by Edward Houk, a native of Denmark. As shown in this aerial view, this bridge, with its graceful arches, has become the subject of more photographers and painters than anything else in Wetumpka. (Peggy Blackburn.)

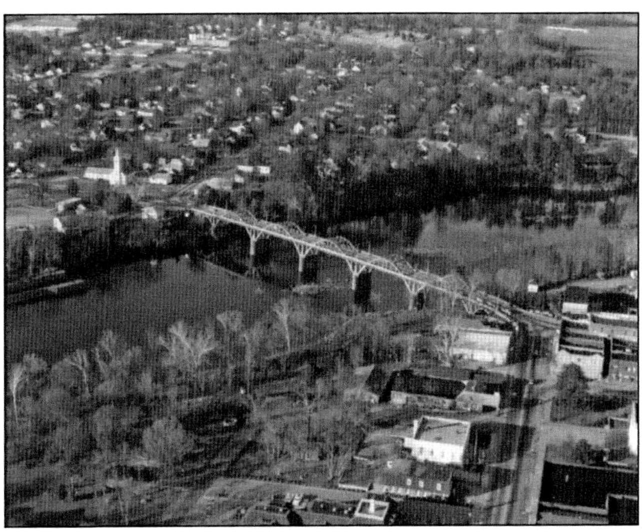

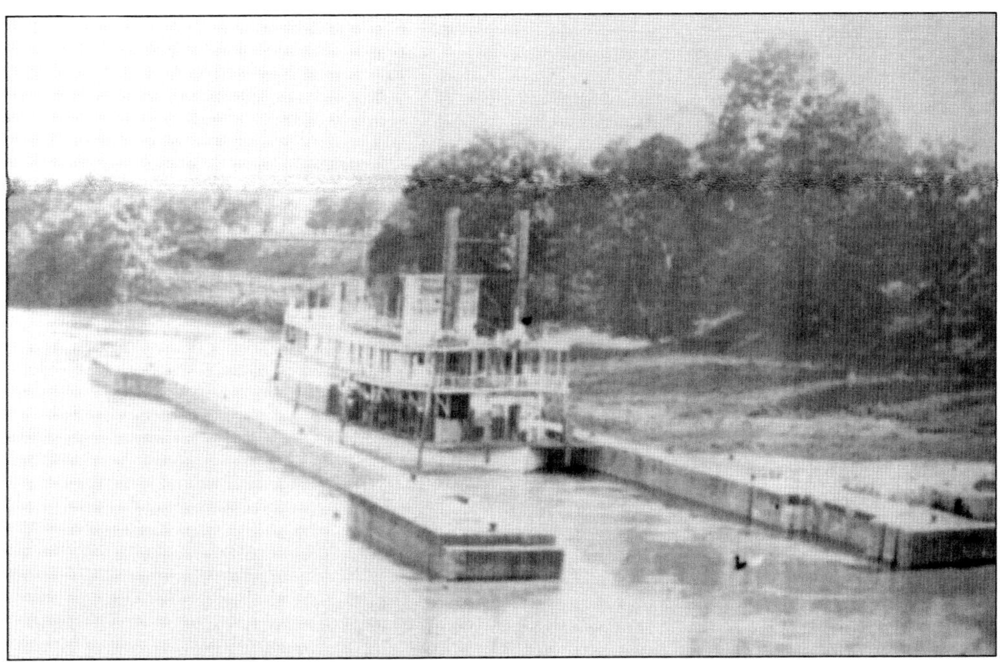

Because of Wetumpka's location as head of navigation of the Alabama River, its antebellum days saw heavy steamboat traffic on the Coosa River. This steamboat is waiting in the lock. After the emergence of the railroad, river traffic slowed to a trickle. (ECHS.)

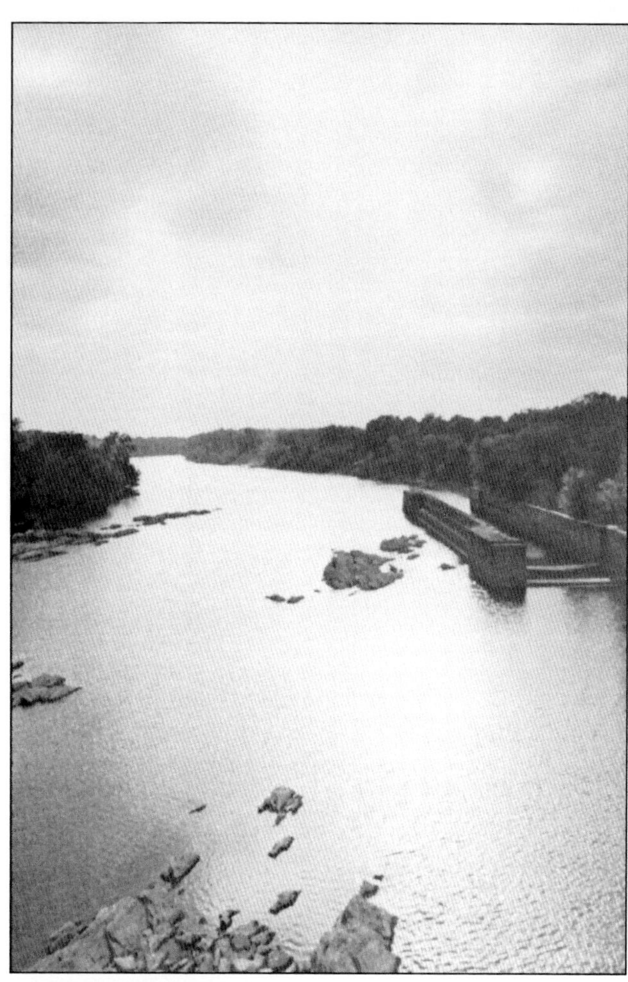

Lock No. 31 stands as a testament to the impact of the advent of the railroad. Completed in June 1896, the lock was to have been one of a system of 31 locks and dams meant to further the development of the Coosa and Alabama Rivers, making them navigable from Wetumpka to Mobile. The project, undertaken by the US Army Corps of Engineers, was estimated to have a total cost of $6.07 million in 1897. Today, the lock is something of a curiosity and is a visual gauge of the height of water rushing down the Coosa. (Peggy Blackburn.)

Bales of cotton stand ready in downtown Wetumpka for shipment downriver to market. (Peggy Blackburn.)

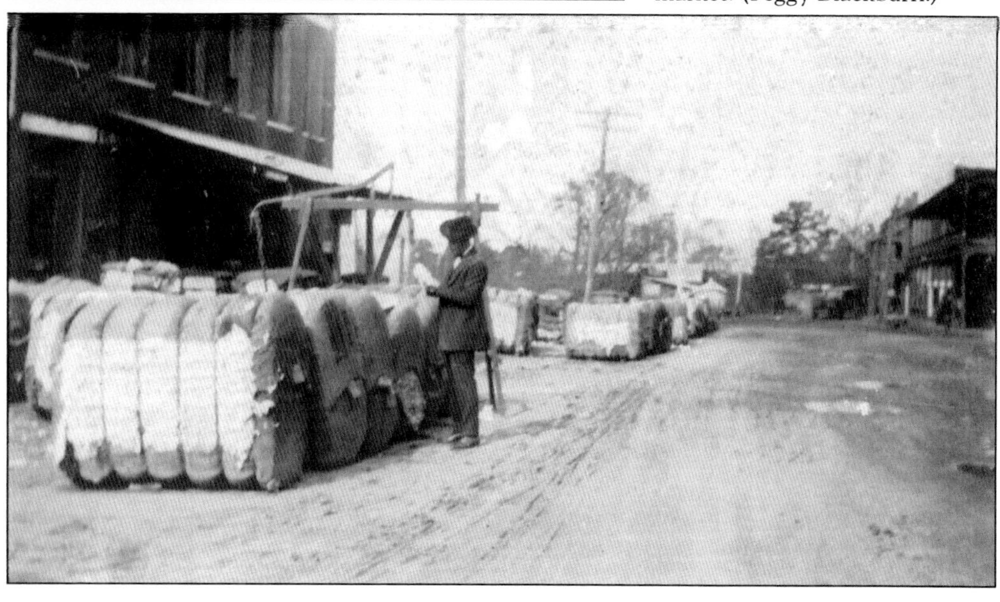

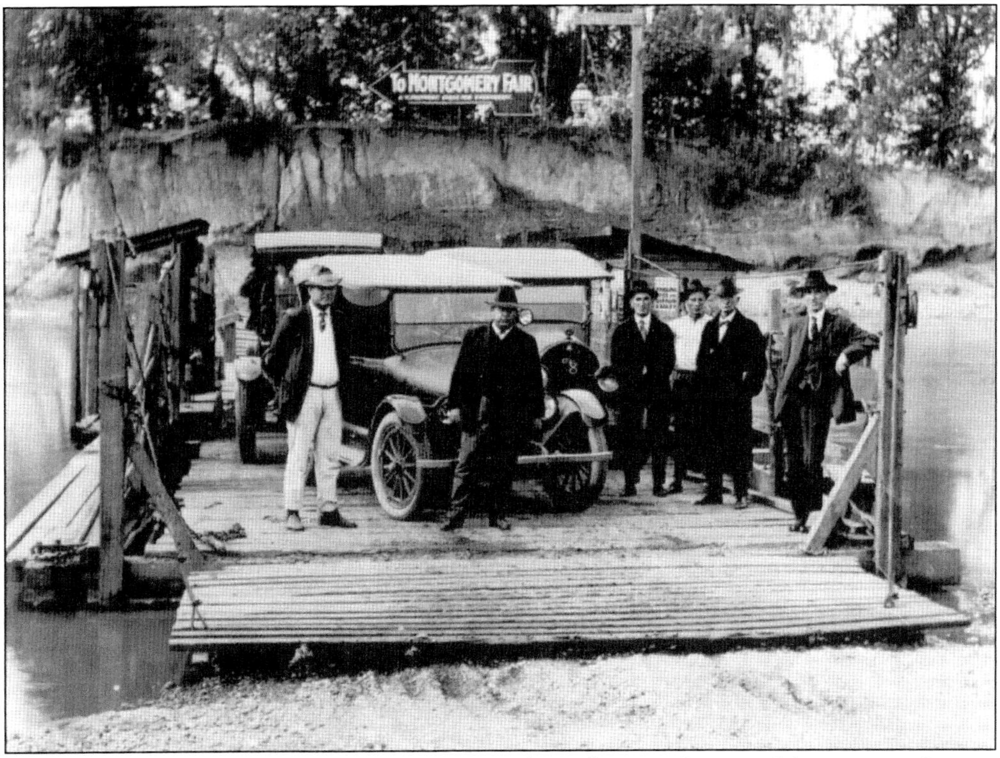

Hughes Ferry was one of several ferries crossing the Tallapoosa River to Montgomery County before the William Lowndes Yancey Bridge was constructed on US Highway 231. Note the sign near the top of the photograph: "To Montgomery Fair." (Peggy Blackburn.)

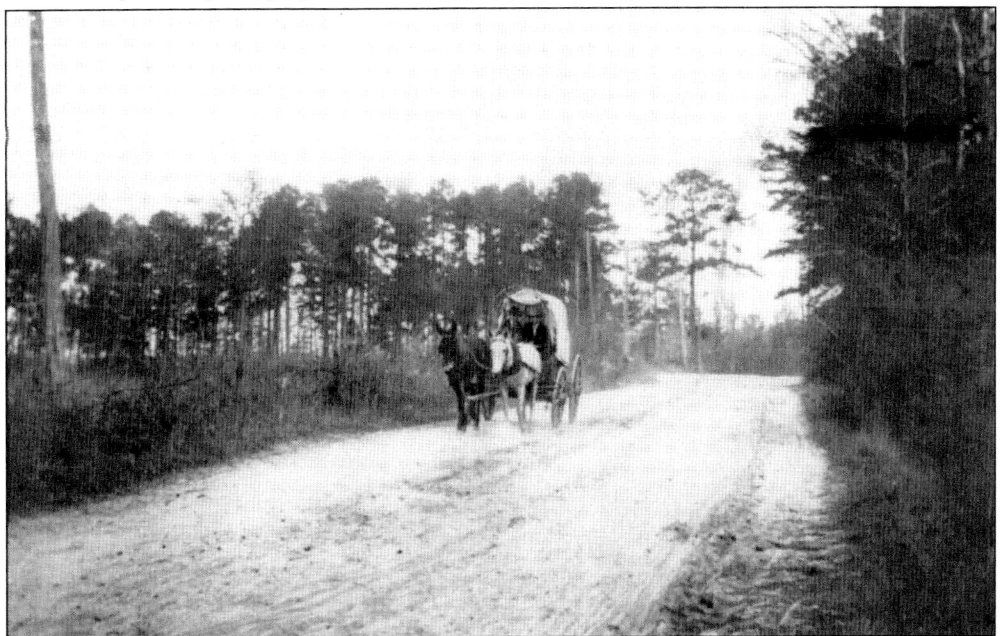

The covered wagon was a common and familiar form of transportation in and around Wetumpka before the start of the 20th century. (ECHS.)

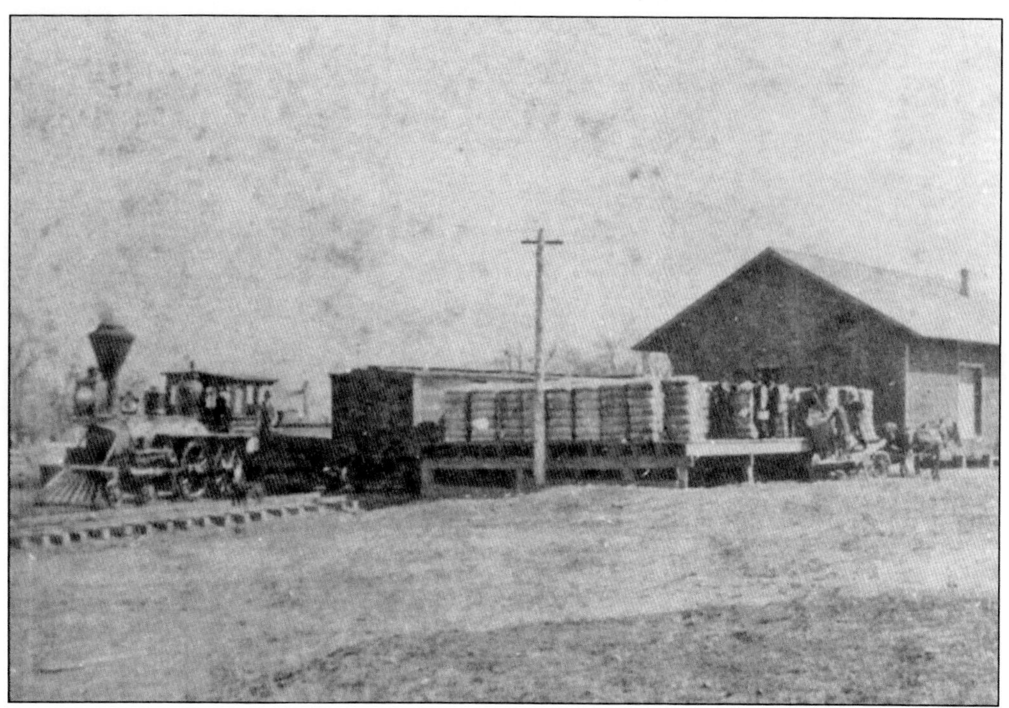

There was no railroad line into Wetumpka until 1878, when a seven-mile track connected it to the Louisville & Nashville Railroad (L&N) at Elmore. Here, cotton is being loaded around 1879–1880. In 1906, the L&N replaced this structure with a new building. (ECHS.)

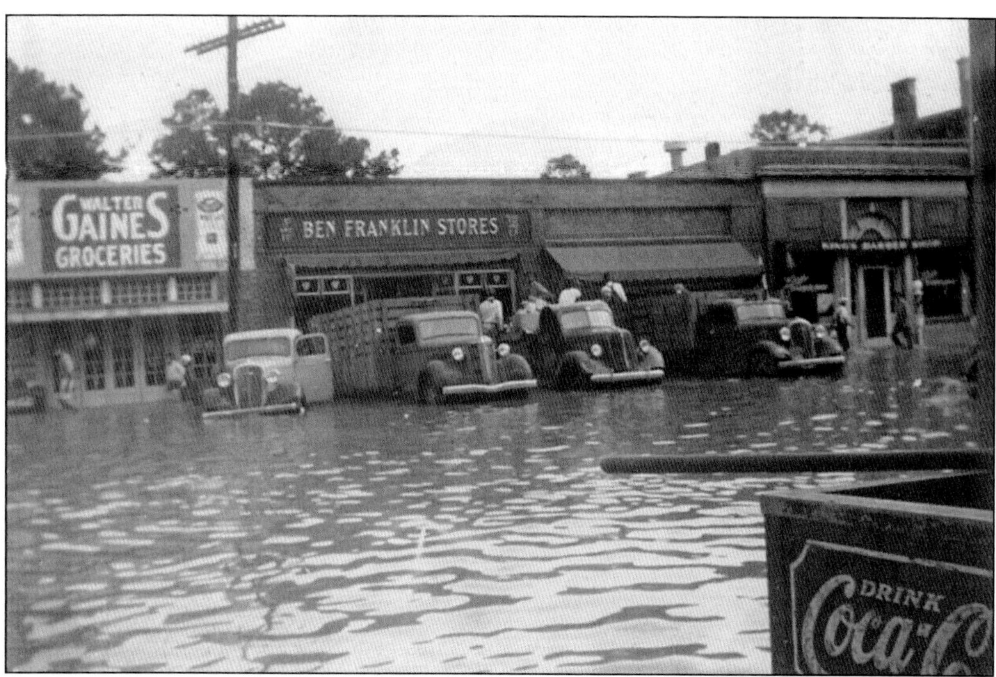


This photograph of a flood in April 1938 shows the level of water that rushed into the businesses along East Bridge Street and demonstrates the efforts to salvage everything possible. (ECHS.)

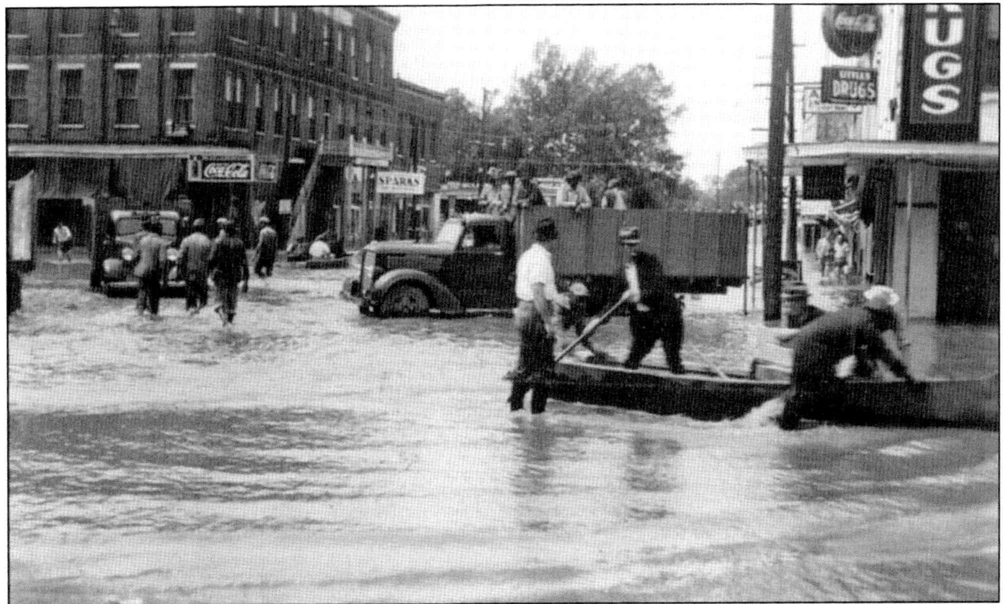


Although the city has seen a number of floods—with those of 1886, 1919, 1938, and 1961 being notable—the most disastrous flood Wetumpka has had since 1886 occurred in April 1938. After heavy rains for several days, the river rapidly rose and crested at 54 feet; flood stage at Wetumpka was 45 feet. Men traveled the downtown streets in rowboats, goods were moved from stores, and residents in low-lying areas had to be evacuated. Property loss throughout the city was estimated to be $100,000. (Peggy Blackburn.)

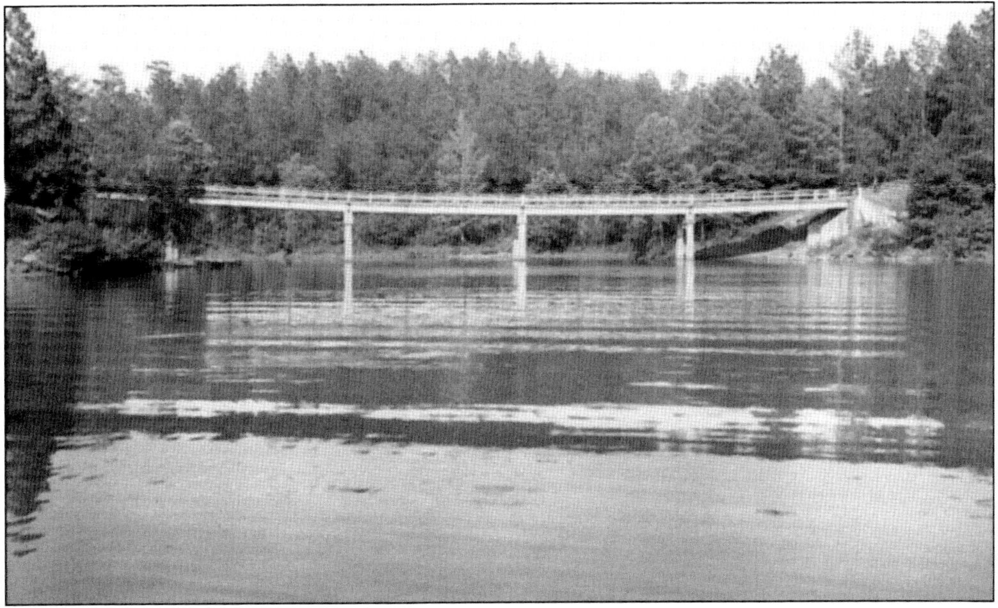

Probably the only "swayback bridge" in Alabama spans Sofkahatchee Creek, which flows into Lake Jordan. In building Lake Jordan, the Alabama Power Company backed up water that covered three wooden bridges. As compensation for that bridge destruction, the company agreed to provide enough money to build an ordinary bridge, but it was constructed a little lower and more narrow, which caused its "swayback" appearance. (Peggy Blackburn.)

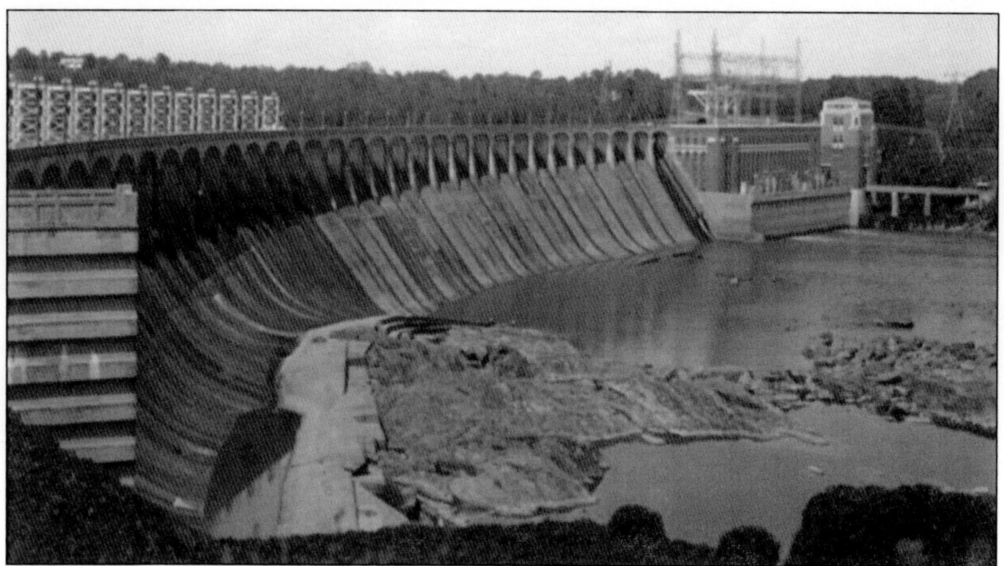

Alabama Power Company has 14 hydroelectric plants in the state. Of these 14 plants, five are located totally or partially in Elmore County. The facility nearest to Wetumpka is Jordan Dam. Work began on Jordan Dam on June 15, 1926. It was dedicated on August 4, 1927, midway through its construction. The plant was put into service on January 1, 1929, and, at that time, was the largest power project undertaken by private capital in the South. The resulting lake spans 6,800 acres and has 118 miles of shoreline. (Peggy Blackburn.)

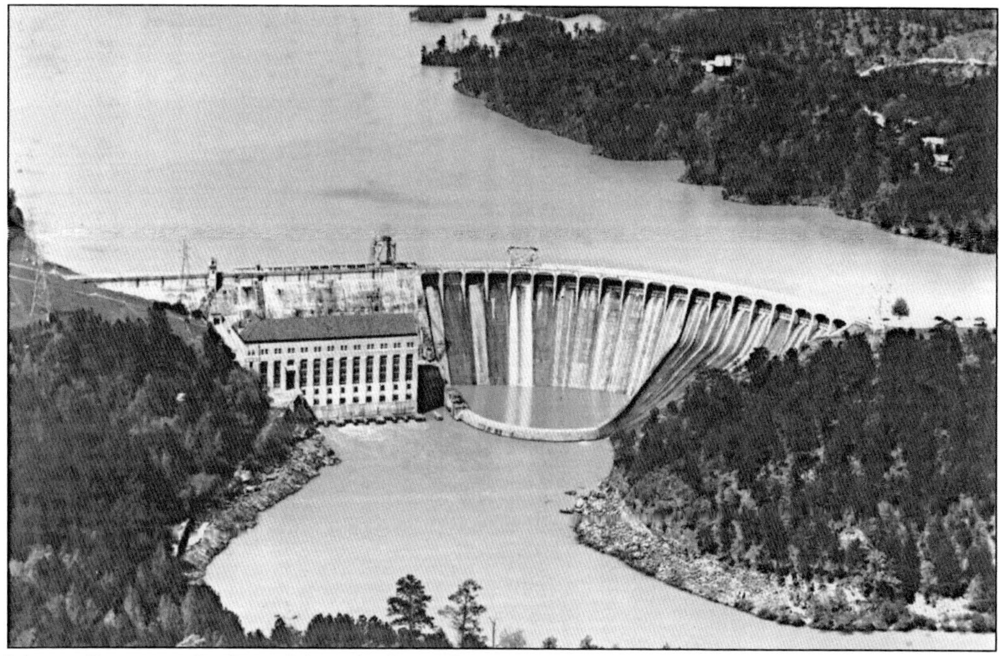

Martin Dam was the first of three built in Elmore County on the Tallapoosa River. The purpose of the dams was to harness the state's water resources for hydroelectric power, flood control, and improved navigation. Requiring 431,000 cubic yards of concrete, construction occurred between 1923 and 1925. The dam stands 168 feet high and is 2,000 feet long. The resulting lake impounds 40,000 acres and has a 700-mile shoreline. (Peggy Blackburn.)

# Four

# Education in Wetumpka

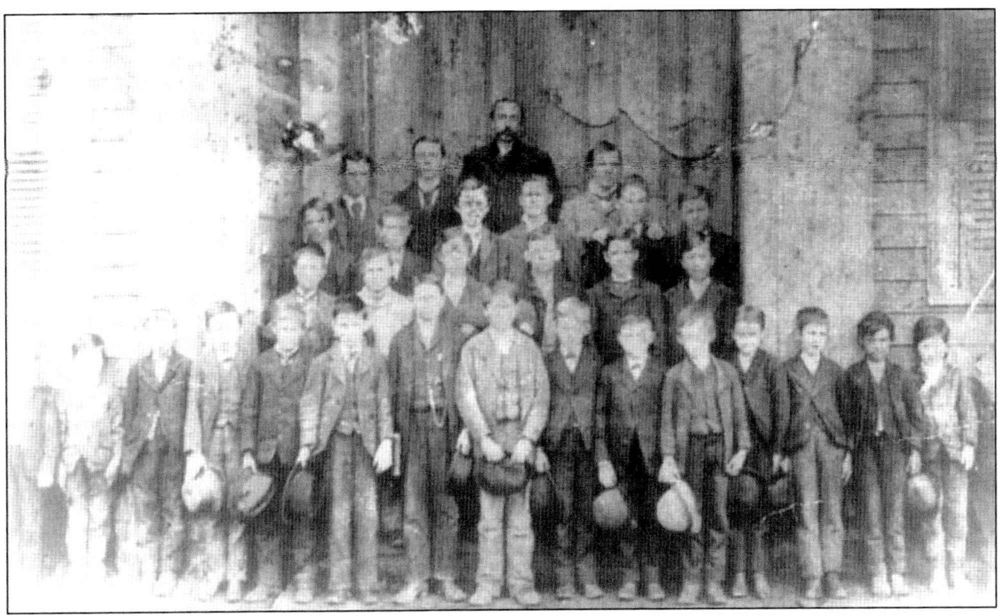

In the days before public education, there were several private schools, some smaller than others. Harriet Johnson kept a small school for beginners in another location. In 1879, Prof. M.B. Dubose was principal of this boys' school located one block north of the river bridge in West Wetumpka. The professor is standing at top center in this image. (ECHS.)

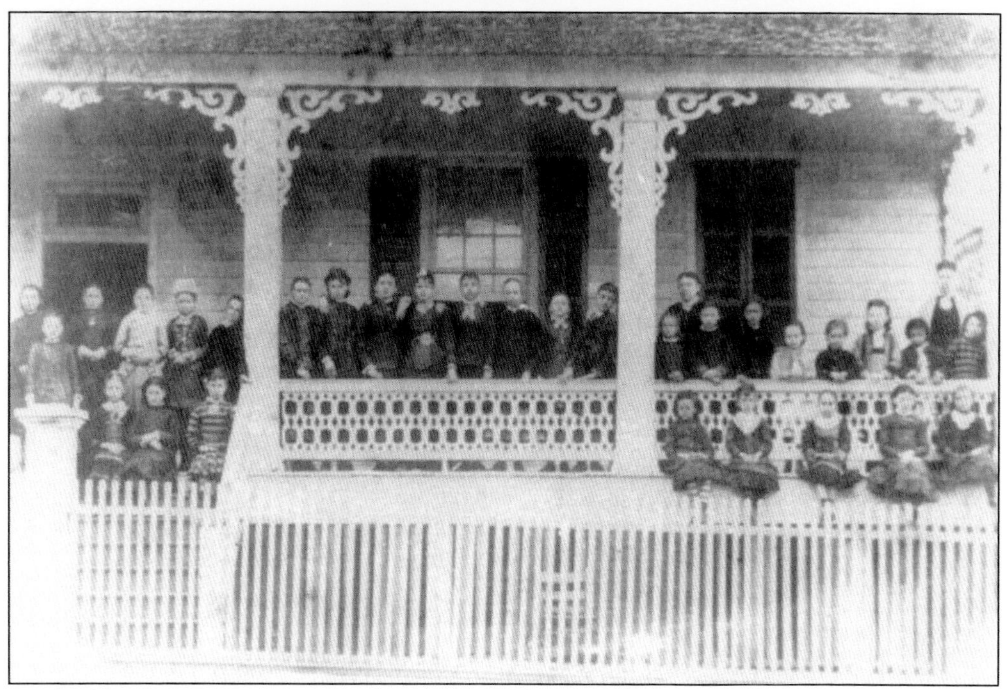

Pupils of the Masonic Female Institute are pictured here around 1880 with teacher Janie McQueen. This photograph was taken on the front gallery of the home of George F. Sedberry. The Masonic Female Institute was to the right of this house. The names are recorded as follows on the back of the picture: "First panel at top of steps: Ledella Kidd; Eleanor Hagerty; Mae Due; Leila McWilliams; Susie Lull. Second row standing: Bessie Samuel; Sitting: Mary Battes; Mamie Smith; Ida Miller. Second panel: Allie Samuel, Flossie Logan; Laura Cain; Fannie Kidd; Emmie Due; Nellie Lull; Lola Cain; Maggie McRae. Third Panel: Miss Janie McQueen, Teacher, Standing at back of pupils: Emma Samuels; Nora Lee McMorris; Mary Lee Taul; Venie McDonald; Tippie Taul; Carrie Sedberry; Myrtle Kidd; Hattie Miller; Mrs. G. F. Sedberry. Standing at back: Sitting outside of baluster: Louisa Thomas; Mary Sedberry; Sallie Seaman; Allie Taylor; Flora Cantelou." (ECHS.)

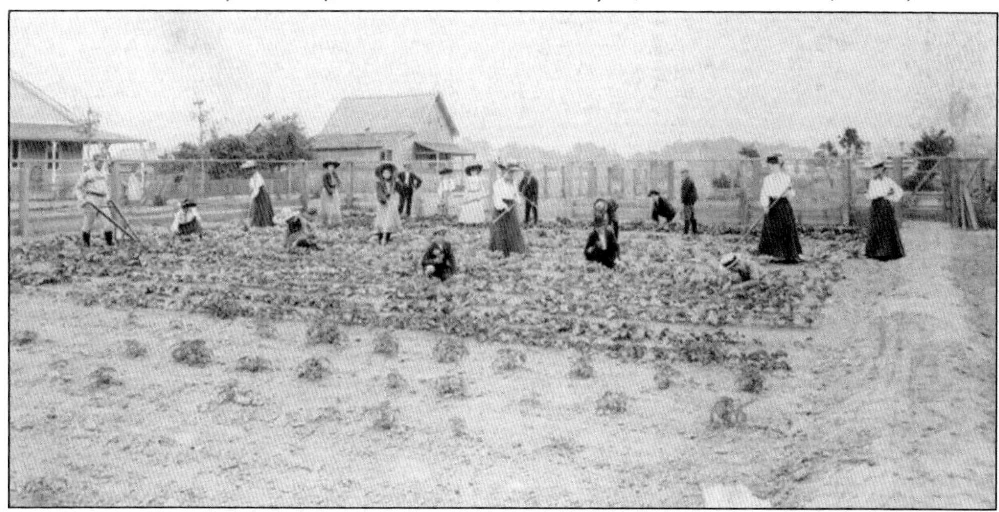

Students work in the vegetable garden on the grounds of the Fifth District Agricultural School. (Peggy Blackburn.)

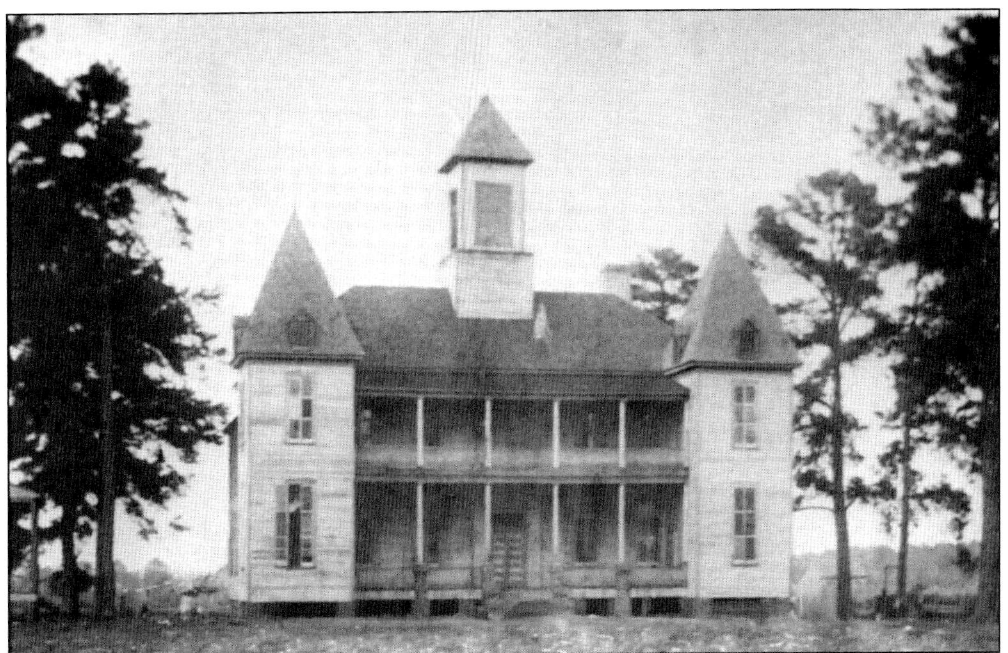

The Fifth District Agricultural School's first building was a two-story frame structure erected in 1897 and destroyed by fire on January 5, 1906. (Peggy Blackburn.)

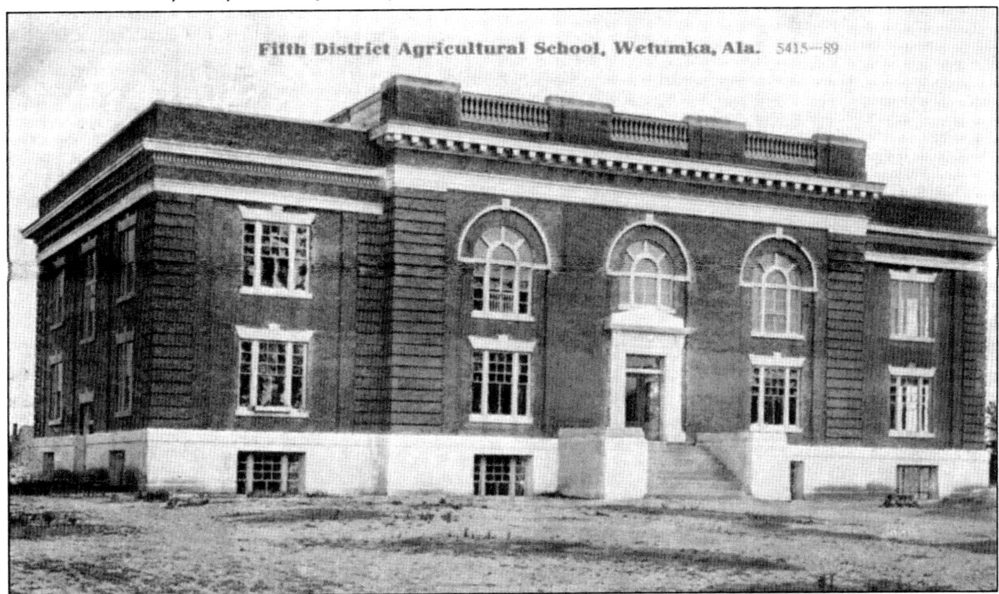


The Fifth District Agricultural School's second building—the three-story brick structure pictured here around 1917—was constructed in 1906, and the class of 1907 was the first to graduate from here. The beautiful auditorium on the third floor had a seating capacity of 1,000. The building also housed classrooms and a large library, an art studio, a music room, an expression room, science laboratories, the president's office, and a gymnasium (in the basement). The entire building was steam-heated, lit by electricity, and well ventilated. The building was surrounded by a campus of about five acres. The last class to graduate from this building was the class of 1938. A new, more modern building was completed in 1939. (Peggy Blackburn.)

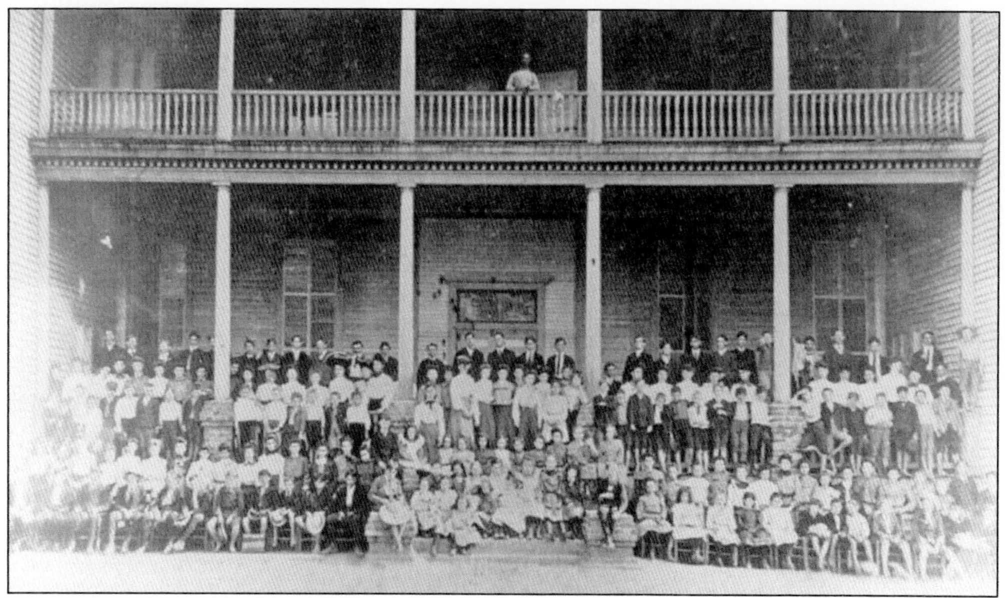

This is the student body of the Fifth District Agricultural School (FDAS). This photograph is dated May 14, 1904, and was in the possession of John Moore. (ECHS.)

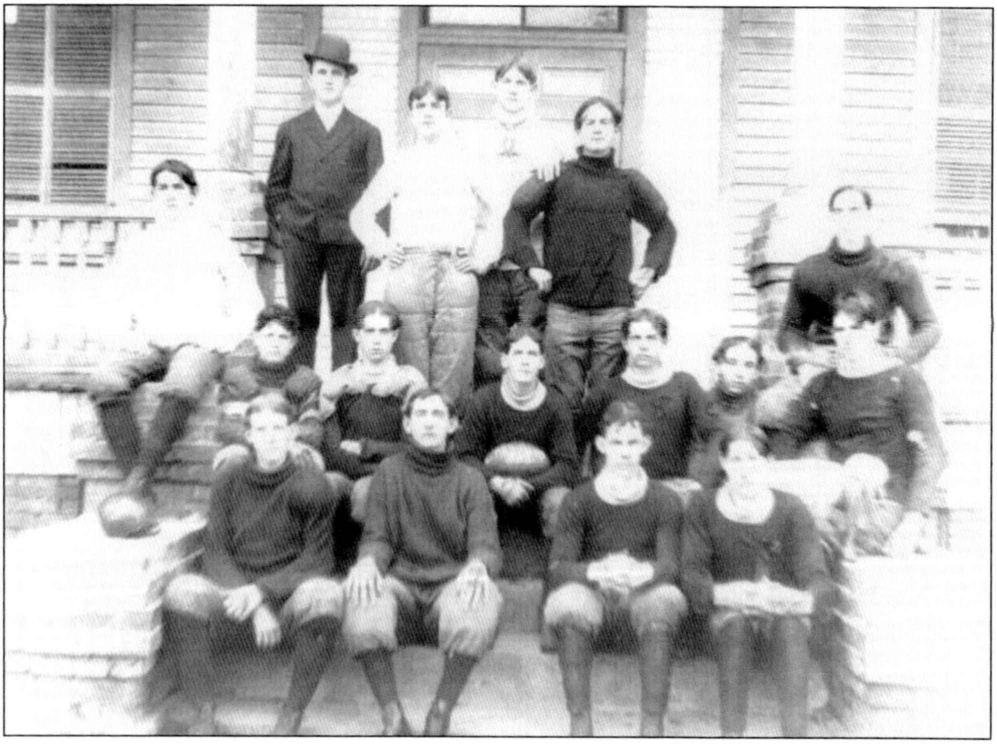

The Fifth District Agricultural School 1905 football team was called the Farmers. Pictured are, from left to right, (first row) Sam Thornhill, Warren Holdbrooks, Charles H. McMorris, and C. O. Pittman; (second row) Peter Temple, Frank Parker, Gordon Robison, Oliver Barker, Claud Ennis, and Briggs Alverson; (third row) Bill Robbins and Graham Thornhill; (standing) Prof. E.E. Tarr, Wetumpka's first football coach, Alva Enzer, Gordon Howle, and Reeves McCullers. (ECHS.)

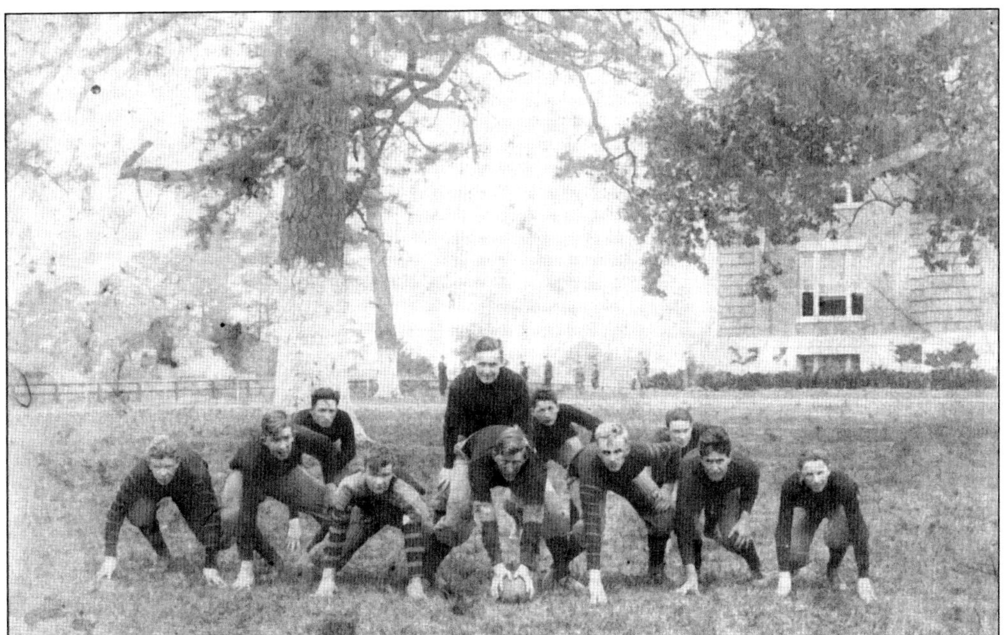

An active football team is pictured in front on the boys' side of the Fifth District Agricultural School campus in 1911. Team includes, in no particular order, Coach ? Peavy, Lawson Speigner, Ehrman Enslen, Ehrman Thornhill, Kyle Holley, Lovick Kimbrough, George Smith, Calvin Weldon, ? Allen, ? Cabinis, and one unidentified player. (John Enslen and ECHS.)

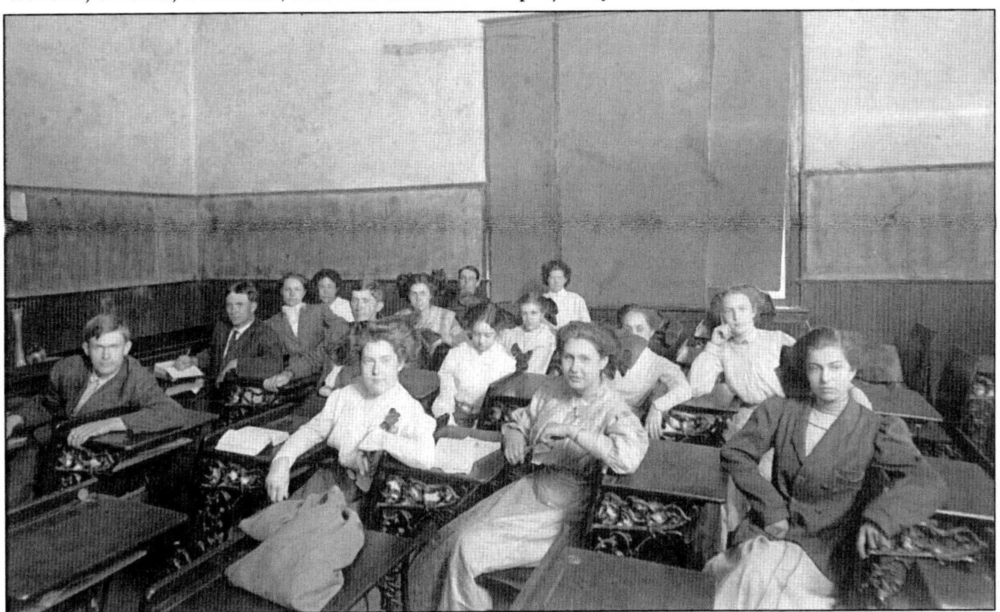

This 1911 image shows a class at Fifth District Agricultural School. Pictured are, from front to back starting from far left, (first row) Clarke Owsley, Grady Lyle, Mary Fannie Sanford, and Bessie Lynn Bilbro; (second row) Oscar Edwards, Lila Mae Britt, and Clarence Ward; (third row) Shell McKee, Eula Cantelou, ? Wallace, and Annie Laurie Cain; (fourth row) Frances Thomas and Genia Gamble; (fifth row) Margaret Enslen and Mary Bateman. The names are recorded in this manner on the back of the photograph. (ECHS.)

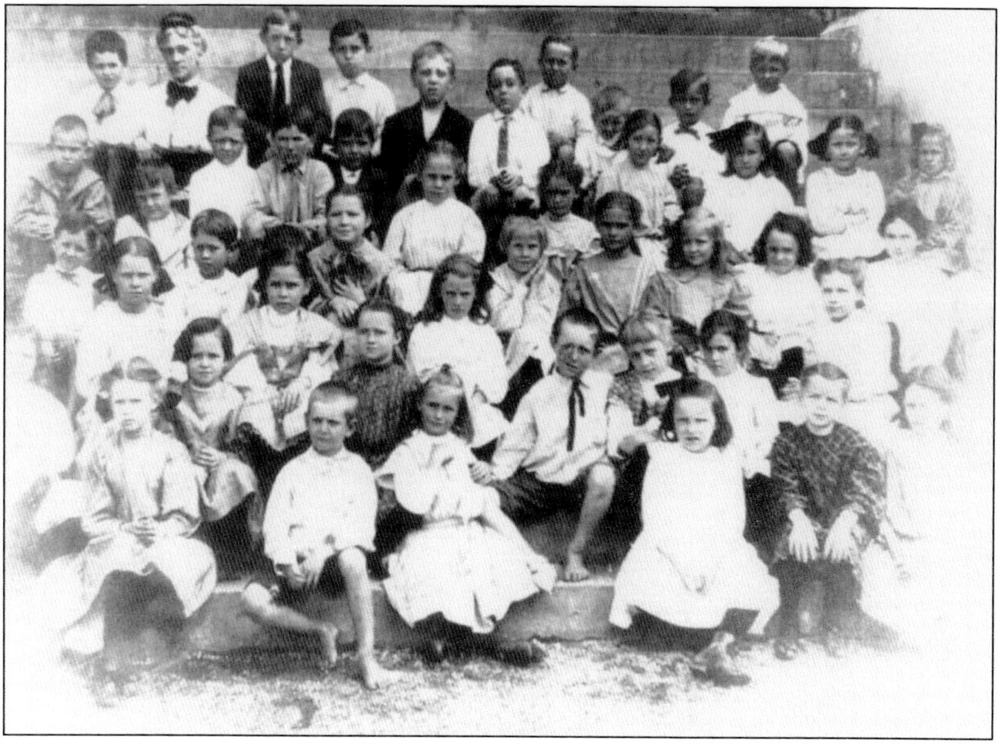

Youngsters in elementary grades of Fifth District Agricultural School are barefoot and sitting on the school steps. (ECHS.)

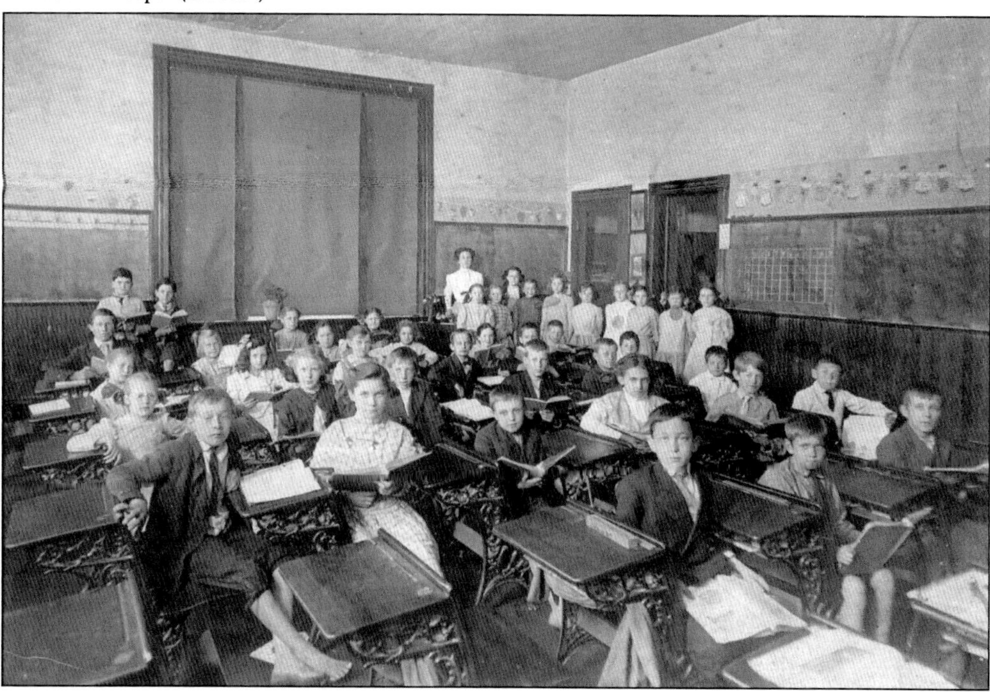

These third and fourth graders are students of Annie Shapard, whose classroom is pictured here on April 13, 1910. (ECHS.)

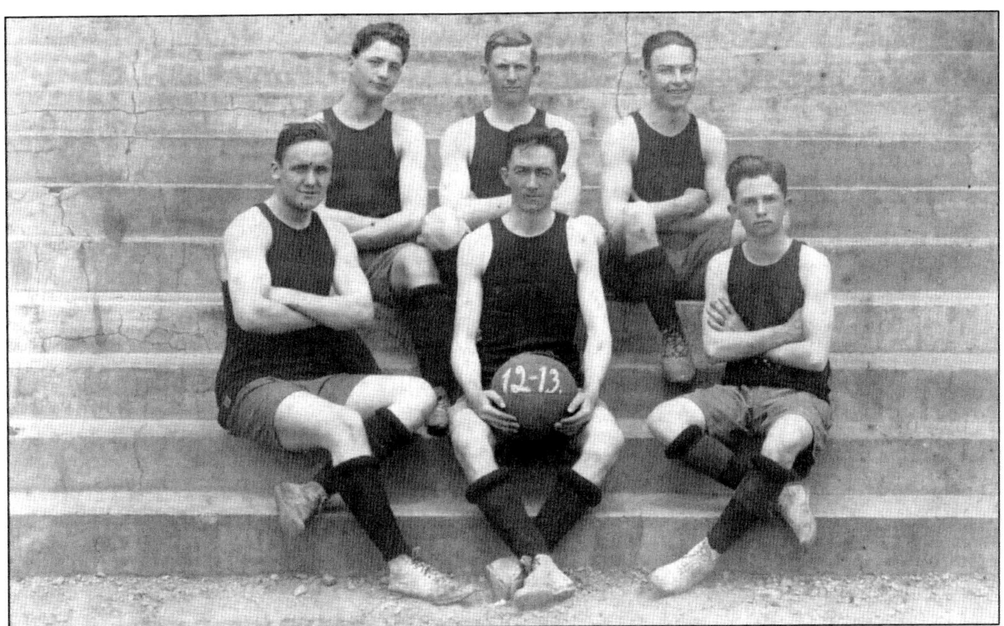


Pictured in a basketball team photograph at Fifth District Agricultural School in 1912–13 are, from left to right, (first row) Coach Ray, Erhman Thornhill, and John Lancaster Gamble; (second row) Goree Johnson, Lovick Kimbrough, and George Bernard Smith. (ECHS.)

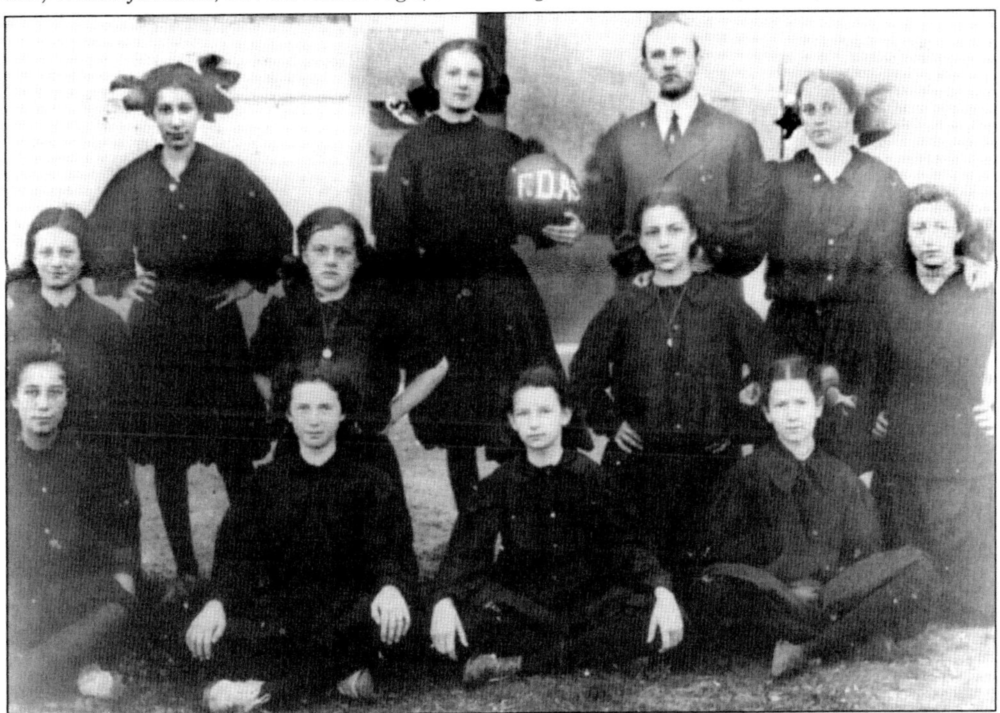


In this image of the 1912 girls' basketball team at Fifth District Agricultural School are, from left to right, (first row) Annie Wall, Thelma Holley, Mason Wall, and Mary Buyck Cain; (second row) Eula Cantelou, Willa Mae Chapman, Annie Chapman, and Pauline Hohenberg; (third row) Bertha Hohenberg, Mary Bateman, Coach E.E. Tarr, and Genia Gamble. (ECHS.)

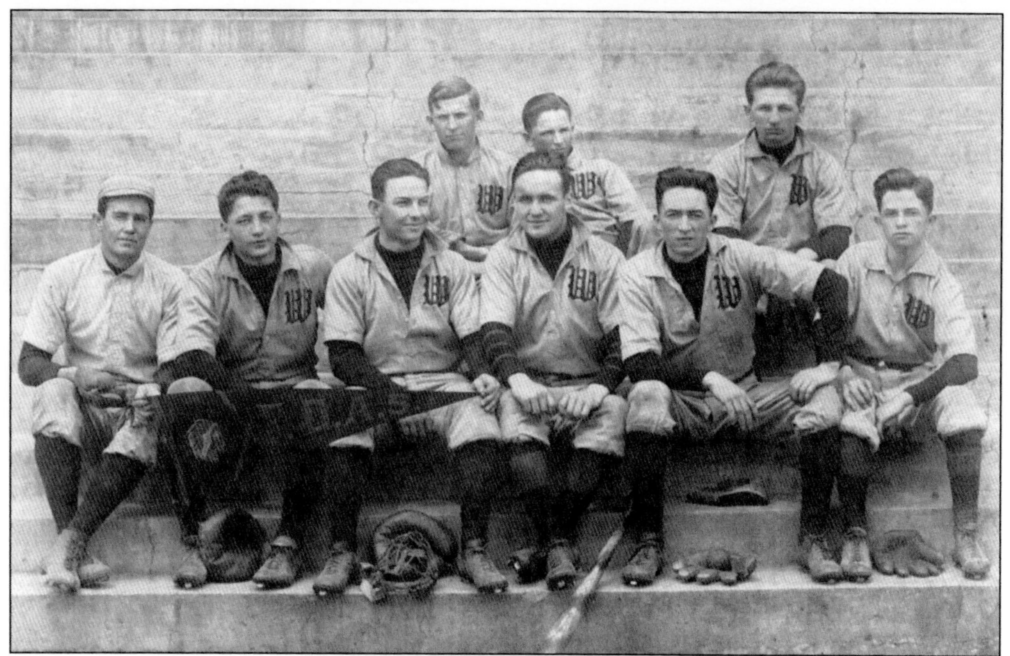

A photograph of the baseball team for the Fifth District Agricultural School includes, from left to right, (first row) Coach ? Peavy, Erhman Thornhill, John Gamble, Lovick Kimbrough, and Calvin Welden, and unidentified; (second row) Herb Chapman, Goree Johnson, and George B. Smith. (ECHS.)

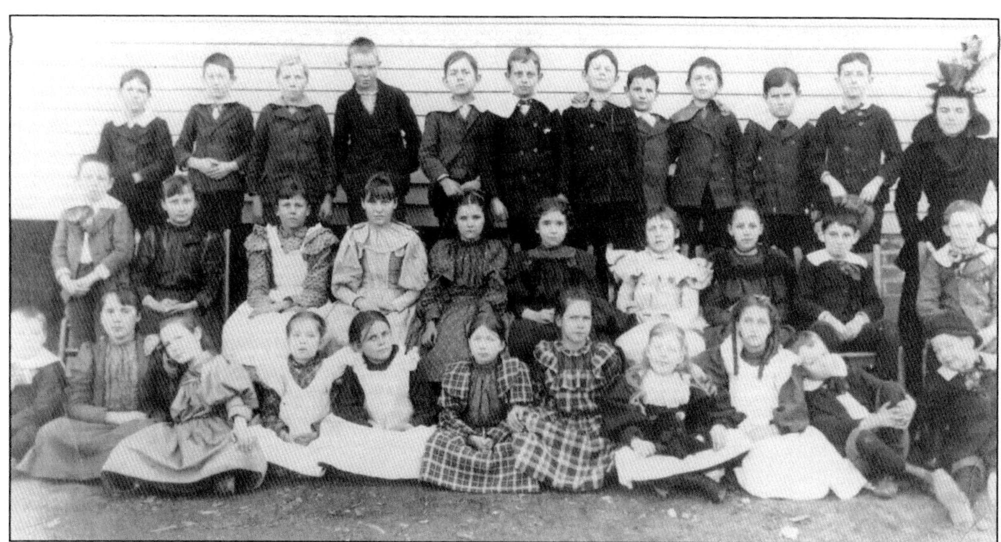

This class pictured includes Kelly Fitzpatrick, Benjamin J. Moon, and an unidentified teacher wearing a very attractive hat. (Ann Moon Lambert.)

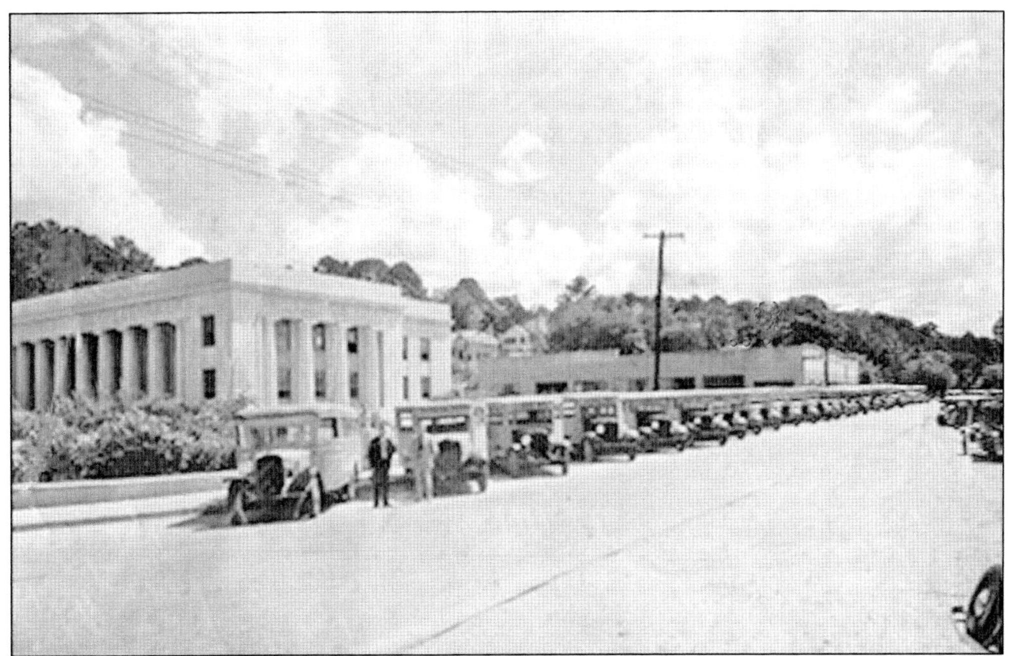

This 1930s photograph of Estes Motor Company shows the Chevrolet dealership. This large number of buses was sold to the Elmore County Board of Education. Lester Estes (dark suit) and his brother Olna Estes (light suit) are pictured. (John Enslen and Peggy Blackburn.)

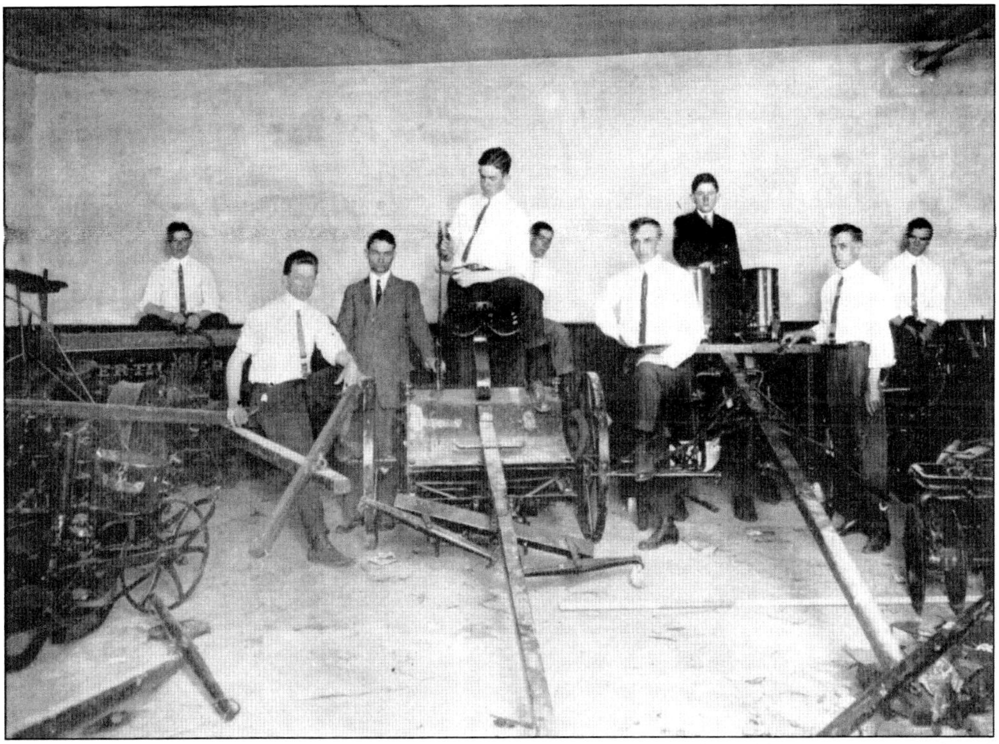

Agricultural students are pictured in class with farm implements at the Fifth District Agricultural School in 1913. (ECHS.)

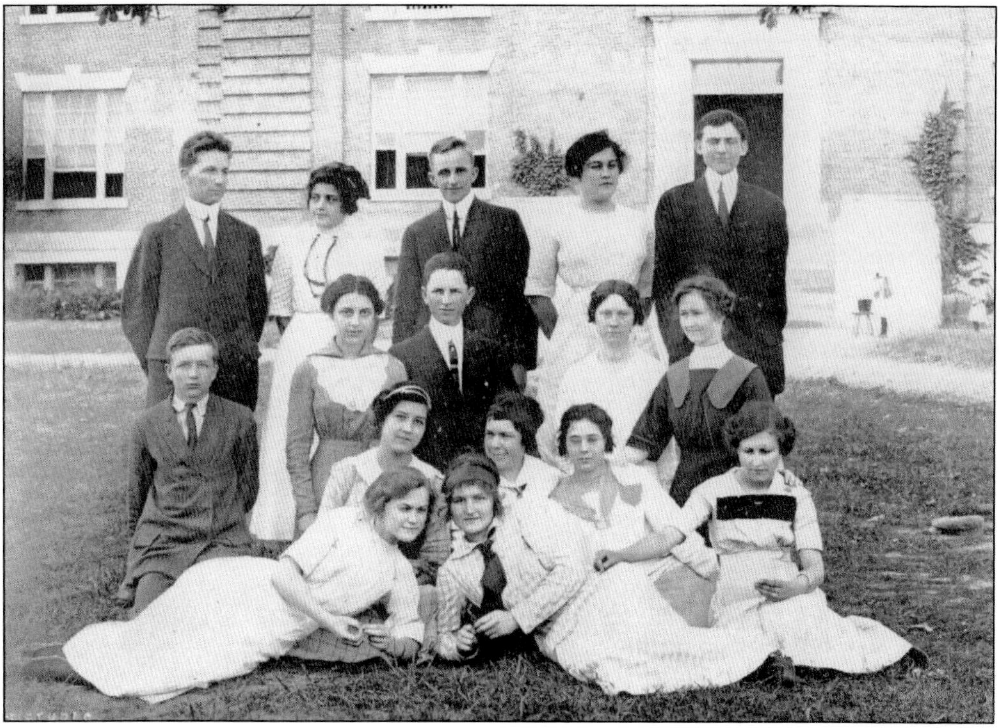

The junior class of 1913 poses outside the Fifth District Agricultural School. (ECHS.)

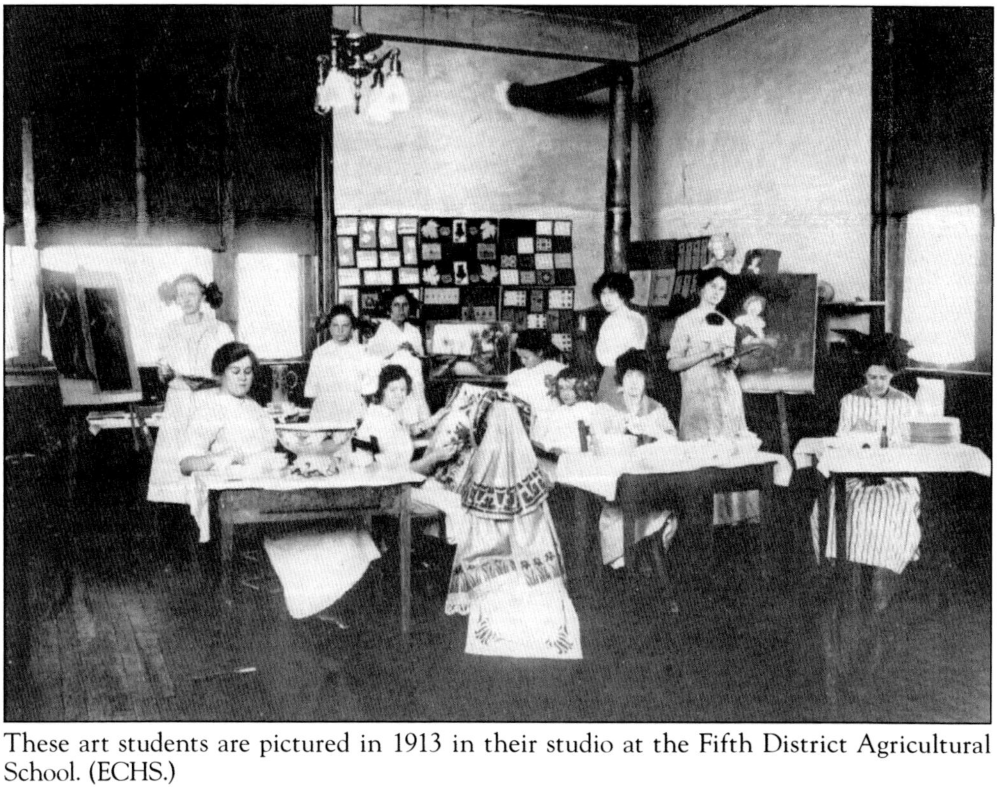

These art students are pictured in 1913 in their studio at the Fifth District Agricultural School. (ECHS.)

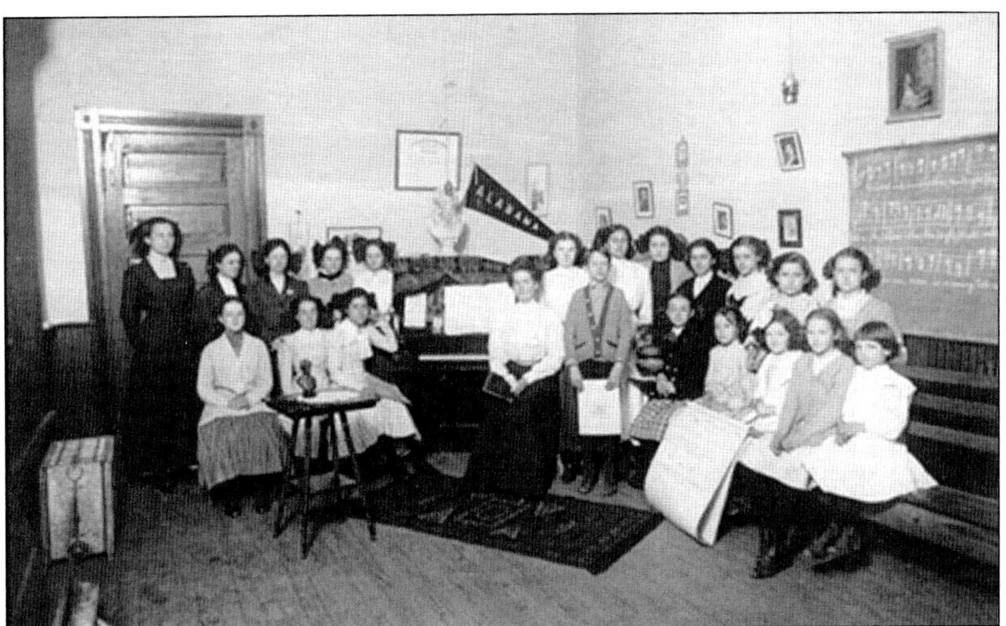

Students of a Miss Allen are pictured in the Fifth District Agricultural School music department in 1910. (Trisha Holloway and Peggy Blackburn.)

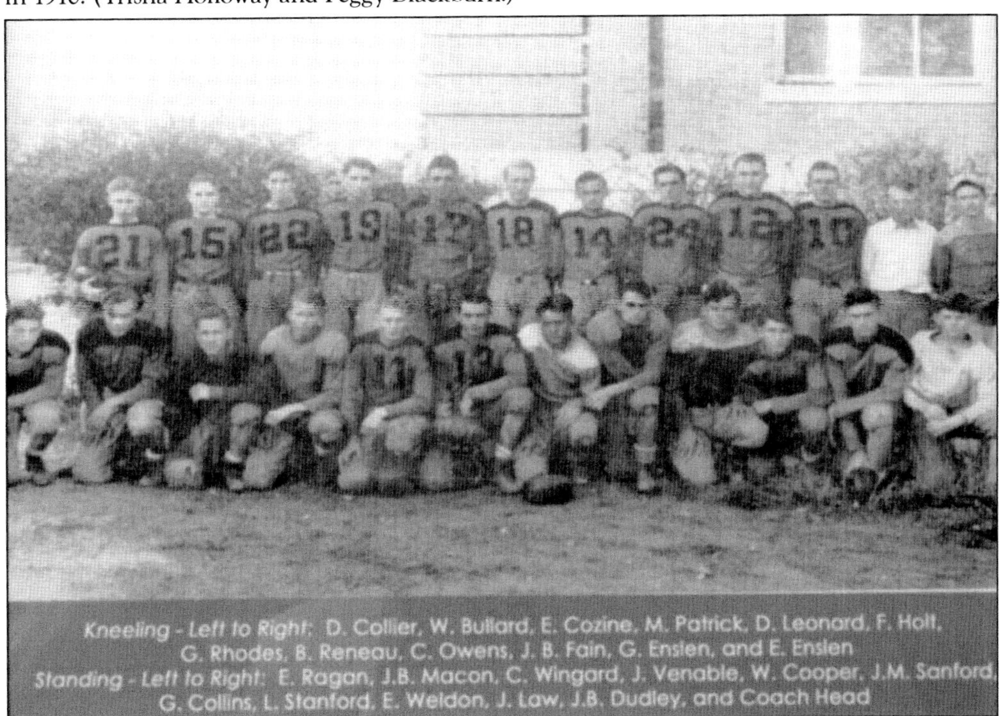


This image shows the 1939 Wetumpka High School football team. Pictured are, from left to right, (first row) D. Collier, W. Bullard, E. Cozine, M. Patrick, D. Leonard, F. Holt, G. Rhodes, B. Reneau, C. Owens, J.B. Fain, G. Enslen, and E. Enslen; (second row) E. Ragan, J.B. Macon, C. Wingard, J. Venable, W. Cooper, J.M. Sanford, G. Collins, L. Stanford, E. Weldon, J. Law, J. B. Dudley, and Coach Head. (ECHS.)

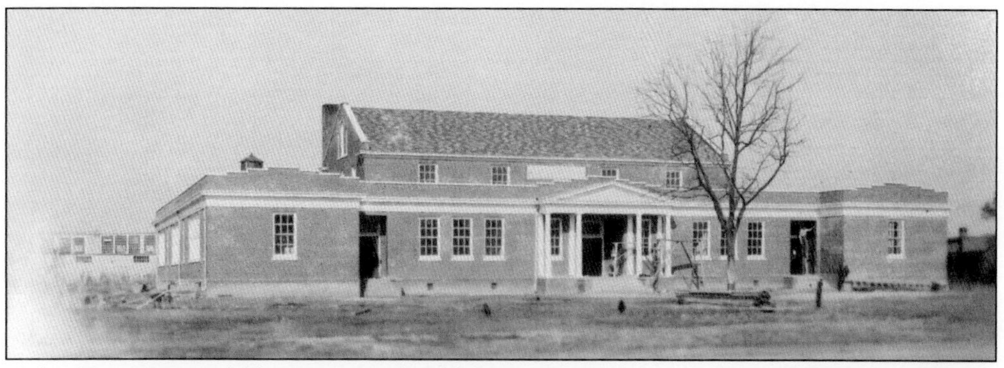

Hohenberg Memorial Elementary School (pictured here under construction) was a welcome addition to institutions in Wetumpka. Recorded in the minutes of the Elmore County Board of Education on January 5, 1931, is: "On July 1, 1923, there were 66 white schools in Elmore County . . . Recounting the various districts—district No. W has a new building, a gift from Mr. Adolphe Hohenberg, the building and equipment costing $27000.00." This school opened in 1929. Due to overcrowding, the elementary grades had been housed in three different buildings in 1927. (ECHS.)

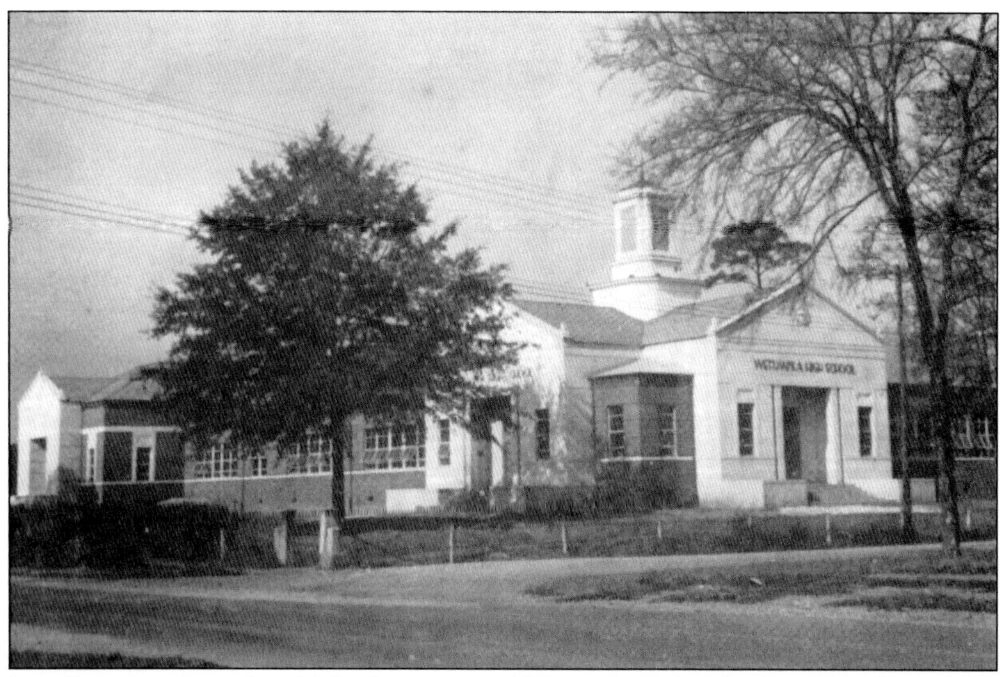

State Secondary Agricultural School was renamed Wetumpka High School in 1936. This building was completed in 1939, and the brick marker in front was placed by the class of 1940. The high school served through the class of 1988 and was then converted to a junior high school. The new Wetumpka High School, located on Coosa River Parkway, was completed in 1988. (ECHS.)

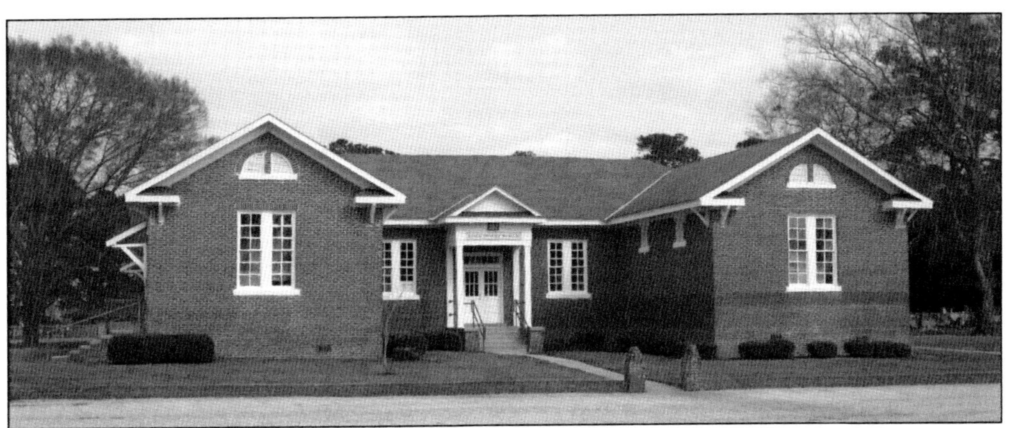

The Elmore County Training School came from "seeds" planted in 1911 when Julius Rosenwald, president of Sears, Roebuck & Co. met Booker T. Washington, founder of Tuskegee Institute. The Chicago millionaire was concerned about the "decadence of rural black educational institutions." He channeled large sums of money into what would become known as the Rosenwald Fund school building program. He gave matching monies to build modern, up-to-date school buildings for rural black children. There were 389 schools, teachers' homes, and training schools built in Alabama. The Elmore County site was built in 1924 as the only such brick structure in the county, and it remains today as the Elmore County Black History Museum. (ECHS.)

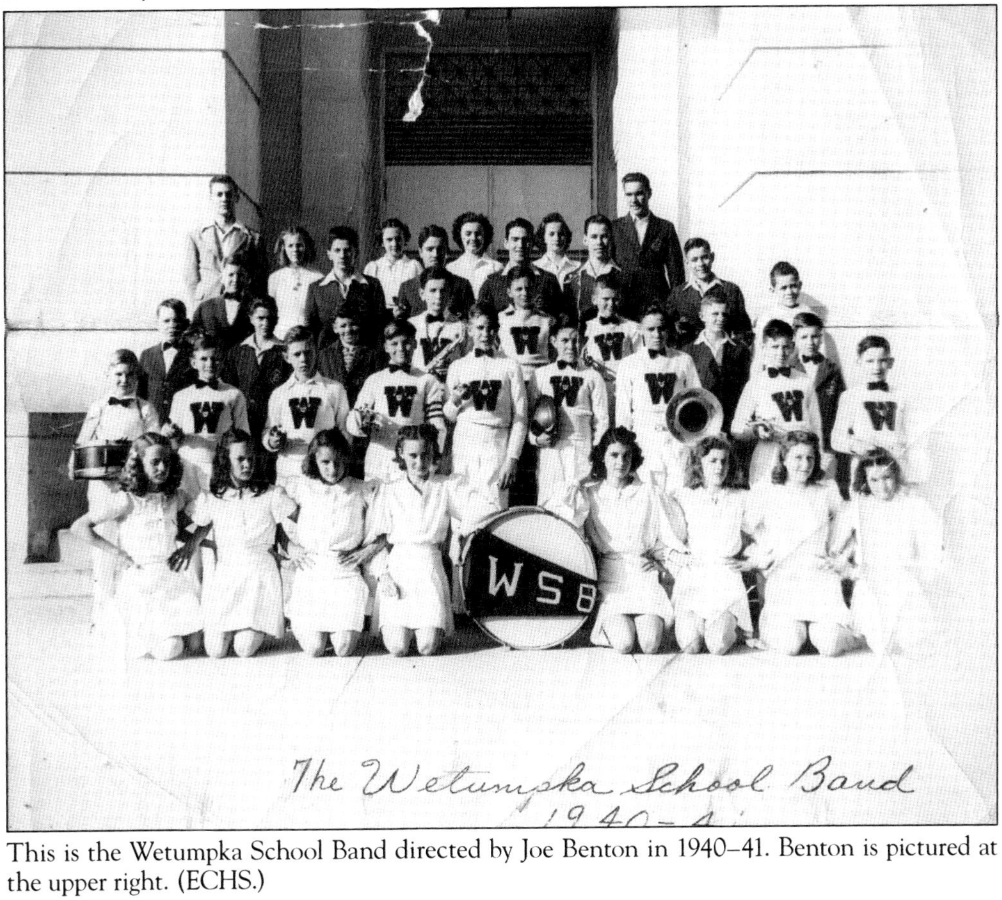

This is the Wetumpka School Band directed by Joe Benton in 1940–41. Benton is pictured at the upper right. (ECHS.)

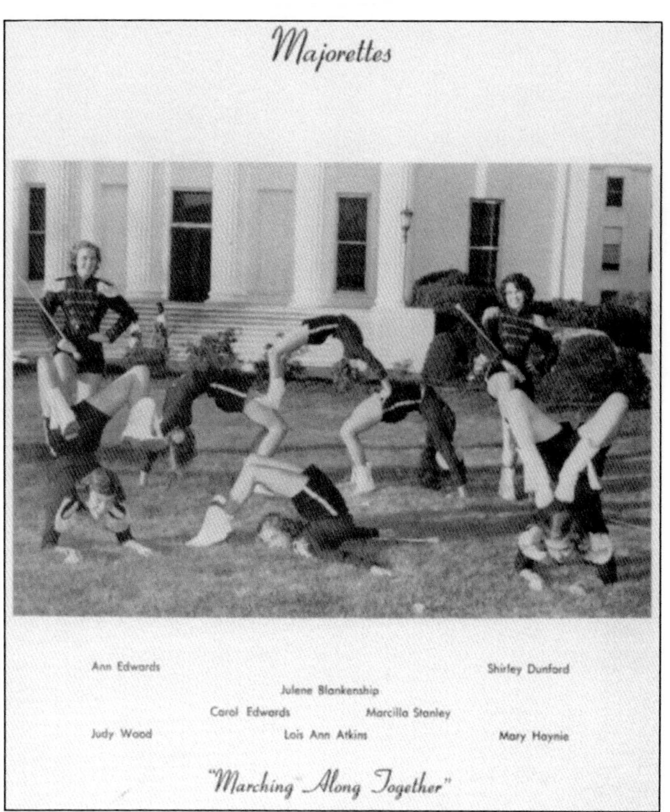


George Truman Welch began his tenure as director of the Wetumpka High School band in 1946. This is the majorette corps as pictured in the 1952 WHS yearbook. (ECHS.)

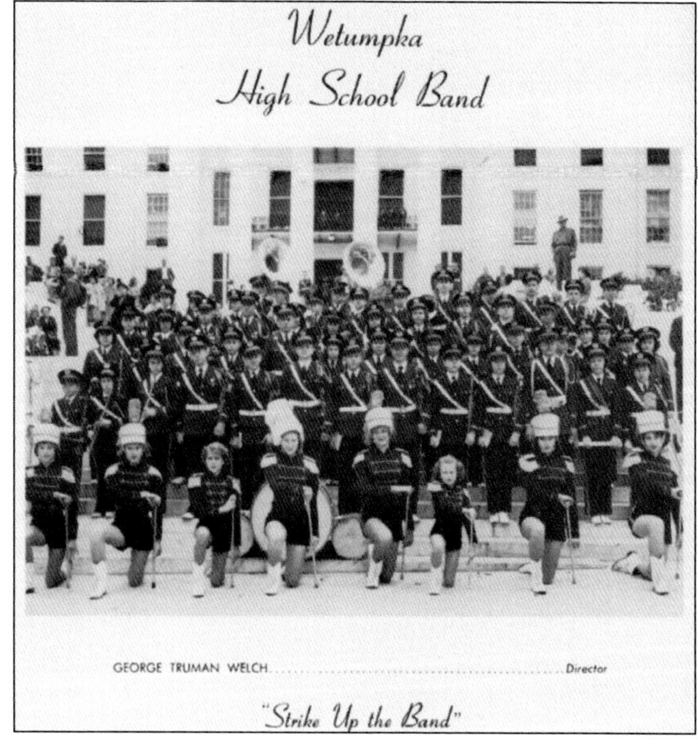


George Truman Welch's Wetumpka High School band is pictured here in 1952. Some of the band's many honors under his direction included playing at the VFW Convention in Philadelphia in 1954 and at the Gator Bowl in 1957 and winning second place in a field of 91 bands in the Lions International Contest in 1959 and fourth place in the same contest in 1960. (ECHS.)

## *Five*

# Institutional Structures in Wetumpka

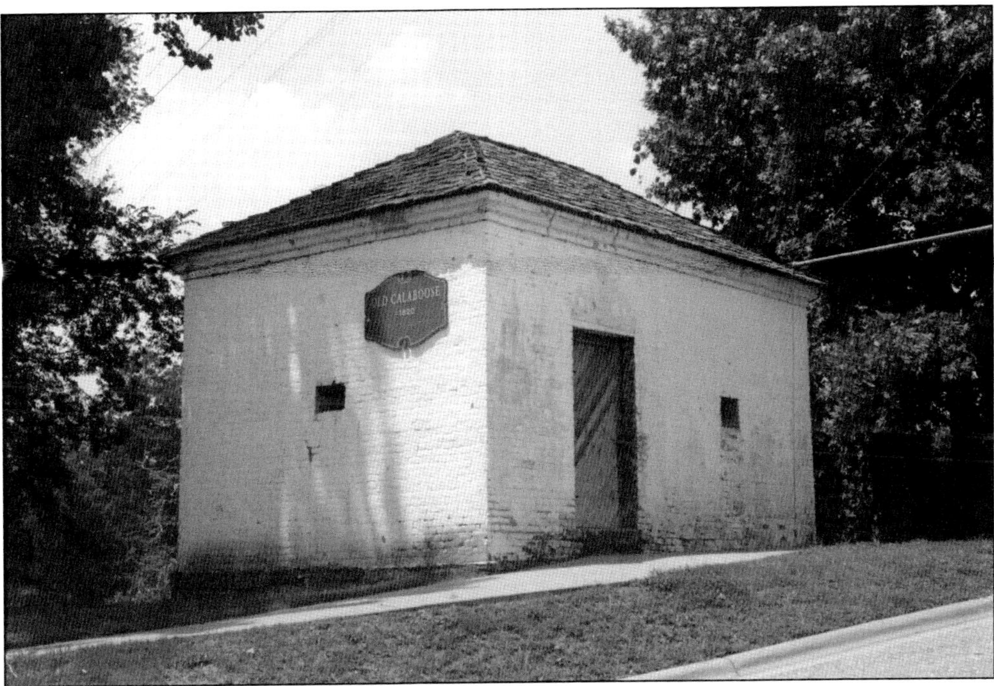


At the foot of the bridge is the Old Calaboose. Built in the early 1800s, it still stands on the east bank of the Coosa River. Traditionally, the calaboose has been regarded as the first jail in Wetumpka and was in use until after the mid-1830s. It is a one-story rectangular brick structure on a fieldstone foundation with a hip roof, small barred windows on three sides, and a heavy wooden entrance door on its eastern elevation. (ECHS.)

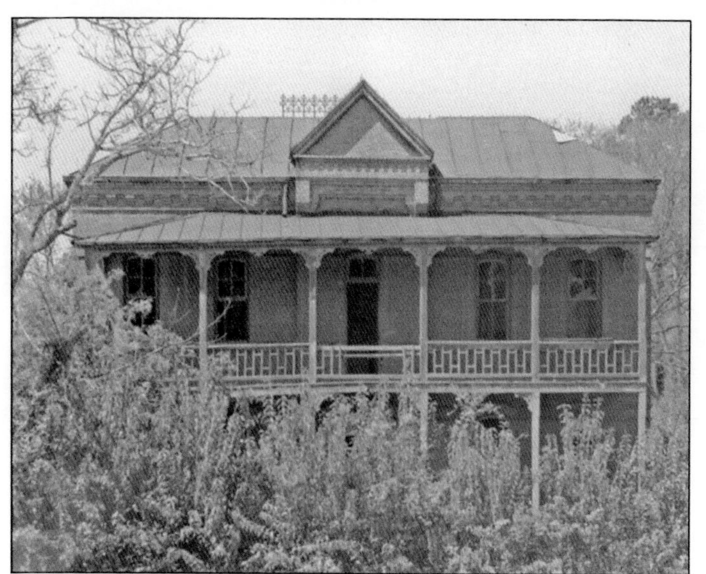

Elmore County was one of 59 counties that had an almshouse or poorhouse, which gave small amounts of money to poor people. The almshouse was a large two-story brick structure formerly used as the county jail and located near the courthouse. G.L. Cooper, the keeper, received $15 per month per capita for boarding and caring for the inmates; the cook got $10 a month plus board. The almshouse was demolished in 1964. (Peggy Blackburn.)

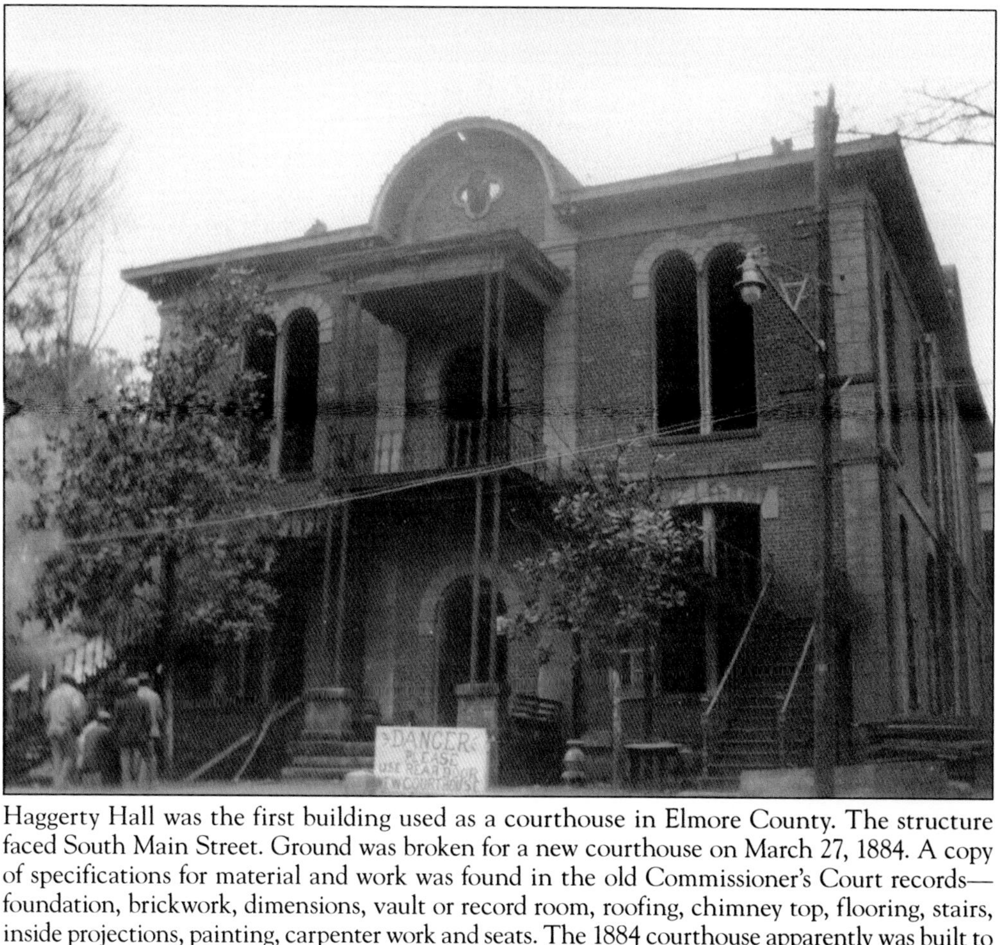

Haggerty Hall was the first building used as a courthouse in Elmore County. The structure faced South Main Street. Ground was broken for a new courthouse on March 27, 1884. A copy of specifications for material and work was found in the old Commissioner's Court records—foundation, brickwork, dimensions, vault or record room, roofing, chimney top, flooring, stairs, inside projections, painting, carpenter work and seats. The 1884 courthouse apparently was built to these specifications and served until the 1931–1932 building was complete. (Peggy Blackburn.)

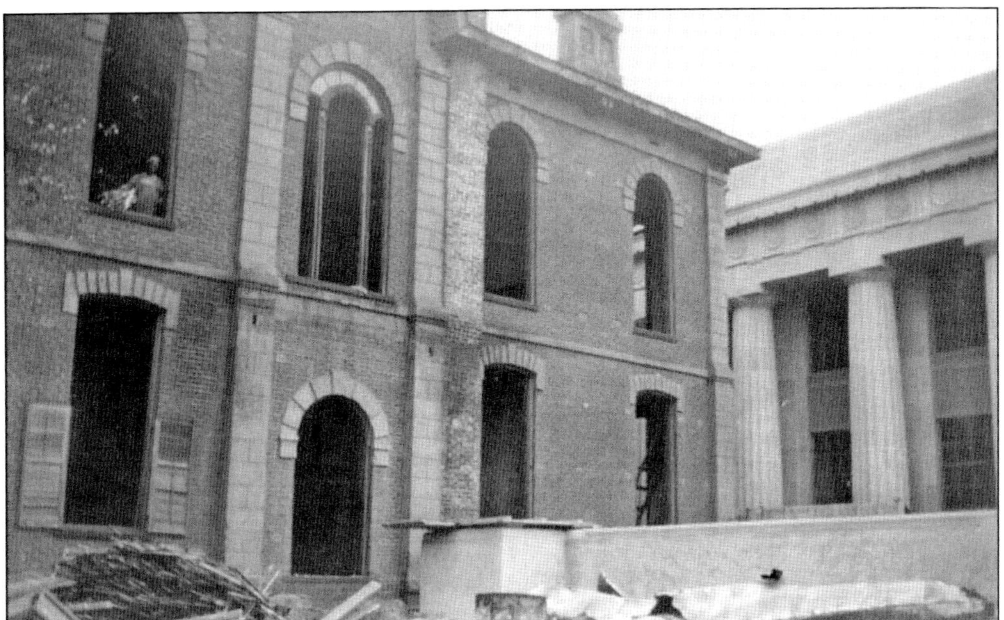

This is an interesting perspective of the 1884 courthouse (left) being dismantled and the courthouse of 1932 (right) being constructed. The two buildings are located quite close together. (Peggy Blackburn.)

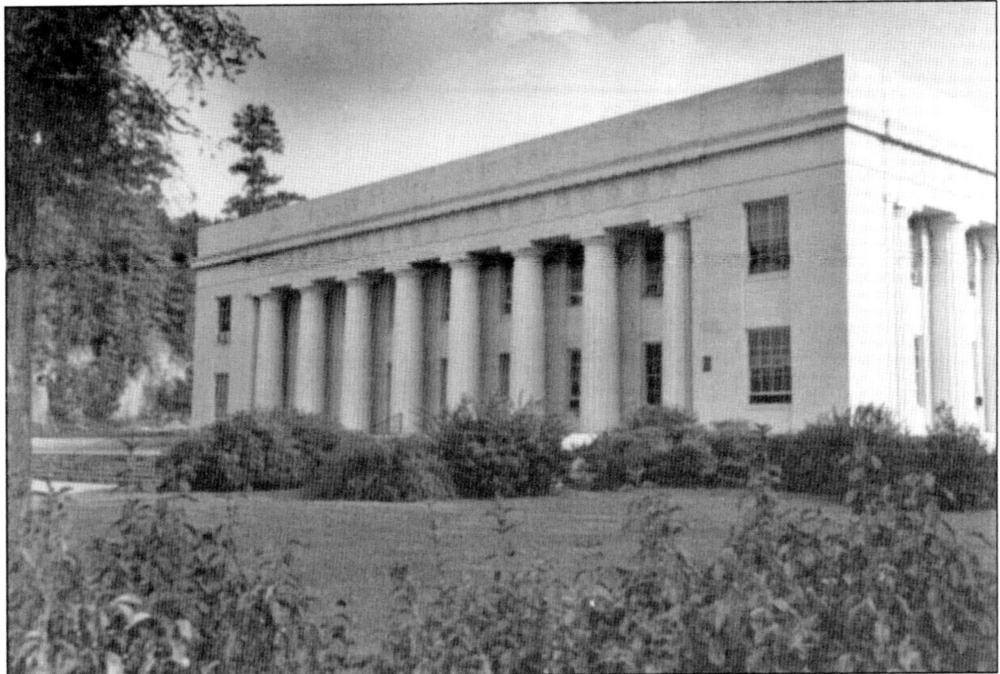

Construction began on this building in April 1931 and was completed in April 1932 at a cost of $240,000. The only wood used in its construction is found in the main courtroom and the commissioner's courtroom and on the stair rails. Built in a Greek Revival style, the foundation is granite and concrete; the outside walls are Indiana limestone, and the marble used inside was from Missouri. (ECHS.)

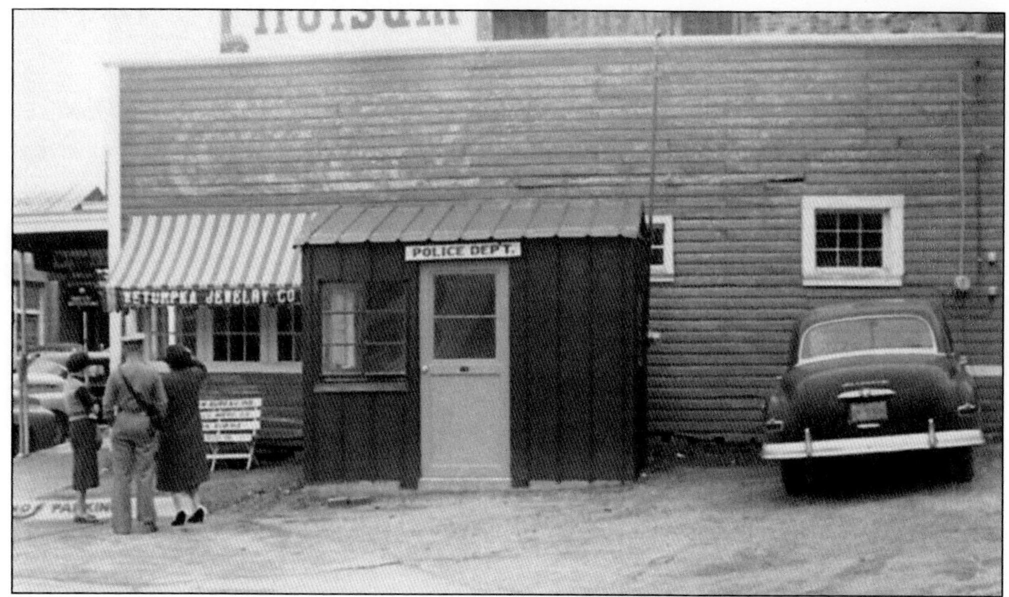


A small gray building displayed for several years in Gold Star Park was said to be the first police station in Wetumpka. This photograph shows Chief Franklin Holt at the police station located at the side of the building at 100 Company Street. Note the police chief's car at right. Later stations were located in the Wetumpka City Hall and on East Charles Street. (Peggy Blackburn.)

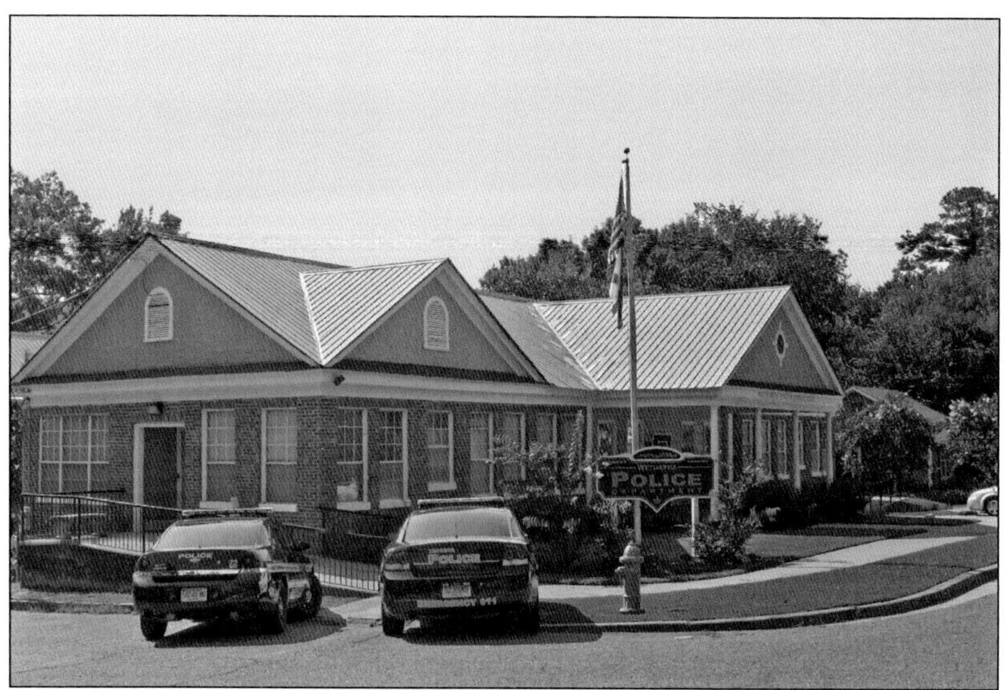


Today's greatly expanded Wetumpka police station is located at 208 Marshall Street in the original building and location of the first official hospital in the city, Wetumpka General Hospital. Dr. John Ferris Sewell opened the hospital around 1935 to serve the needs of the people of the city and surrounding areas. (Peggy Blackburn.)

This white building constructed in July 1912 served as the Elmore County Jail and was located behind the existing courthouse. The building was remodeled during Lester Holley's term as sheriff (1946–1967) and later replaced by a new structure. The county jail was moved to the location of the new Elmore County Judicial Complex completed in 1995. (Peggy Blackburn.)

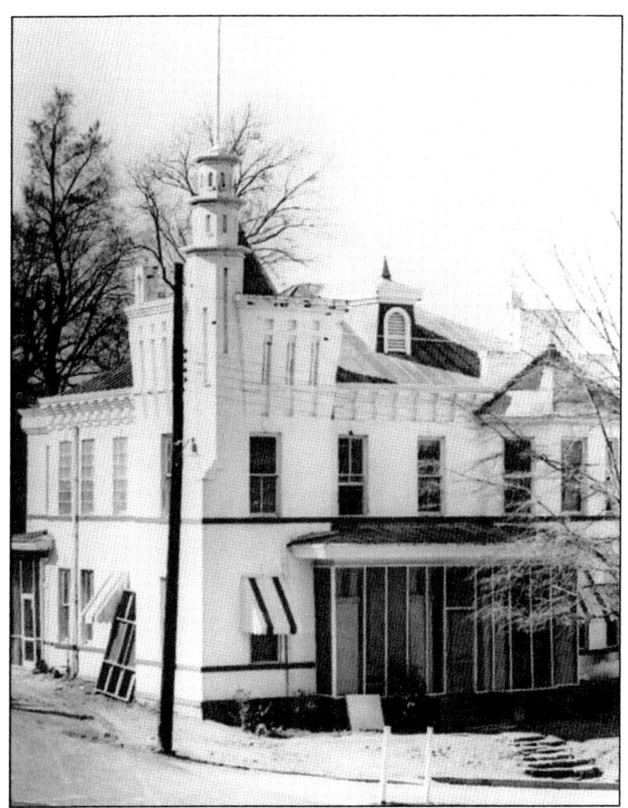

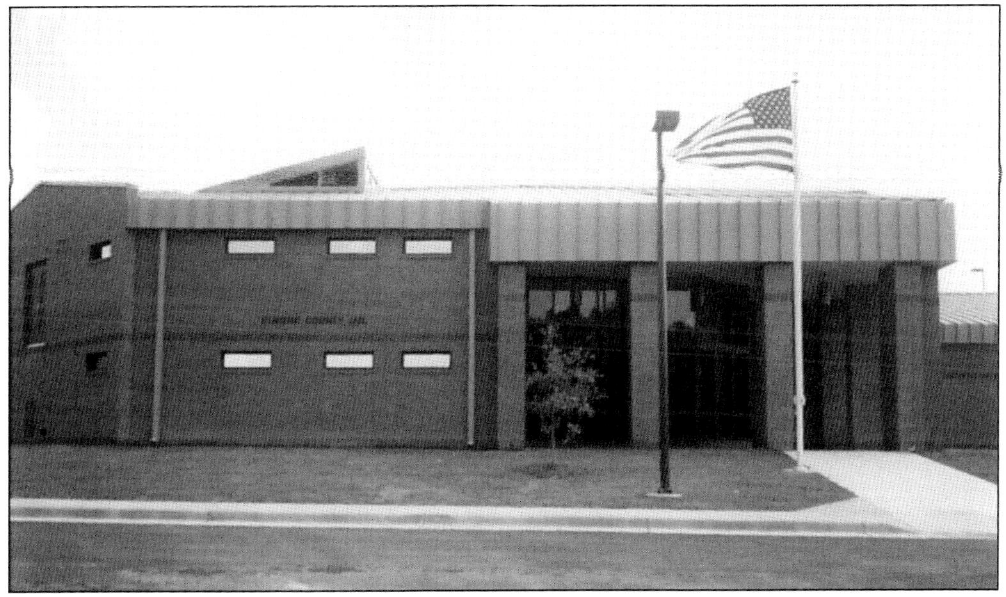

The present-day Elmore County Jail is located on US Highway 231. The complex includes two major buildings, the sheriff's office, and space for jail staff, along with a six-pod jail facility that houses adults and a limited number of juveniles. The judicial building houses three courtrooms, offices for the district attorney and staff and court judges, a circuit clerk's office, and E-911 offices, among others. (Peggy Blackburn.)

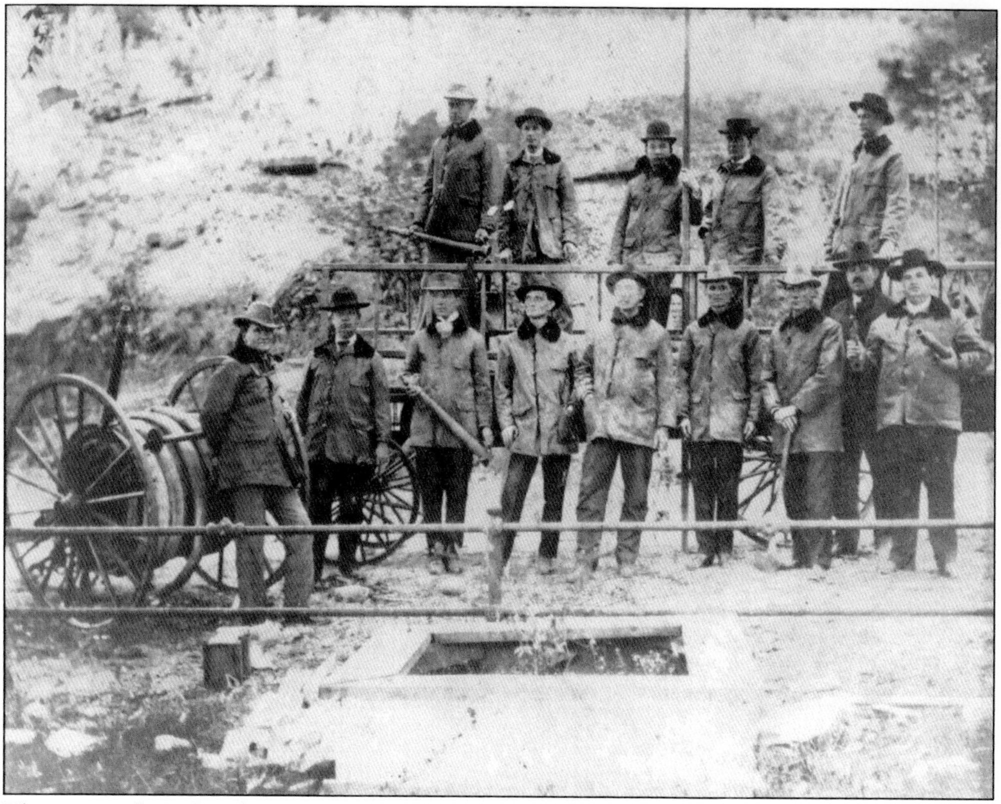

This image from October 13, 1907, shows the Wetumpka Fire Department with Chief James Augustus Wall. Pictured are, from left to right, (first row) Millard J. Ramsey, John Harris, W.A. (or Leonard?) Calloway, James Augustus "Gus" Wall, Joe Clifton, Dawson Asque, Lloyd Tate, John Collier, and Walter Thomas; (second row) Bob Ward, E.C. "Ed" Fain, Hunter Golson, George Smoot, and Mark D. Still. (ECHS.)

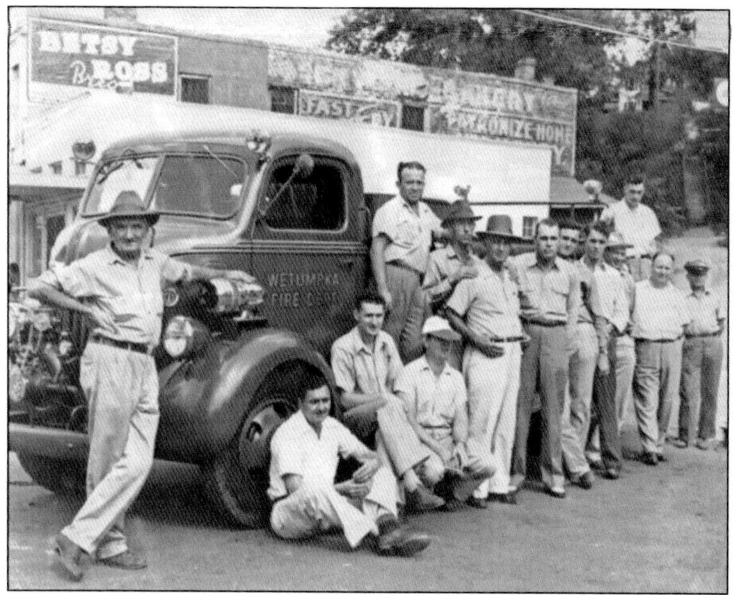


This c. 1940 image shows the Wetumpka Volunteer Fire Department. Pictured are, from left to right, (first row) fire chief O.R. "Dick" Warner, F.L. Hayes, Franklin Wingett, Ed Ragan, Henry S. Taylor, Ed Turner, Ben H. Jones, Raymond Gantt, Frazier Williams, Lloyd Fain, and Clifton Turner; (second row) Durell "Geechie" Grier, O.W. McDonald, and W.E. "Will" Lacy Jr. (ECHS.)

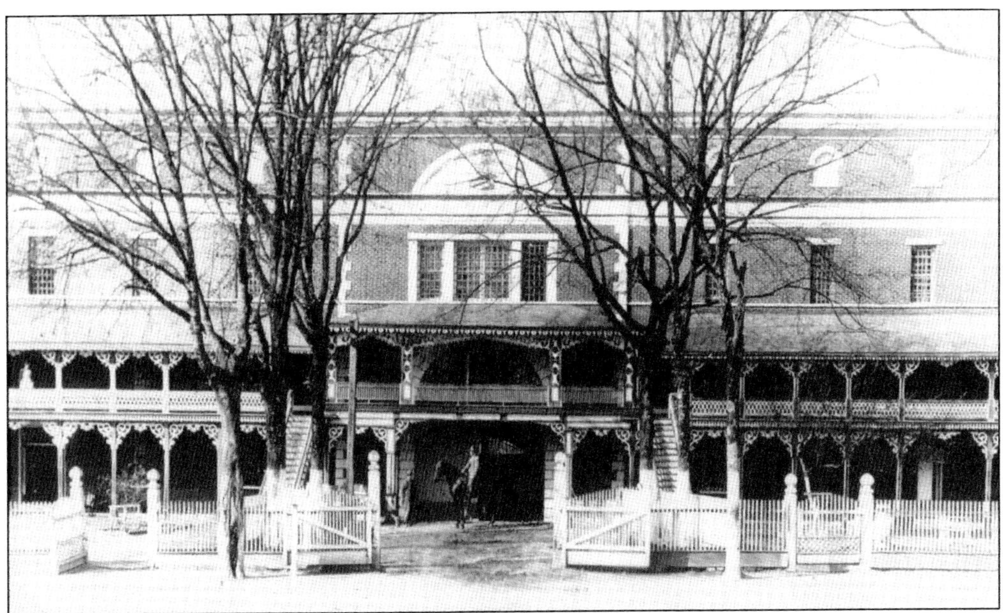

This is the Administration Building of the Alabama State Penitentiary founded in 1841. On January 26, 1839, the Alabama Legislature passed a law establishing a state penitentiary. Its location was to be not more than 50 miles from the center of the state. A site was selected in East Wetumpka, which was in Coosa County at that time. Wetumpka was divided by the Coosa River, and West Wetumpka was in Autauga County. (ECHS.)

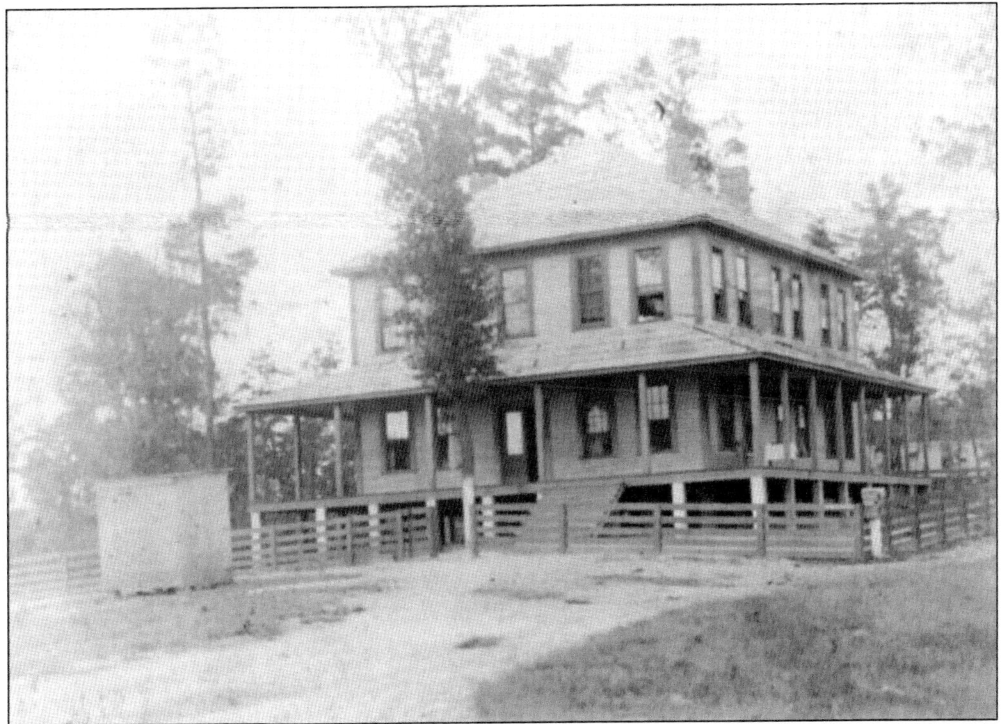

This house served as the home for several wardens of the Alabama State Penitentiary and their families in the latter part of the 19th century. (Peggy Blackburn.)

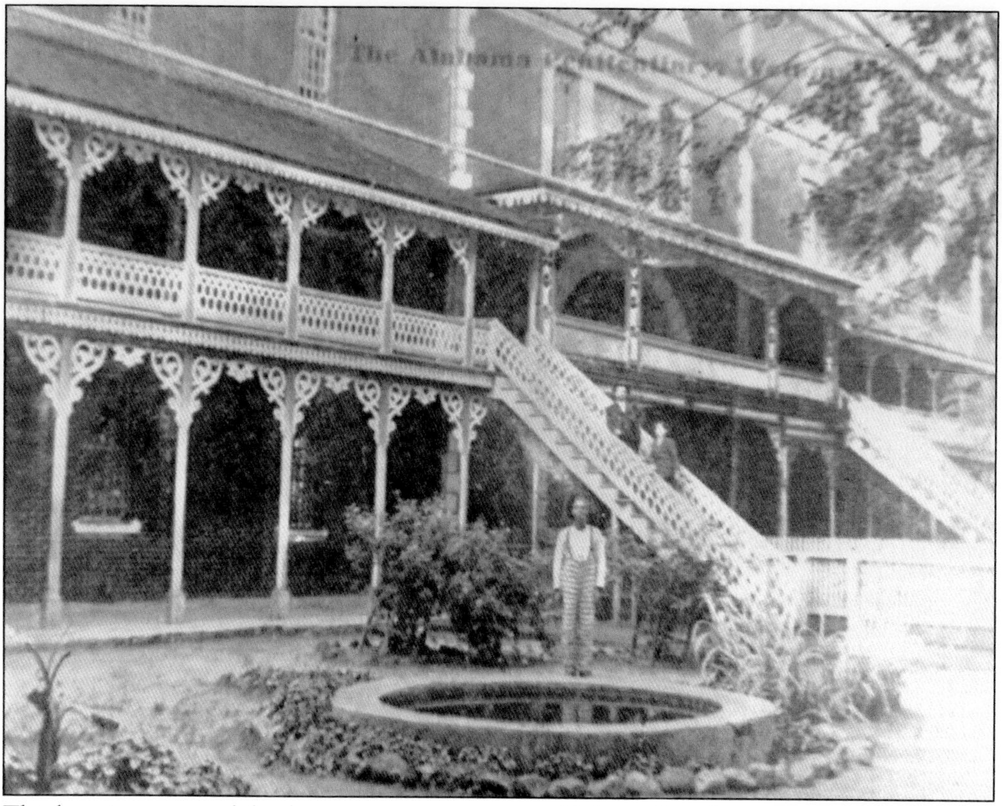

This lone inmate stands by the ornate entrance to the Alabama State Penitentiary. A contract for the construction of the buildings was let to W.H. Thomas for $84,999. The cornerstone was laid during an imposing ceremony by the Masons on March 4, 1840. On October 27, 1841, the keys to the state penitentiary were formally turned over to the county commissioners. The occasion was marked by a dinner for all in attendance, which included many state dignitaries such as Alabama governor Arthur P. Bagby. (ECHS.)

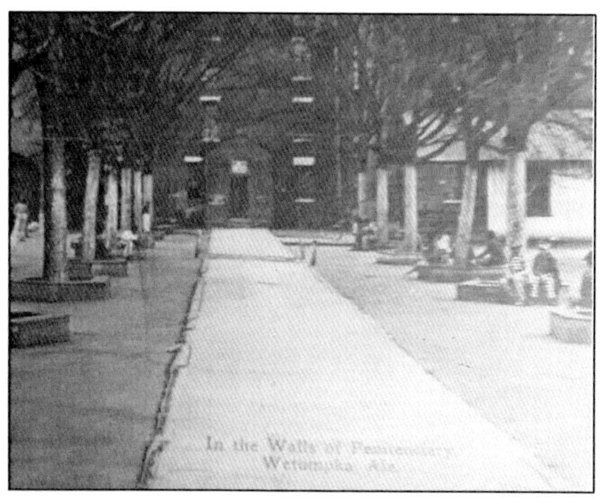

Inmates sat on these benches and passed the time in the prison known as "The Walls." In the beginning, it housed only male inmates, but later female inmates were housed there in segregated quarters. By late August 1922, most of the male inmates had been transferred to the newly constructed Kilby Prison in Montgomery. (ECHS.)

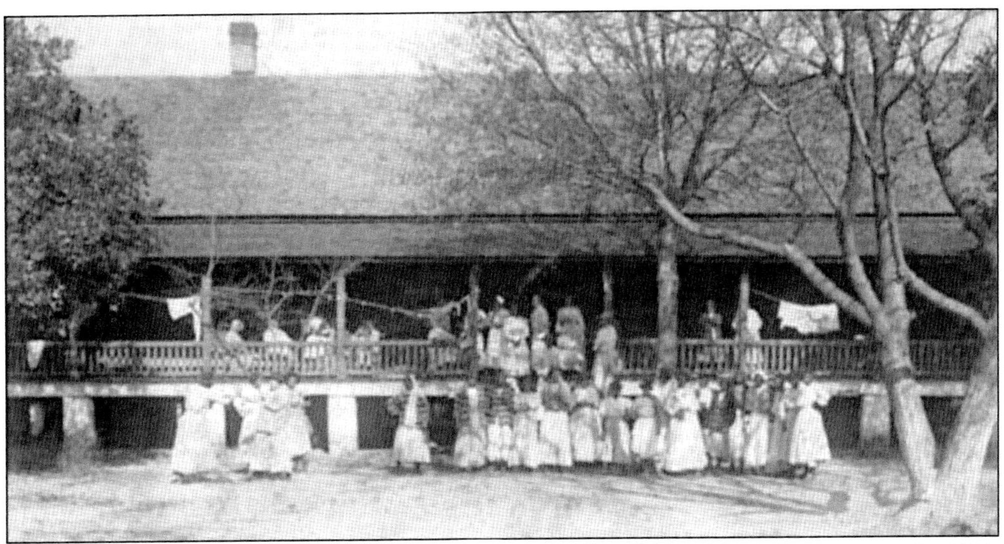

These female inmates are shown doing laundry at the old Alabama State Penitentiary. In 1941, this prison housed only female inmates. In 1942, a new building for female inmates was completed and the name was changed to Julia Tutwiler Prison. The old prison building was closed in 1945. The site was used by the Elmore County Commission as a workshop. By the mid-1950s, most of the buildings had been demolished, and they were completely gone by 1990. (Peggy Blackburn.)

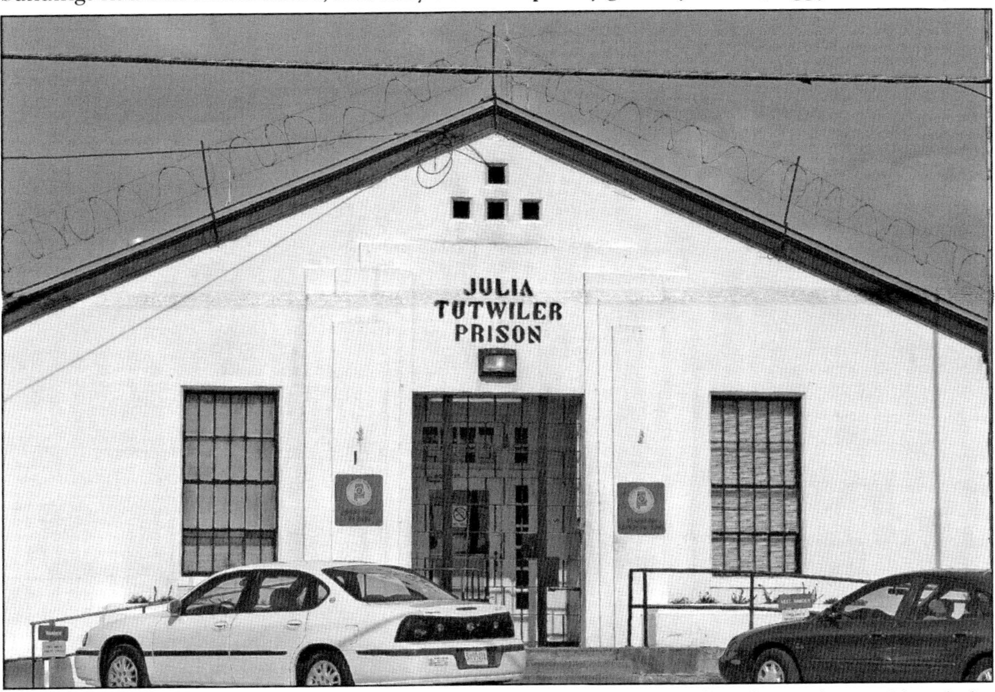


Julia Tutwiler Prison was created in 1942. Nell Farrar was the first female warden and headed a staff entirely of women, a first in the nation. The prison was named for Julia Tutwiler, the noted educator and crusader for the improvement of prison conditions. The prison contained a sewing factory and a beauty parlor. The inmates were taught craft trades such as rug weaving and making of draperies and bedspreads. Julia Tutwiler Prison is the only state prison for women. It has a death row and is therefore classified as a maximum-security prison. (Peggy Blackburn.)

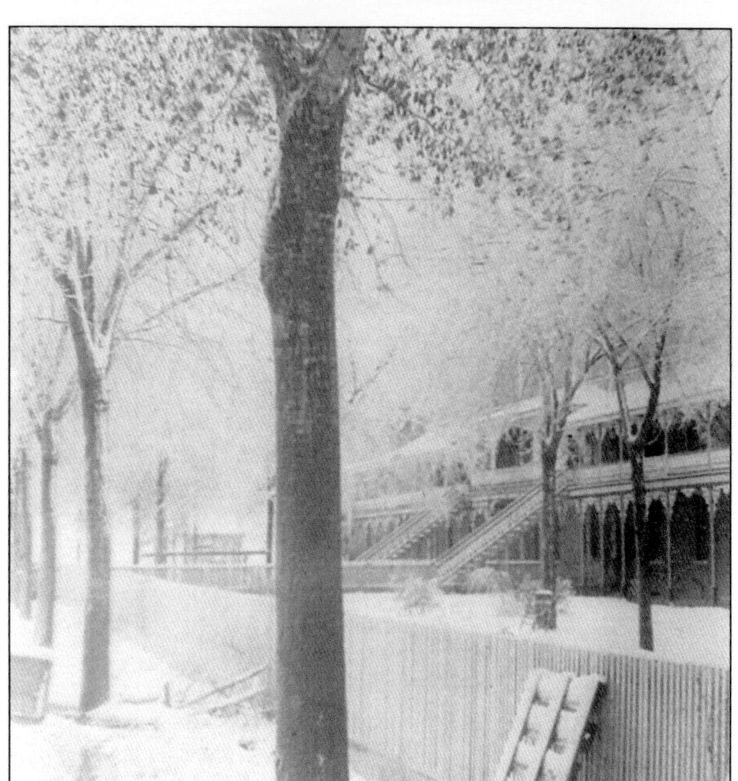

Here, the entrance to the Alabama State Penitentiary is covered with snow. (ECHS.)

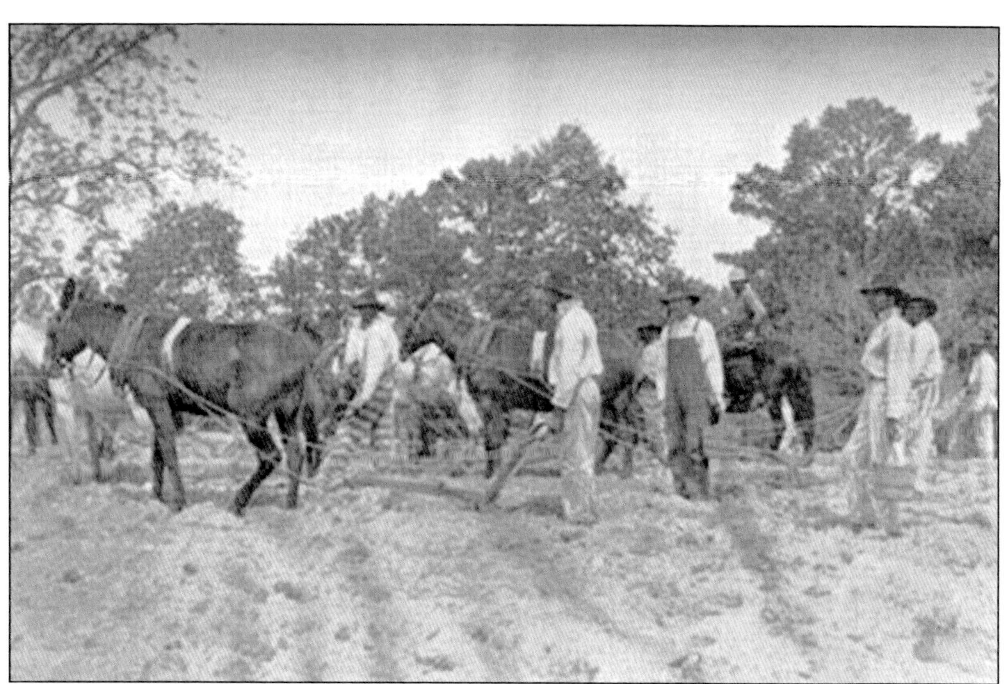

This is a male "plow squad" working at the Tubercular Hospital around 1900. The hospital was part of the Alabama State Penitentiary. (Peggy Blackburn.)

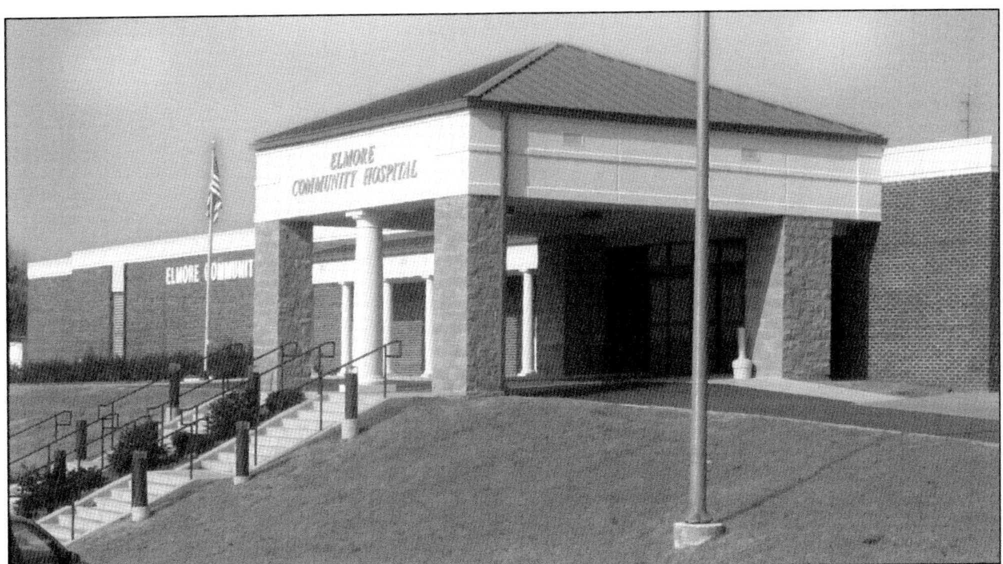


Elmore Community Hospital, located at 500 Hospital Drive, was built in 1959 and has experienced many reorganizations. The hospital was originally constructed to house 36 patients, and a new medical surgical wing was added later. Beginning in 1971, a $2 million renovation and expansion took place. Emergency and outpatient services were greatly expanded. New innovative services include dialysis, a helipad, computerized tomography, and rural health services, among others. New management agreements have been utilized, and an increased staff of active consulting physicians continues to meet challenges. (Barry Chrietzberg.)

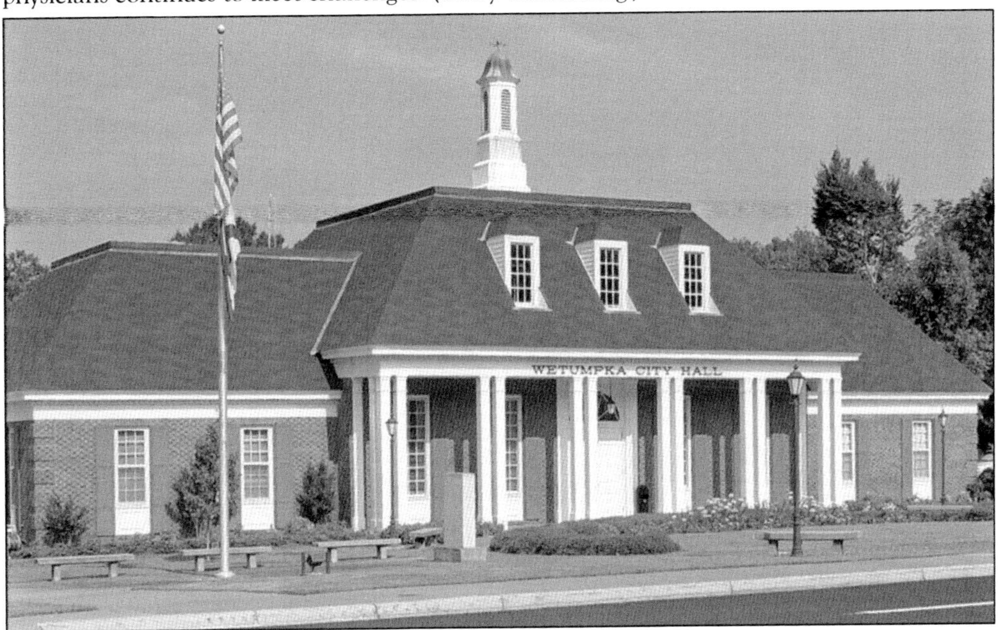


Wetumpka City Hall is located at 212 South Main Street. This location was the site of the livery stable and Riverside Inn. It was also the Cantelou and Law Cotton Gin and Warehouse location. This building, constructed from revenue-sharing funds, was completed in 1974. Wetumpka City Hall currently houses the city court offices and the Wetumpka Public Library and serves as the venue for city council meetings. (Peggy Blackburn.)

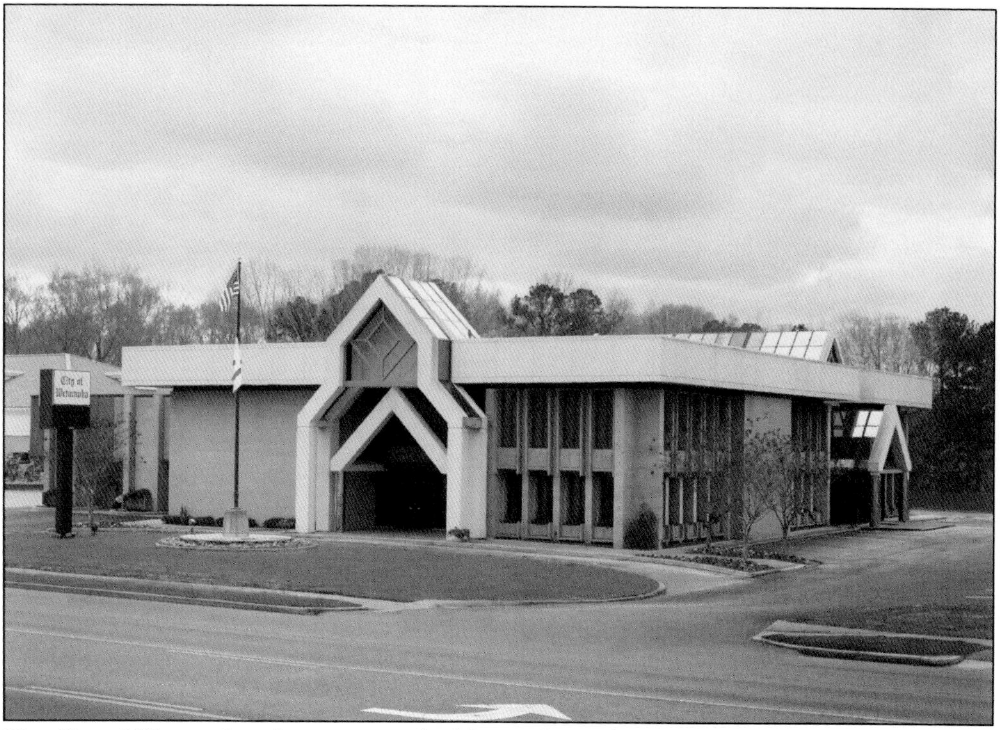

The City of Wetumpka administration building is located at 208 South Main Street and was originally constructed as the First National Bank in 1967. City staff moved into this building in September 2006. (Barry Chrietzberg.)

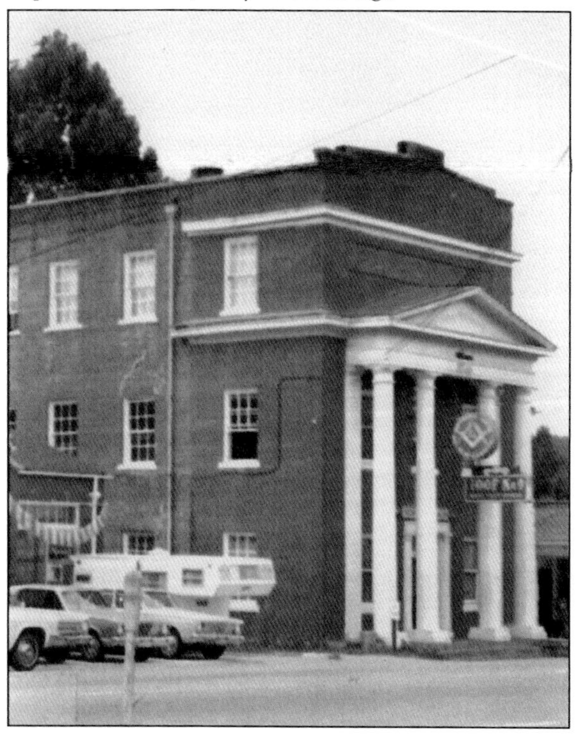

The Masonic lodge has been in several locations through the years. The one pictured was built in 1926 and was demolished and replaced by a smaller structure in 1976. Fraternal organizations have been a part of Wetumpka since the town's earliest days. The Masons' lodge was instituted in April 1837. The Independent Order of Odd Fellows was organized in 1845 and the Knights of Pythias in 1879. Other organizations included Woodmen of the World, Order of the Eastern Star, Lions Club, and Kiwanis Club. (ECHS.)

# *Six*

# Homes, Churches, and Cemeteries

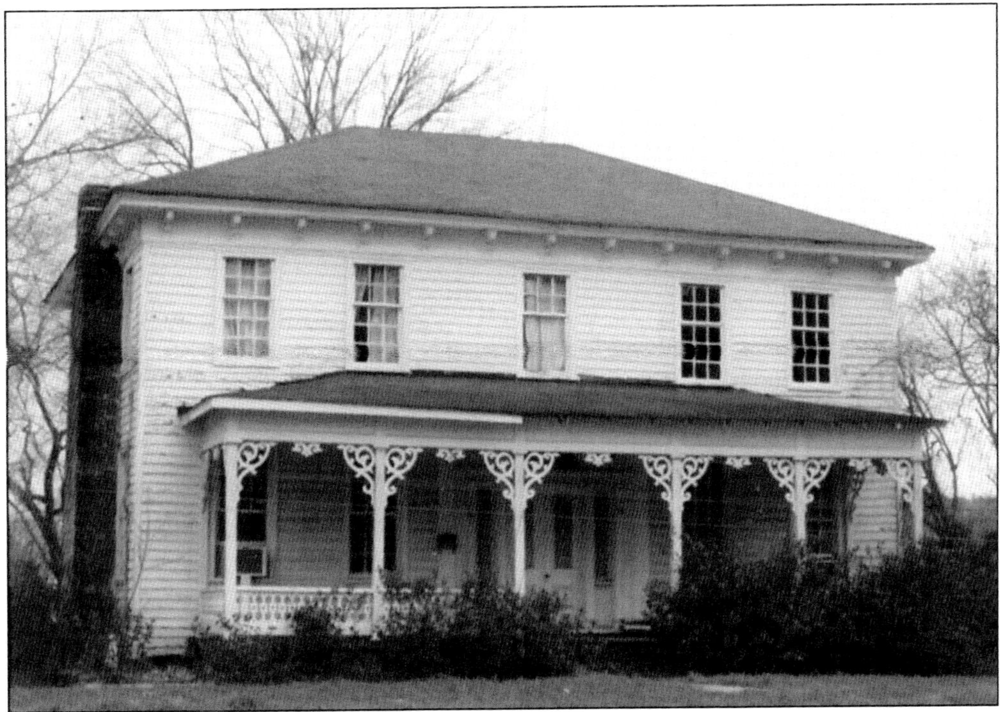

This house, located on the southeast corner at 508 West Main and Osceola Streets, dates to around 1850 and was built by Sam Adams. Dr. William Carey Penick, an early Wetumpka resident, lived here starting in 1835. The rectangular five-bay-front frame house has two stories with a one-story extension at the rear, a one-story porch, hip roof, and exterior end chimneys. Its 1850s Italianate style is similar to that of the First White House of the Confederacy in Montgomery. The double-leaf front doors, with semi-elliptical fanlights, are an interesting feature of the house. The Sellers and Davis families have also lived here. (Kristin Myers.)

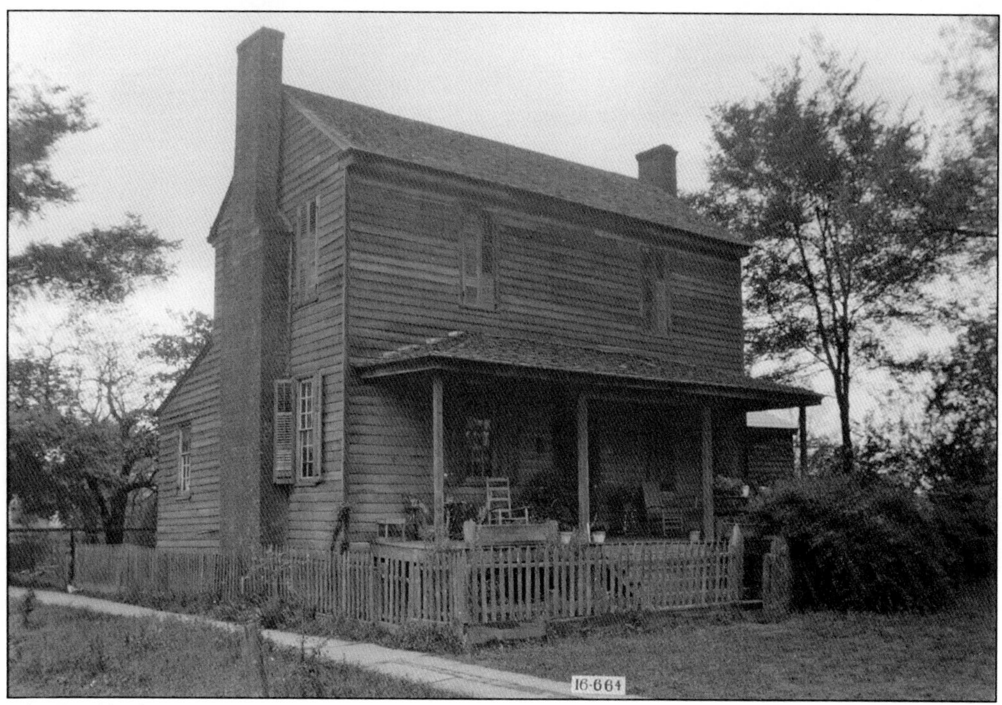


The Bradford-Stowe House, located at 401 West Main Street, is believed to date to the late 1820s, making it one of the oldest homes in town. Local lore says that James M. Bradford operated a trading post here and later converted it to his residence. The frame house with clapboarding has a three-bay first story and a two-bay second story. There is a one-story shed extension at the rear. It has a gable roof and two exterior end chimneys. The floor plan style originated in Virginia and the Carolinas and is seldom found in this area. The interior is simply designed, and the stairway is enclosed and tucked away. (Peggy Blackburn.)

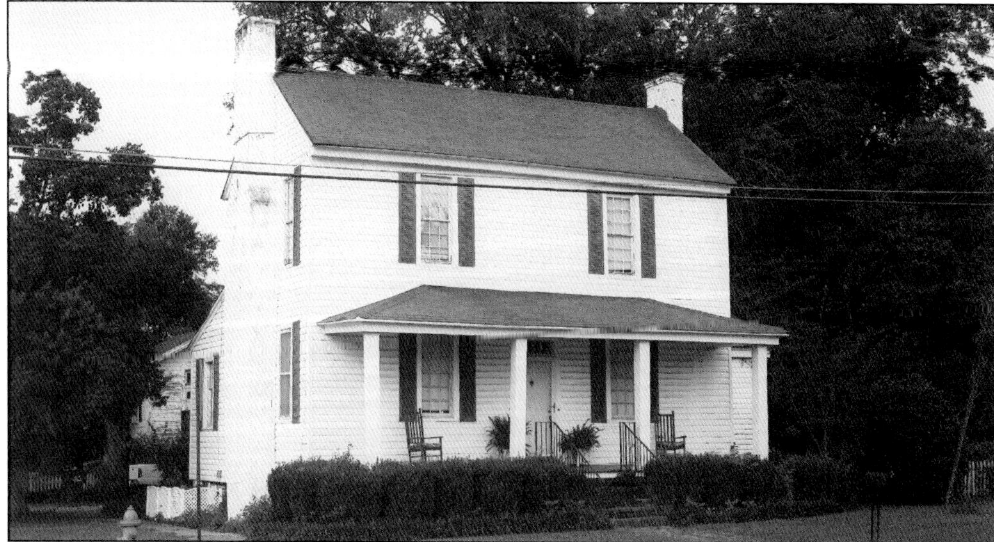

The Tom Stowe family was careful to make renovations to retain the integrity of this historic home. Another generation of the same family still resides in this location and has continued to make improvements to the family home. (Kristin Myers.)

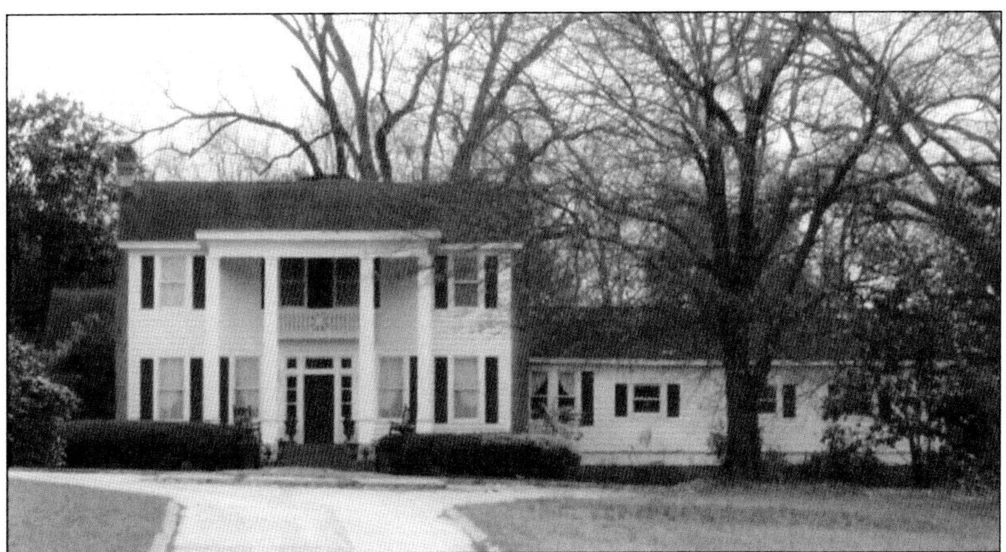

This stately Colonial-style home, located at 1 Penton Lane, was recorded to W.E. Arant in 1842. The next owners were Dr. and Mrs. S.F. Penton. The next owner began an extensive restoration and remodeling project. Throughout the years, this home has slowly taken on a new facade. The current owners have continued the tradition by remodeling, building additions, and decorating the historic home. As a result, it has evolved into a stunning work of art. (Kristin Myers.)

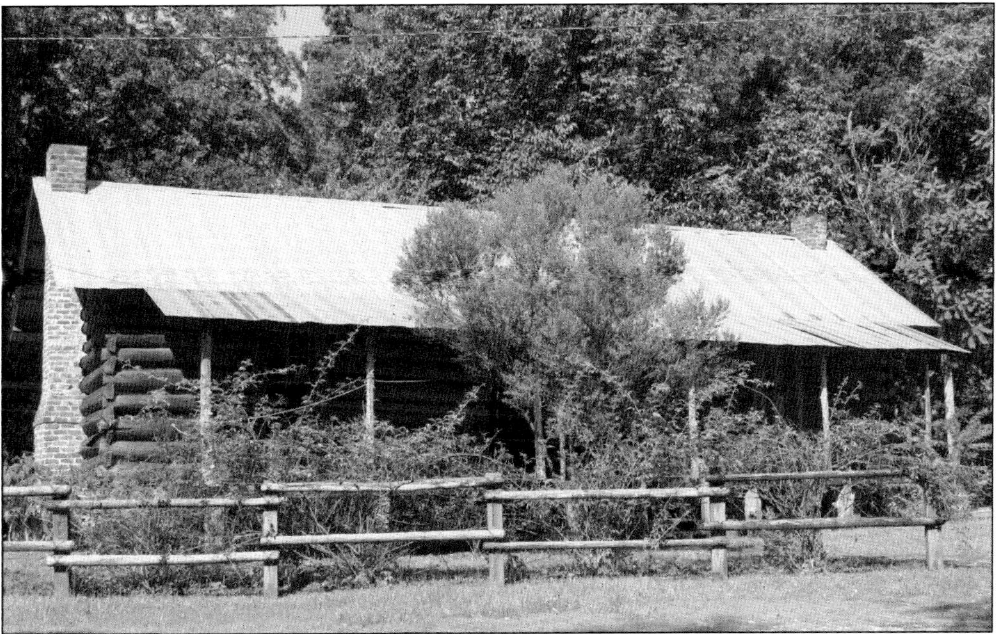

William Edmond Brown constructed this dogtrot home two years after his marriage in 1879. He lived there until his death in 1922, but Martha Nobles Brown his wife lived there until 1950. Eleven of their twelve children were born in the house. Stones used in the reconstruction of the chimneys were salvaged from along the Coosa River and around the area where the house was relocated. Heirs of Willie L. and E.W. Holt donated the cabin, built around 1881, to the Elmore County Historical Society. In July 1992, it was moved from its site in Deatsville to 299 Wharf Street in Wetumpka. (Kristin Myers.)

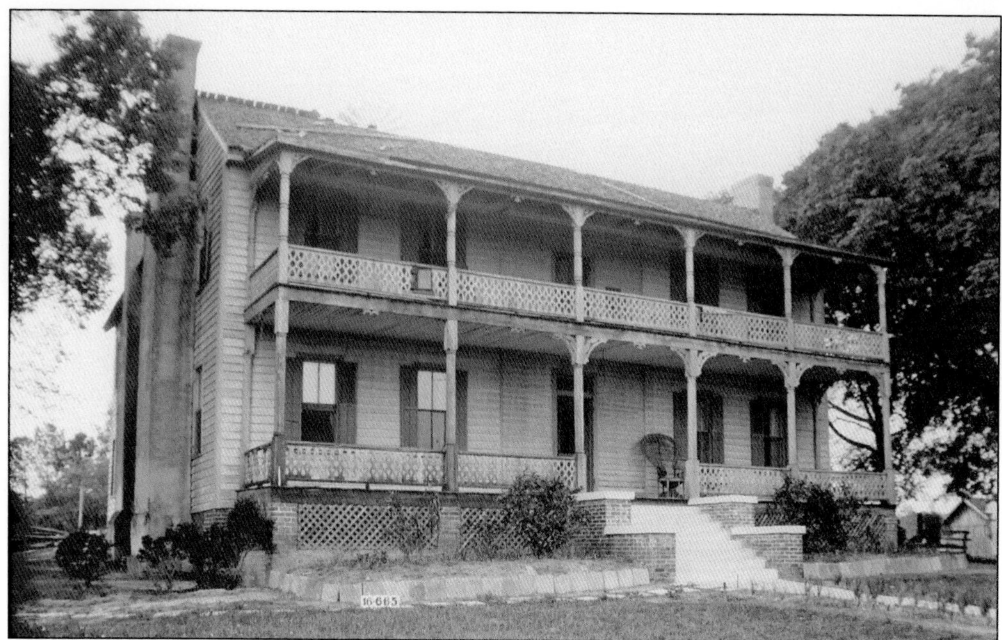

Built around 1823, this Bullard plantation home on Sugarberry Road was occupied by several noted Alabamians: Marie Bankhead Owen and Peter Brannon, both directors of the Alabama Department of Archives and History, and retired Adm. Henry Crommelin and his wife, Sally. Now called Sugarberry Hill, it sits high in the Blue Ridge foothills. The house is white clapboard, two-story, post-Colonial style with Federal influence, exterior end chimneys, and a two-story full width porch and veranda. (ECHS.)

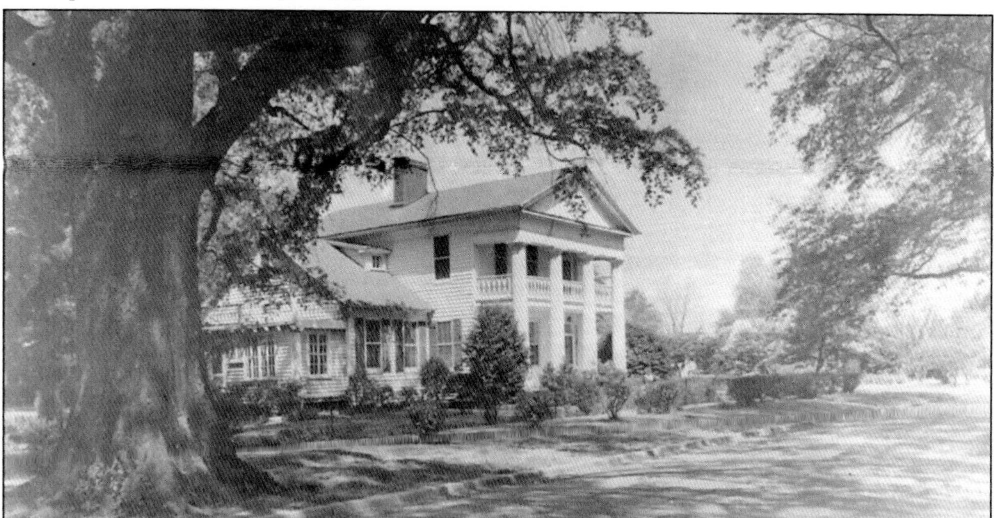

This stately Greek Revival with its massive columns, known as the Northrup-Bateman House, was a gift from Elisha Milton Cain, who built it around 1842 for his daughter Martha Cain Northrup and her husband, John Northrup. Following Martha's death in 1847, there was a succession of occupants and renovations. The most notable occupant was Florence Golson Bateman, who lived there from 1936 to 1987. Mrs. Bateman lost her sight at a young age but continued her dream and became a renowned voice teacher, composer, and vocalist. The home is located at 311 Government Street. (ECHS.)

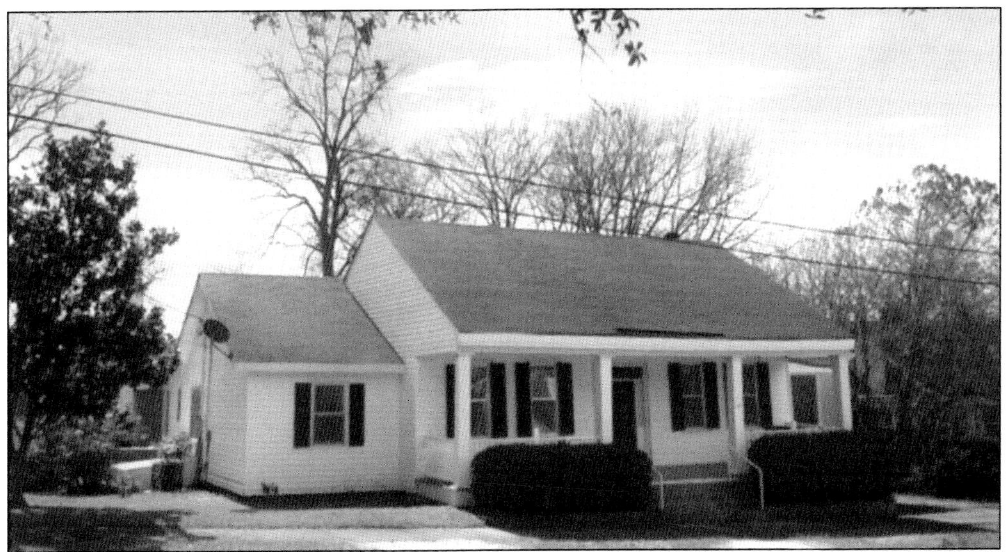

Following the War Between the States, Lamar Cantelou and his bride moved to Wetumpka, where he established a mercantile business. In 1869, they bought the house, and family members lived here for the next 104 years. Through the years, the home has been known as the Cantelou-Macon-Moody House at 207 West Tuskeena Street. This interesting mid-19th-century residence has one and a half stories and a gable roof extending over an inset full-length balustrade porch with four square columns. The house was the birthplace of artist Kelly Fitzpatrick. Louis Cantelou was associated with his father and inherited the home. He was also a director of the Bank of Wetumpka, organized in 1905. (Kristin Myers.)

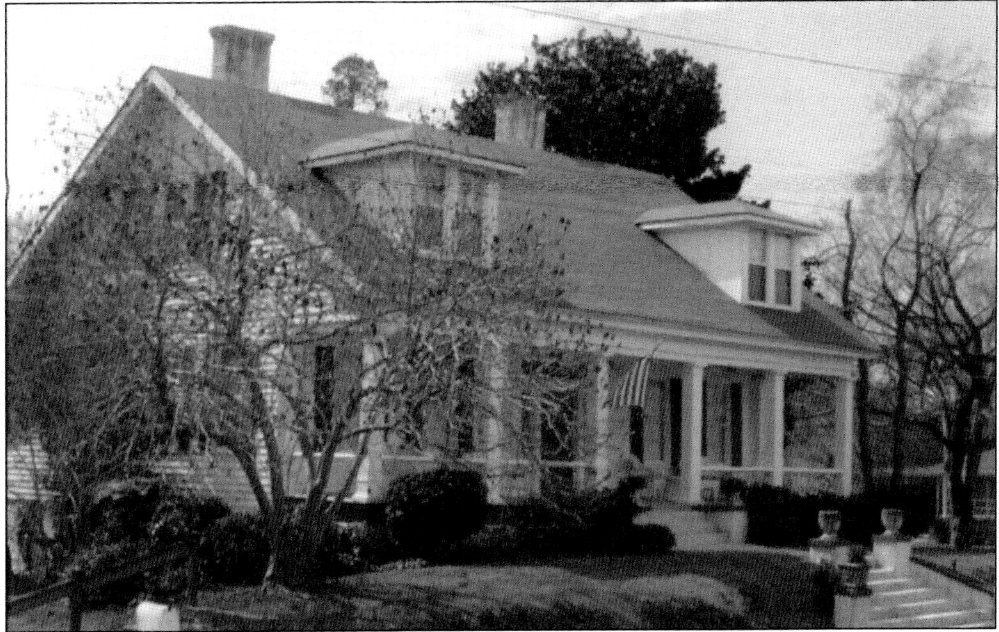

The W.B. Cooper House, built about 1840, is located at 209 West Coosa Street. Dubbed the social center of Wetumpka, this stately antebellum home was a frequent place of respite for Cornelia Wallace (second wife of Gov. George Wallace). Her hostess was Mary Hogan Williams, who adoringly owned the home from 1945 until 1995. (Kristin Myers.)

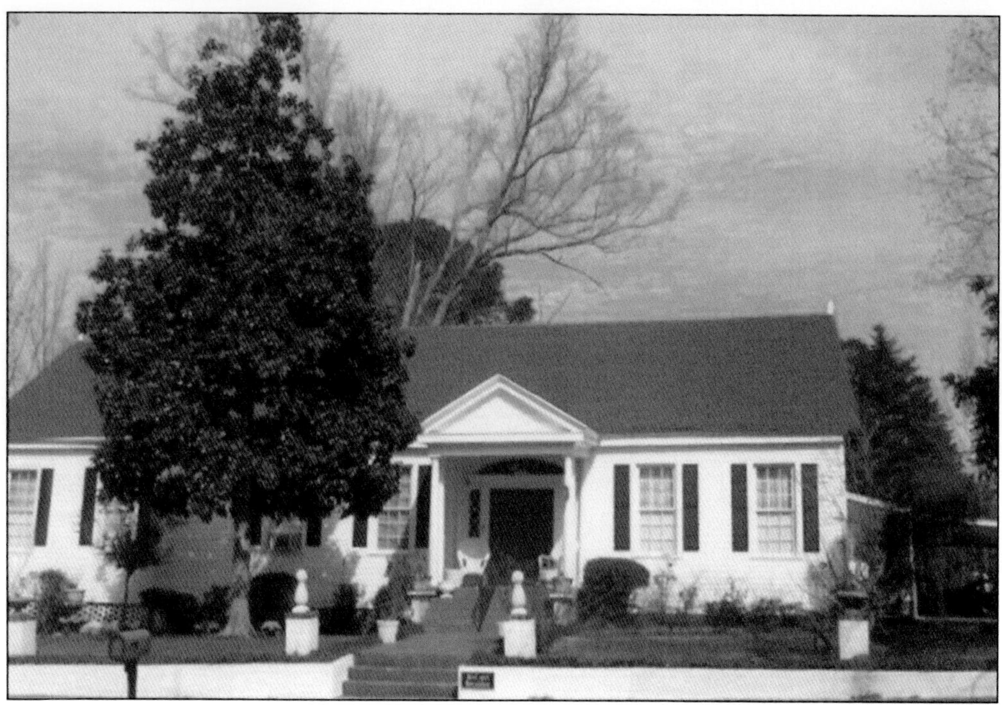

This home at 600 West Tuskeena Street is one of a group of interesting mid-19th-century houses along one of the older residential streets on the west side. The home was constructed by Alexander Gordon Due around 1849. The original part of the house is a white clapboard Greek Revival–style cottage with double front entrance doors, transom, and sidelights. Four generations of the Freeman family, whose ancestors came to Alabama in 1816, lived in the home until its purchase in 2006. In later years, this home was a bed-and-breakfast, and it is featured in a 2007 episode of the HGTV show *If Walls Could Talk*. (Kristin Myers.)

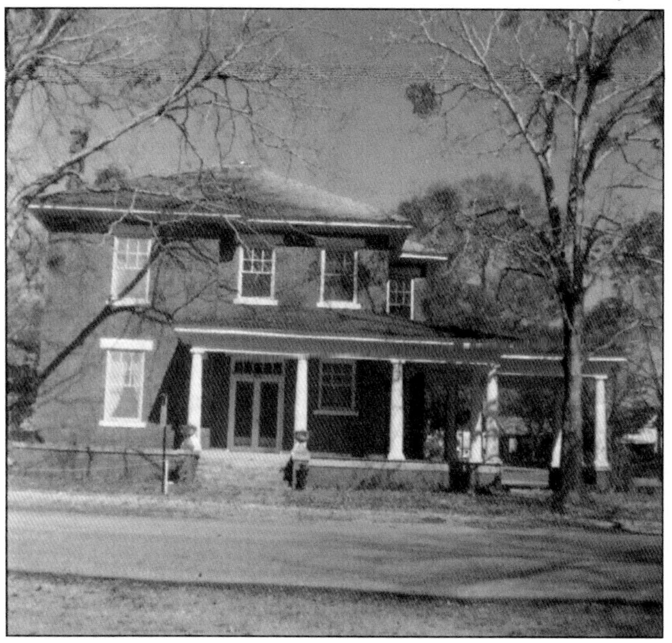

This stately Greek Revival house, built by Eugene "Genie" Edwards around 1917, has undergone renovations that have enhanced its beauty. Upon entering the foyer, to the left are a parlor, a dining room, and a beautifully remodeled kitchen. A den and bedroom complete the first floor. The striking stairwell leads to four spacious bedrooms. This house is located at 506 West Street. (Kristin Myers.)

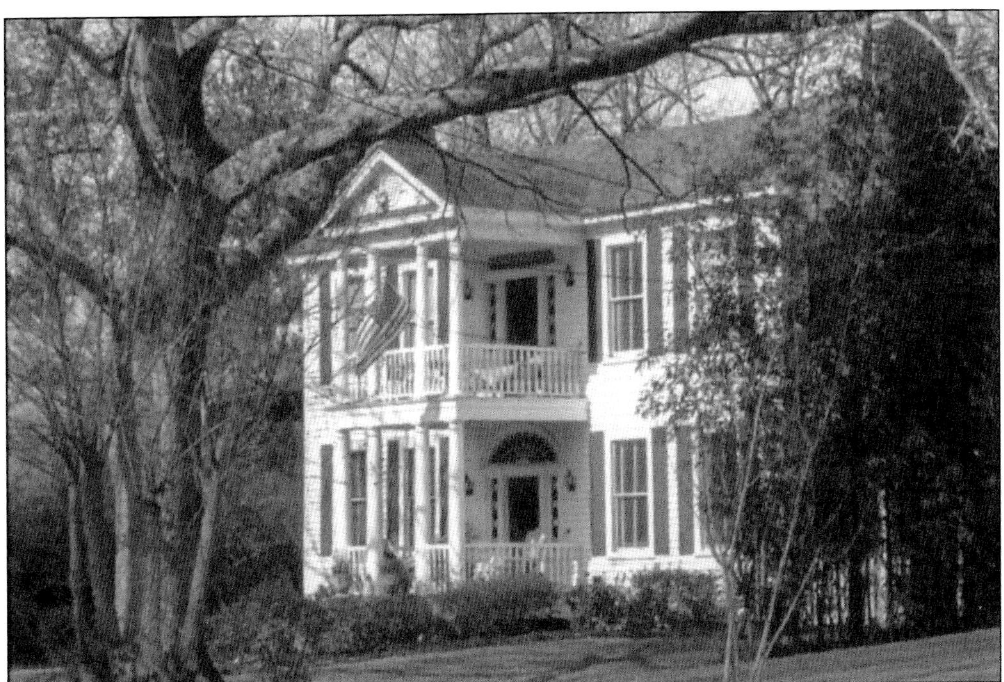

After moving from Georgia in 1834, Dr. Ruben Fitzgerald purchased land in Wetumpka and built this home at 709 Mansion Street between 1835 and 1843. Many families have lived here, including that of Frank Lull, whose daughter Lucia was a Broadway actress in the 1930s. Recent renovations have helped return it to near its most original state. (Kristin Myers.)

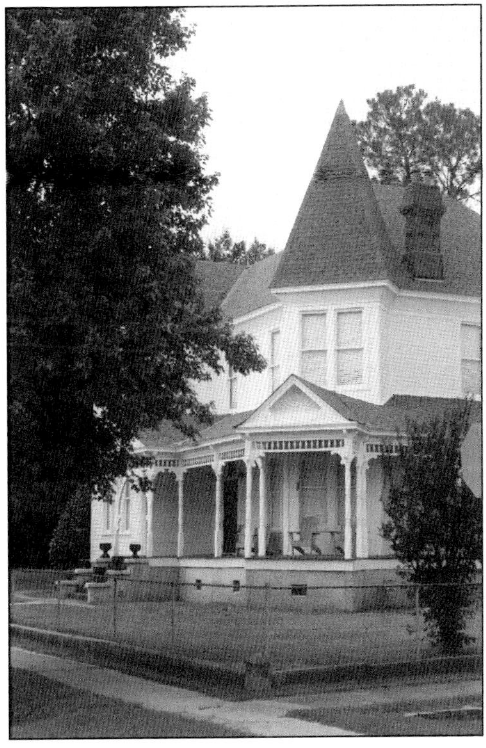

The structure known variously as the Fitzpatrick-Thomas-Hohenberg-Sewell House is located at 402 West Tuskeena Street. The Queen Anne home at Tuskeena and Broad Streets was built in 1892. Benjamin Fitzpatrick, an attorney in Wetumpka who held the office of circuit solicitor, constructed the house. He was the youngest son of Benjamin Fitzpatrick, the ninth governor of Alabama, and the father of Benjamin Fitzpatrick of Jasmine Hill Gardens. It was reported in the *Times Democrat*, a local newspaper, that "the house will have ten rooms and will vie with any city residence in point of finish and equipment when completed." Adolphe Hohenberg, a local merchant and cotton buyer, lived here with his family until December 1929. The house was later purchased by Dr. and Mrs. J.F. Sewell, who renovated the house and landscaped the grounds. (Kristin Myers.)

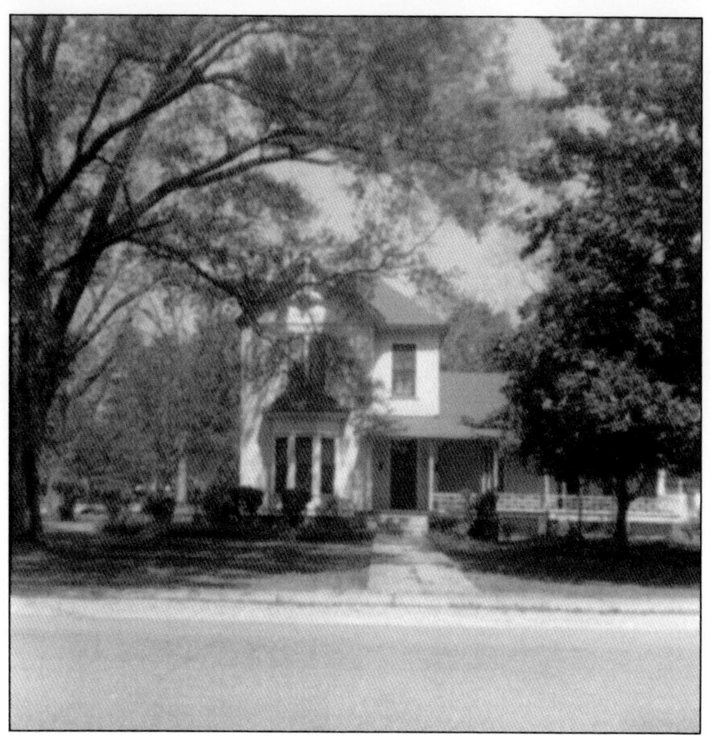

The Hohenberg-Lancaster House, a tall, two-story Victorian home with a one-story east wing, stands at 108 West Tallassee Street, on the corner of Government Street. It was built by Morris Hohenberg, the elder of two brothers who were successful Wetumpka businessmen. Probate judge Henry J. Lancaster bought the house around 1910, and it has remained in the Lancaster family until the present day. A third-generation descendant of Judge Lancaster now owns the property, which is maintained as an apartment house. (ECHS.)

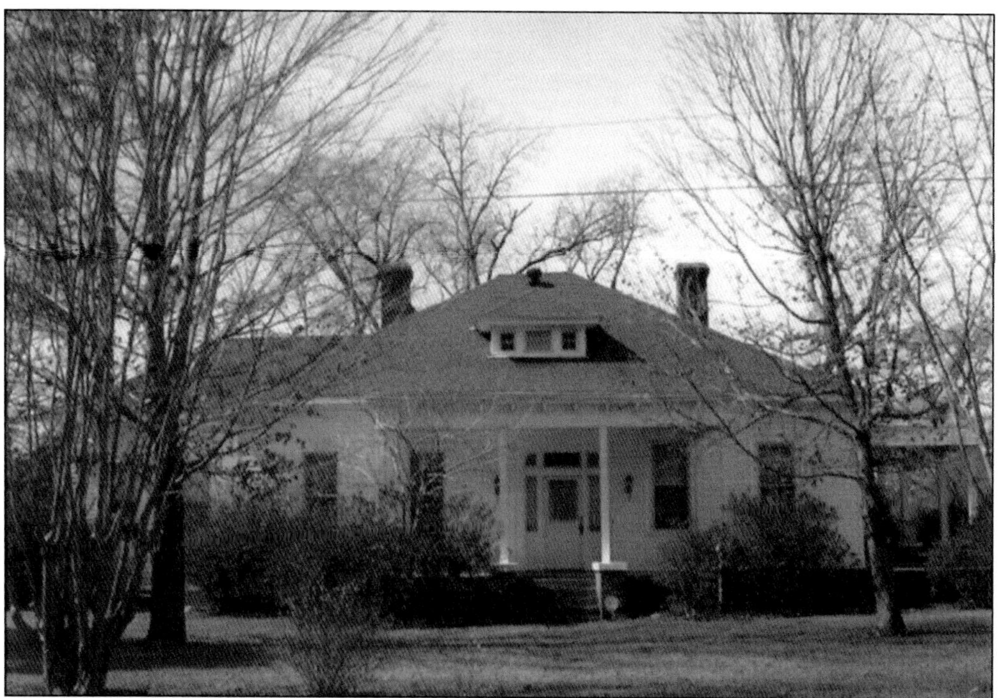

The names of many prominent Wetumpka residents have been attached to this home located at 108 East Tallassee Street and constructed around 1850 by Samuel House. Longtime residents remember it as the Martin House, where the late Wetumpka artist Austin Martin grew up. The yard and home are beautiful attractions in the historic area. (Kristin Myers.)

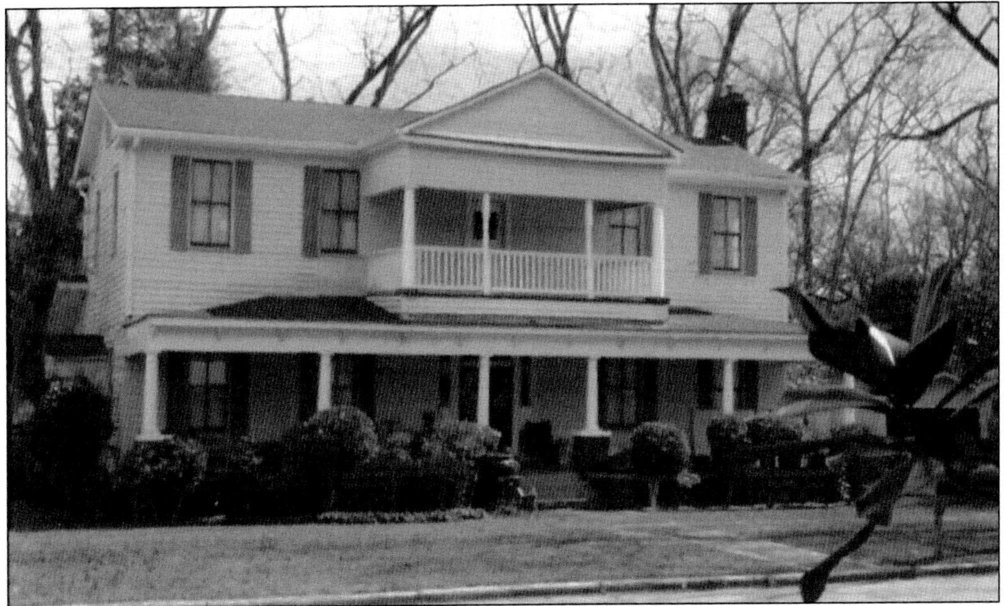

This Victorian home, located at 306 Government Street across from the Bateman home, is much less ornate and formal than the Bateman home. This house was built in 1848 by Dr. Thomas Mason, a prominent physician in mid-19th-century Wetumpka. Alterations were made to the porches—originally built in post-Colonial style—with a full-width porch across the front downstairs. The triangular gable is supported by columns on the upstairs portico and downstairs front porch. (Kristin Myers.)

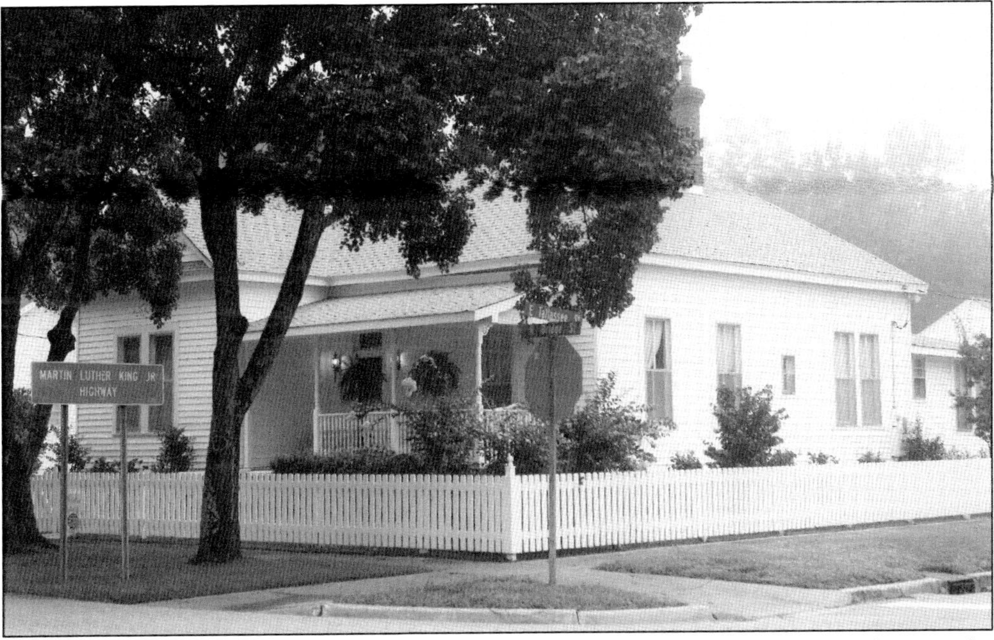


Spencer James McMorris constructed this home at 400 North Bridge Street around 1904. The original hand-carved front door with Victorian hardware opens to a six-fireplace home. A beautiful 1934 brass and copper radiant heater still warms the living room. The six-foot windows throughout the house are original. A charming white picket fence has been added. (Kristin Myers.)

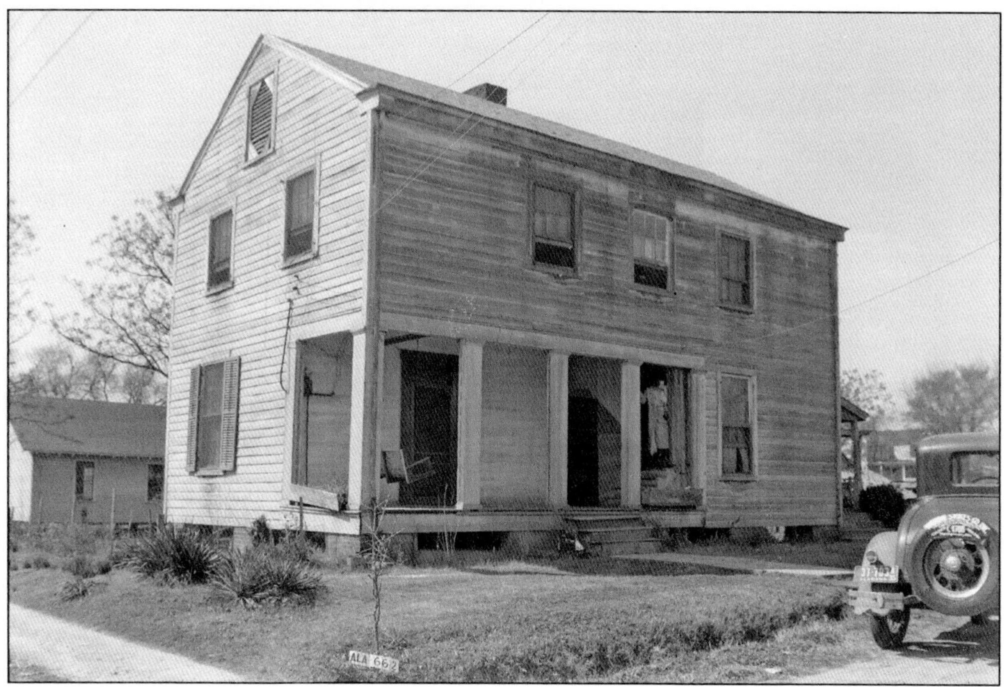


This house on the corner of West Bridge and Broad Streets was demolished in 1979. It was a rare example of antebellum Alabama architecture. The floor plan was arranged around a single central chimney. The two-story, rectangular frame house with clapboarding, a gable roof, and a central chimney faced east. It had an inset one-story, two-thirds-length porch on the front with four square columns. The house was built in the mid-19th century as a stagecoach inn and tavern but was later converted to a residence for the Norman McQueen and J.L. McCullers families. (Peggy Blackburn.)

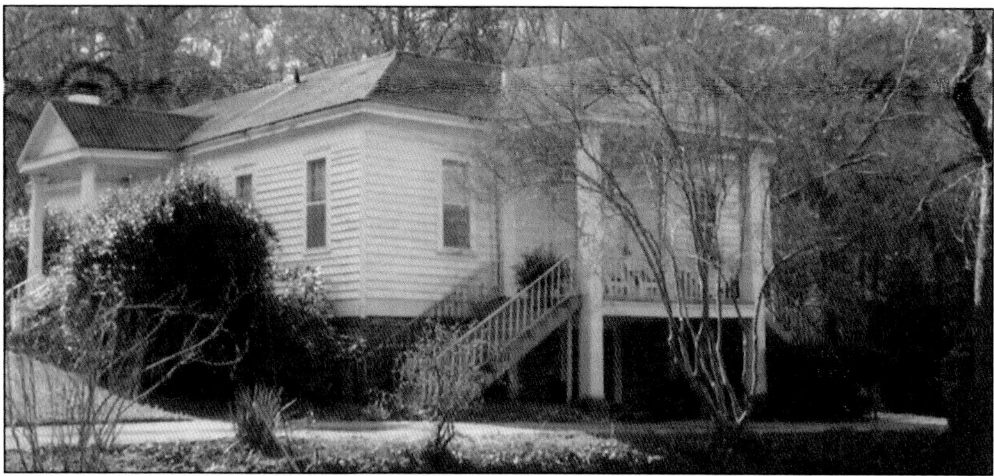

One of the most interesting houses in Wetumpka was constructed around 1855 as a combined tavern and stagecoach stop along the Old Federal Road. Located at 500 Green Street, it sits on a nearly vertical slope. Its main entrance opens off a porch with steps at either side. The lower floor has ground-level doorways opening beneath the porch. There are two entrance doors, side by side on the first and second levels. The McQueen and Ray families did extensive restoration work to preserve the original character of the house. (Kristin Myers.)

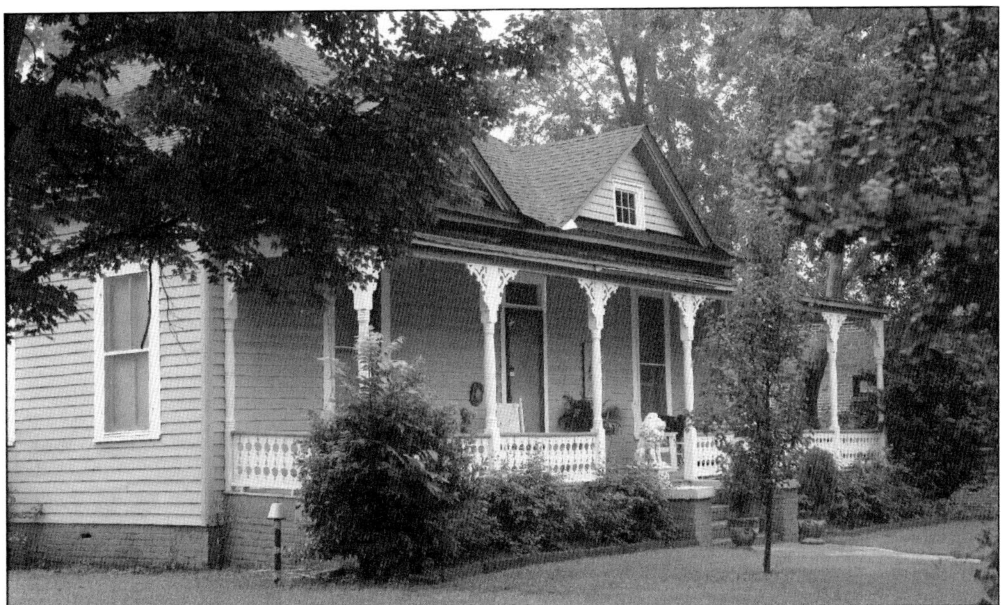

George Parker constructed this Victorian home at 106 North Bridge Street around 1905 for his son, Homer, and his son's bride, Fannie Lou, as a wedding gift. The beautiful crape myrtles lining the east side of the street further enhance the beauty of the "pink house." Fannie Lou's father, M.L. Fielder, was the founder of Eclectic, Alabama. (Kristin Myers.)

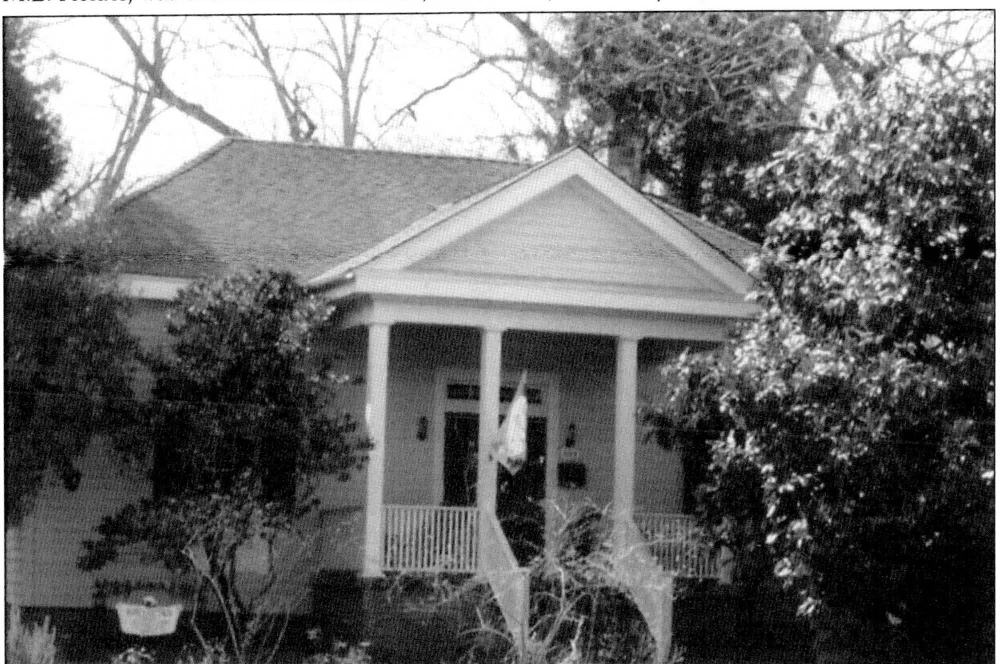

The Rose Cottage, located at 301 West Tuskeena Street across from the First United Methodist Church, served as the Methodist meetinghouse from 1843 to 1854. A very important session of the Alabama Methodist Conference was held in this house in 1845; delegates voted that the churches of this conference would become a part of the Methodist Episcopal Church, South, thus separating from the General Conference. (Kristin Myers.)

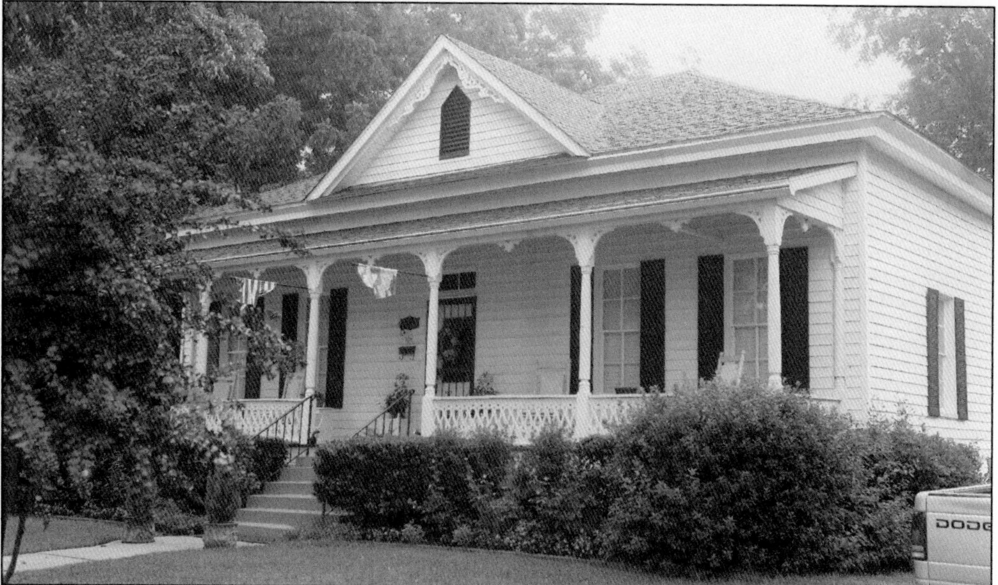

The Charles Sedberry House, built around 1902, is located at 108 North Bridge Street. This was the site of Wetumpka Male Academy. The home is now used as a business that provides private dining, cocktail parties, and intimate weddings. The largest magnolia tree in Elmore County lies to the north side of the house, thus this five-star establishment became Magnolia Cottage. (Kristin Myers.)

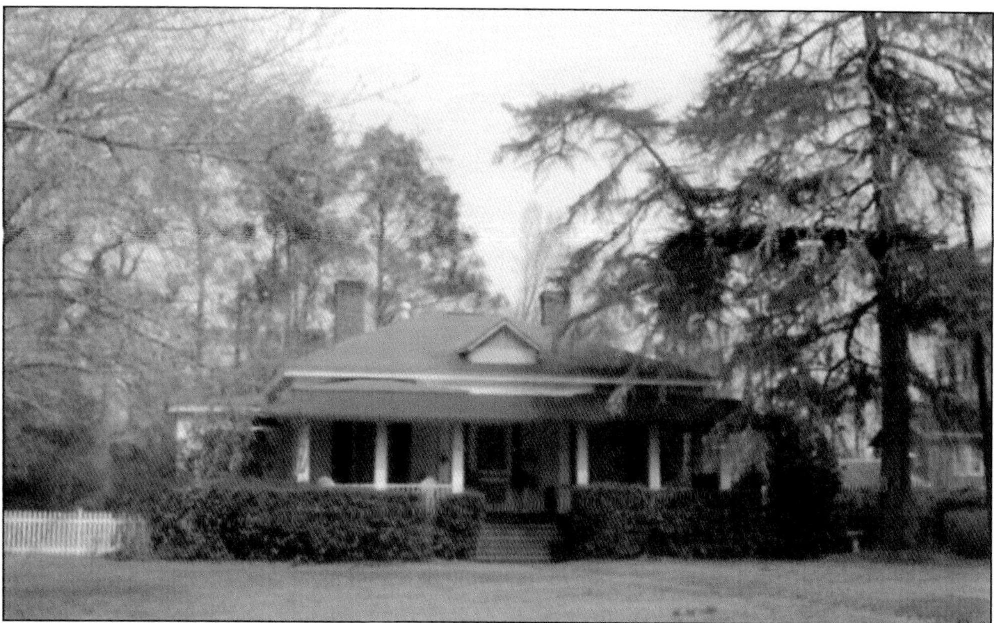

The E. Seman/Cain/Moore House, built around 1827, is located at 204 West Tallassee Street. It began as a combination of two homes joined together. The back part of the residence was originally a small house thought to be the oldest occupied home in the city. Its walls are made of solid home-burned bricks about 18 inches thick. Its timbers were hewn by hand, and sturdy wooden pegs hold them together. This part of the home was later joined to the Moore house. (Kristin Myers.)

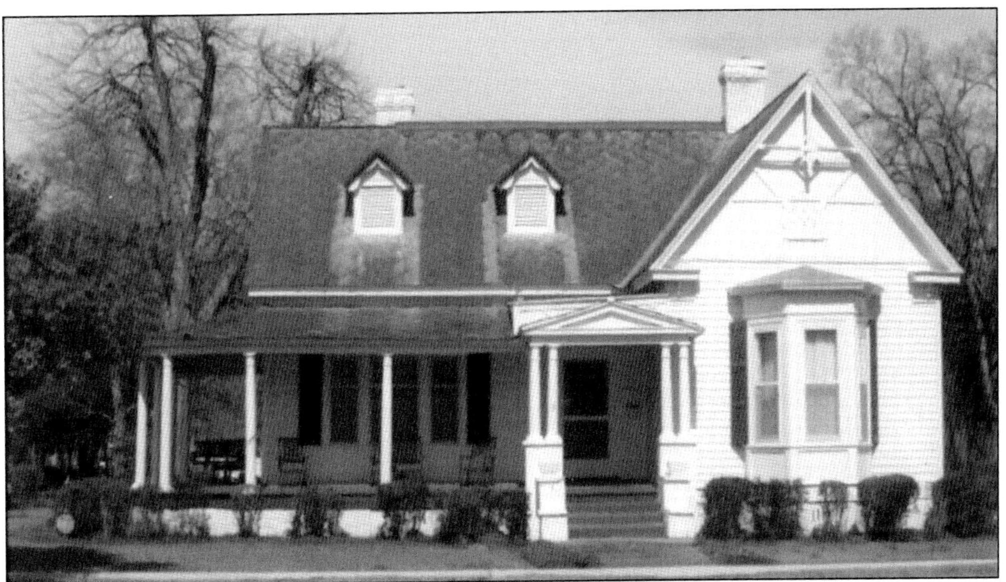

Judge F. Loyd Tate House, located at 408 West Tallassee Street, was built around 1880. As an original central-passage cottage, this home was a two-family dwelling. The D.C. Spivey family moved into the residence in 1947, then purchased it in 1964. That family made it into a single-family home in 1969 and filled it with heirloom antiques. (Kristin Myers.)

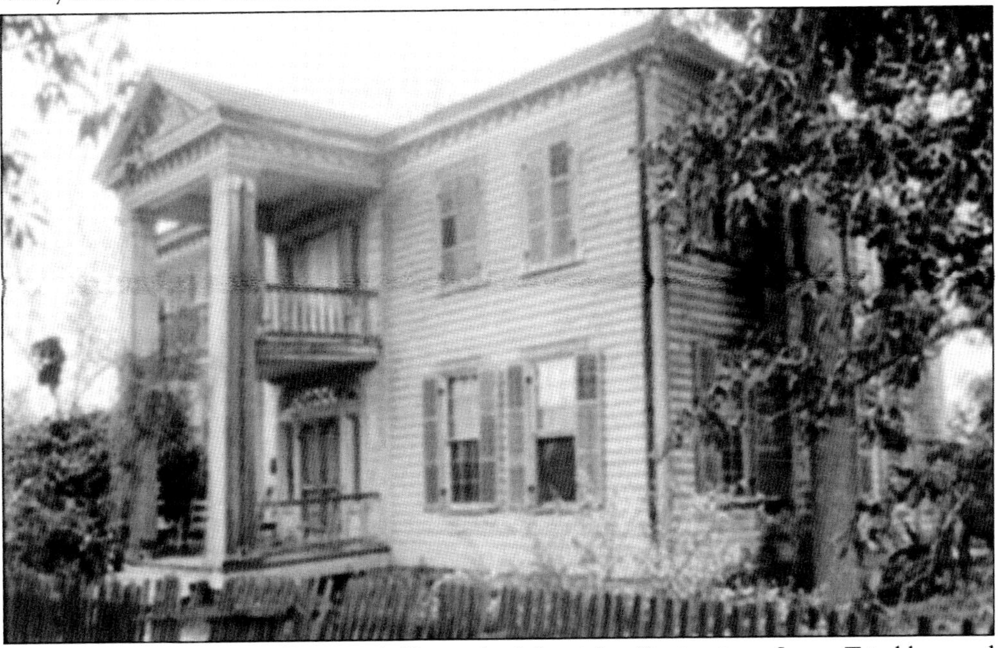

The c. 1840 Trimble-Rose-Fitzpatrick House, built by either Benjamin or James Trimble, stood on Autauga Street in Wetumpka. Col. Howell Rose purchased the property in the late 1850s. By 1876, the house had become the home of Prof. George F. McDonald, a music and dancing teacher. He and his brother Thomas Sherill McDonald built the famous McDonald Opera House in Montgomery. The house was purchased by Dr. Phillips Fitzpatrick in the late 1890s. It was the childhood home of Kelly Fitzpatrick, a noted Southern artist. Kelly lived there until his death in 1953. The house was sold and demolished in 1955. (ECHS.)

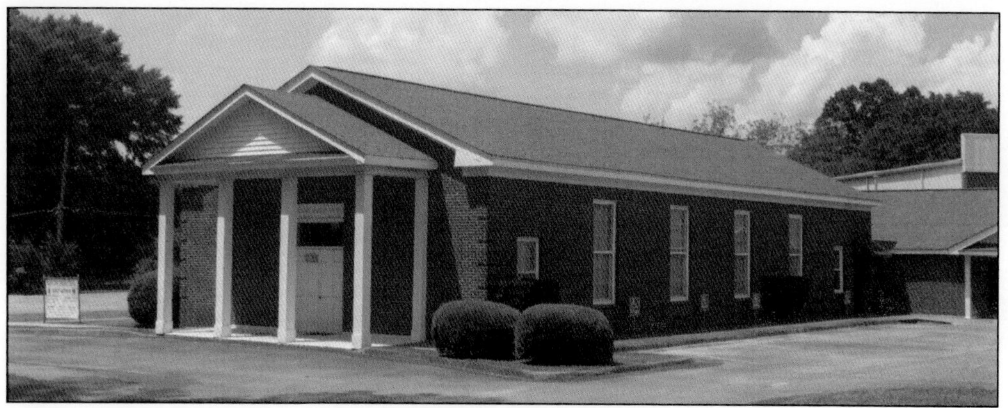

Calvary Baptist Church is located at 504 West Osceola Street. Its unique origin story is that it is a Baptist church founded by Methodists and built on property donated by a Presbyterian. Locals realized the need for ministry for children of the local textile mill village in 1937. The new building was named Union Chapel. Most of the people attending this eclectic church were Baptist, thus 1940 saw the gathering constituted as a Baptist church. In 1962, a new sanctuary was built and adjacent lots were purchased. The name was changed in 1976 to Calvary Baptist Church. (Barry Chrietzberg.)

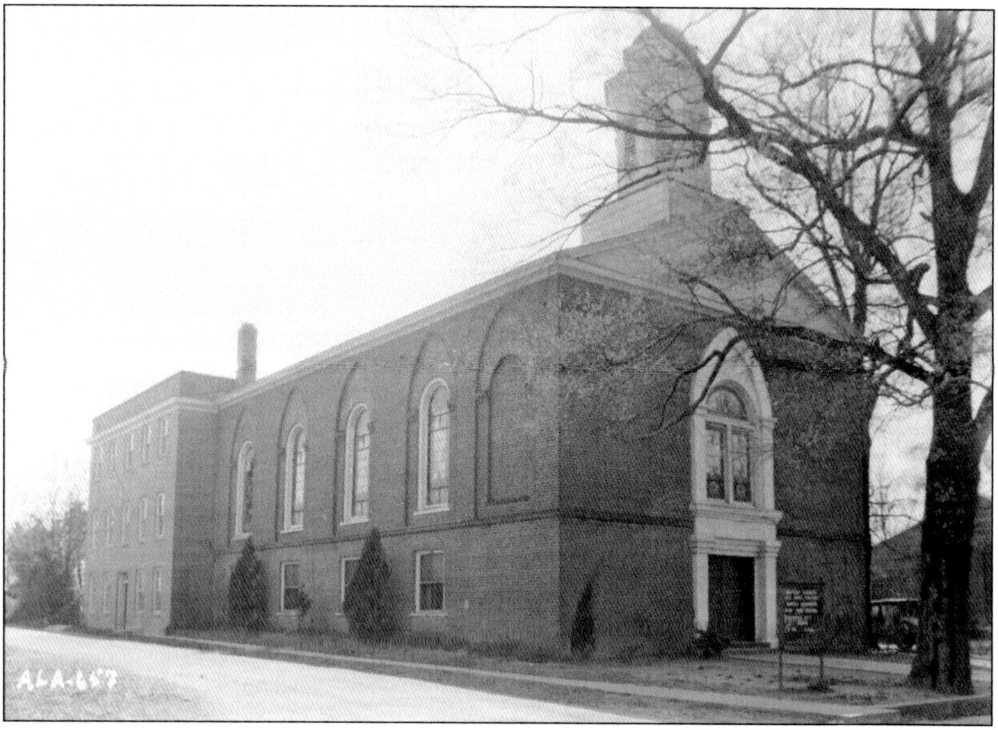

First Baptist Church of Wetumpka is located at 205 West Bridge Street, was organized in 1821, and was originally known as the Coosa River Baptist Church. After having occupied several locations in the countryside west of the Coosa River, the church settled at the Coosa River community several miles west of Wetumpka. Due to doctrinal differences, the church split. One group moved into Wetumpka, joined a small group of like-minded Baptists, and formed the First Baptist Church of Wetumpka. By 1847, members had begun work on a permanent house of worship. The building was completed and dedicated in July 1852. (ECHS.)

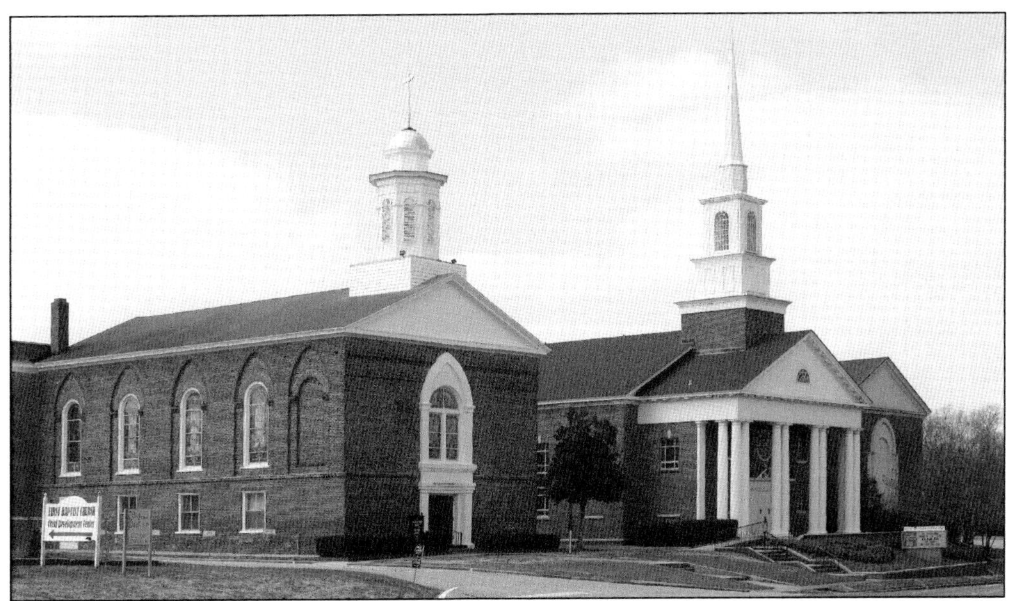

In 1909, when redecoration of the sanctuary began, Corinthian pilasters and other decorative moldings were added to the walls and ceilings. In 1929, Sunday school rooms were added along with a Moeller pipe organ. A two-story educational building was dedicated in March 1960. Ground was broken for a new sanctuary in 1966, and for a new educational building in 1991 with office suite, conference room, music suite, kitchen, fellowship hall, and 17 classrooms. (Barry Chrietzberg.)

First (United) Methodist Church, located at 306 West Tuskeena Street, was organized in 1819. It occupied two or three locations around Wetumpka before settling in a small wooden structure on Tuskeena Street in 1843. In 1853, plans for a new building were made. The small building the congregation had been meeting in was moved across the street and construction of the new building was begun and completed in 1854. (ECHS.)

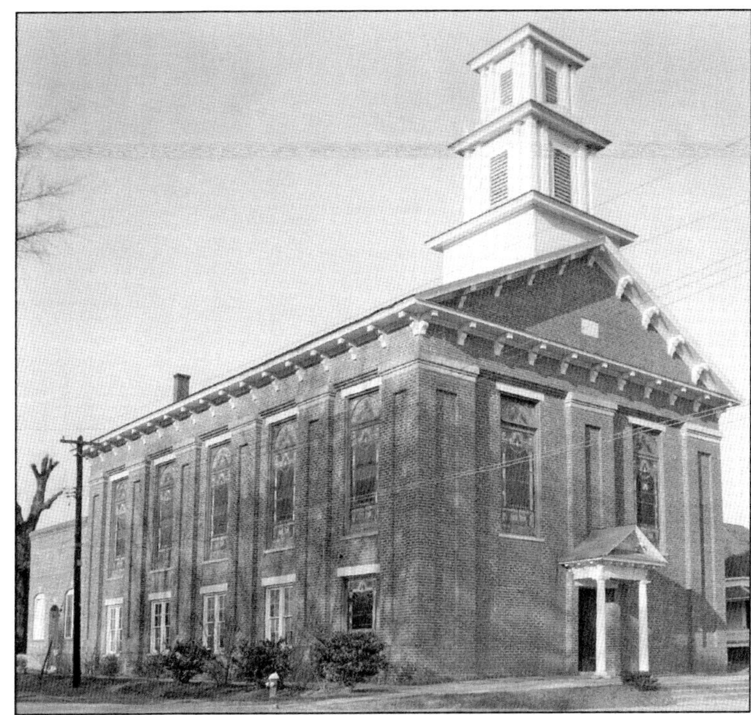

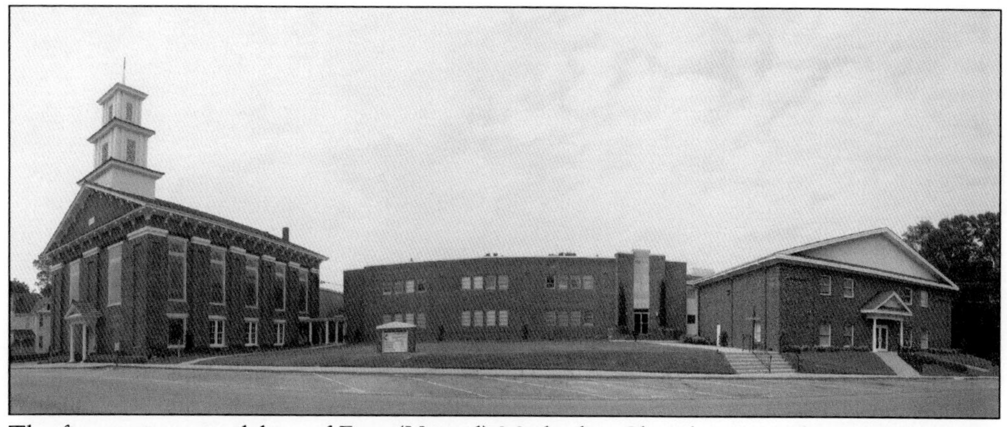

The first major remodeling of First (United) Methodist Church occurred in 1909 with the addition of light fixtures, a hot-air furnace, a hand-pumped pipe organ, new pews, and stained-glass windows. A new educational building was completed in 1957. In the 1970s, $75,000 was put into preservation, restoration, remodeling, and repairing. In 1984, a classroom was converted into a beautiful memorial chapel. This was followed by the 1999 Family Life Center connecting the educational building by means of an elevator. Other enhancements include a modern kitchen and downstairs fellowship hall. (Barry Chrietzberg.)

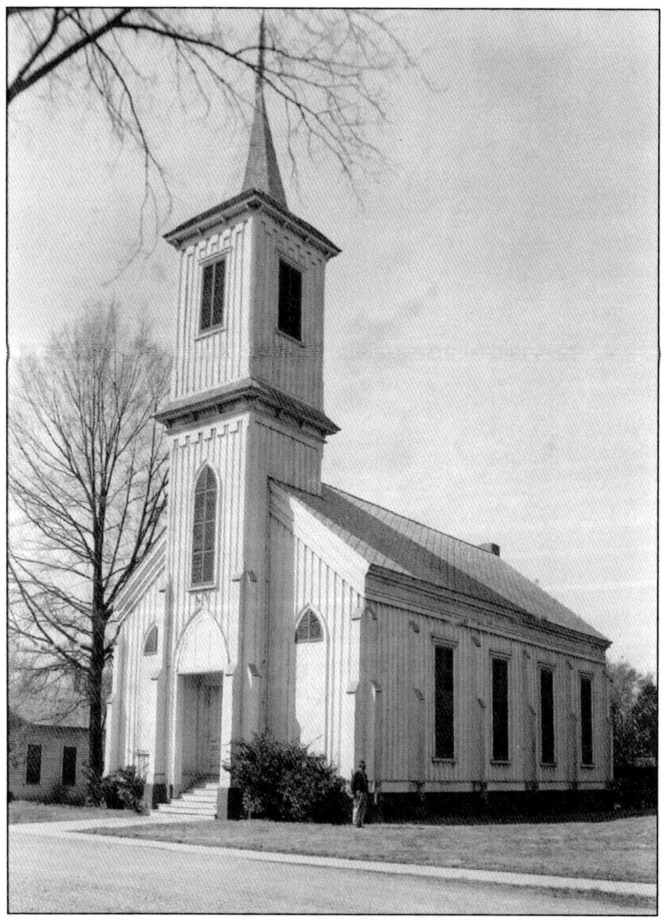

First Presbyterian Church, located at 100 West Bridge Street, was founded in 1836 and built its first church in 1857. This structure is an early Carpenter Gothic style. The exterior has a classic window treatment with stationary blinds. The new church was dedicated in 1857 and prospered before the Civil War. On April 27, 1861, some 141 young men—members of the Wetumpka Light Guard—heard a farewell sermon here before they left to join the 3rd Alabama Regiment of Infantry. (ECHS.)

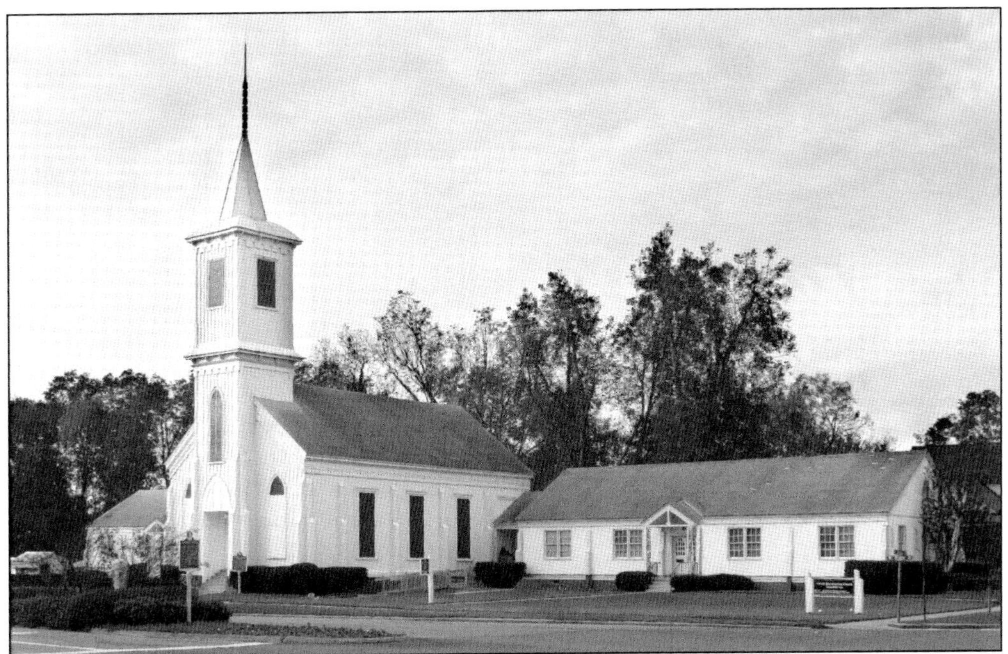

In 1933, the church was restored to its original beauty. It celebrated its 100th anniversary in April 1936. An educational or east wing was erected in 1947; classrooms, recreational hall, and kitchen were included. A Baldwin organ was bought in 1949; a new manse was purchased in 1951 though sold later on, and the house and lot west of the church were added to church property in 1956. The "west wing" was completed in 1955–56. First Presbyterian Church has now celebrated more than 177 years. (Barry Chrietzberg.)

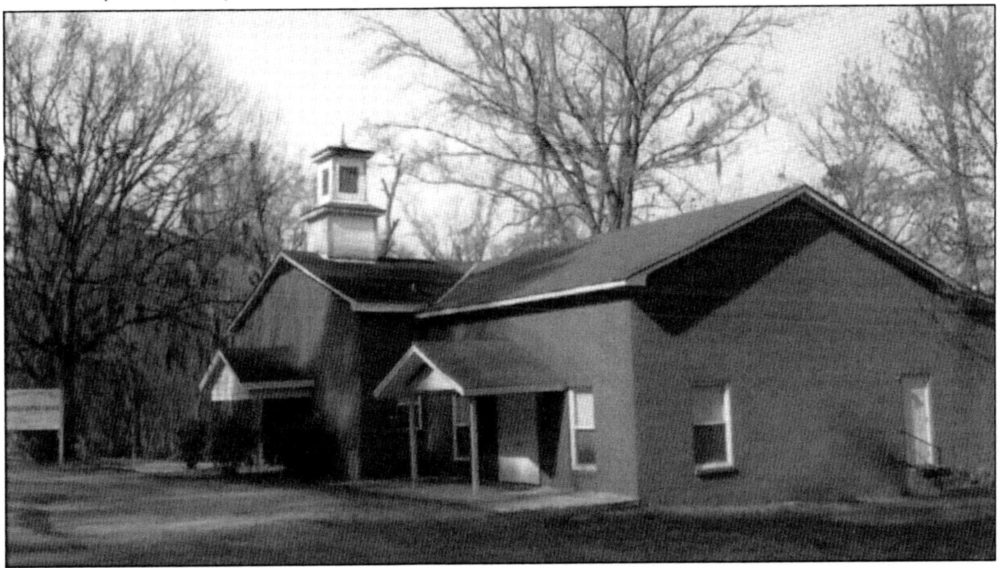

Guilfield Baptist Church, founded in 1870, is located at 421 Company Street. In 1869, Thomas Williams, a Representative in Congress, gave this property to the black members of the First Baptist Church for the purpose of building a house of worship. The name Gift Field was selected because the property was indeed a gift of love. Through the years, the name has evolved into Guilfield. It continues to serve the members of its community. (Kristin Myers.)

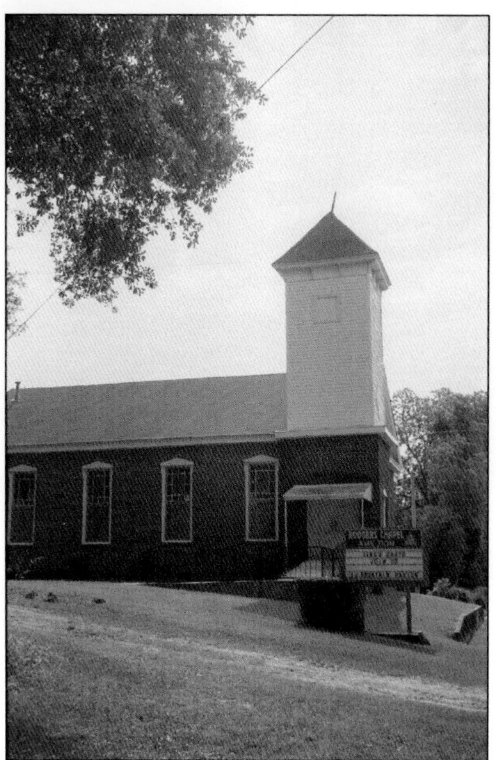

Rodgers Chapel AME Zion Church is located at 609 West Bridge Street. A group of former slaves from the Methodist church founded this church in 1863. They erected their first building in 1884 on the site of the old Wetumpka Ice and Coal Company. The growing church was destroyed by a tornado, and the foundation for the new church was formed from stones that were hauled from the banks of the Coosa River. The frame church, dedicated in 1902, was named for a beloved pastor. In 1965, the building was bricked, and the entrance was moved from the front to the side. (Kristin Myers.)

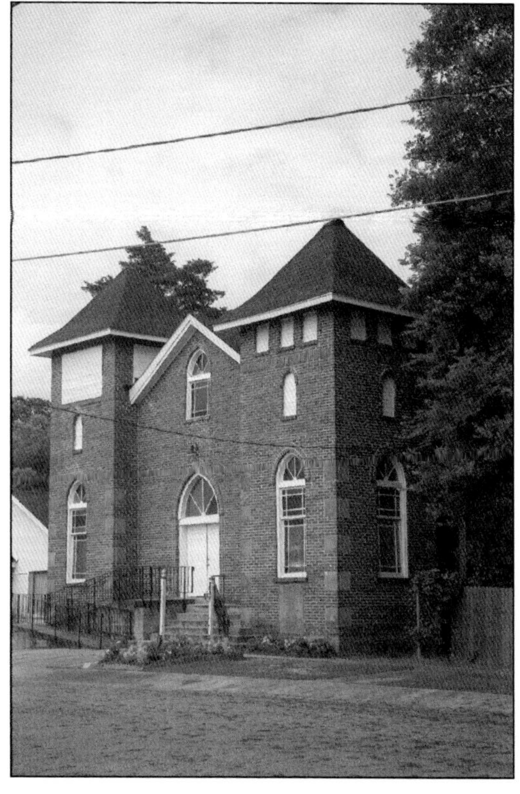

Second Missionary Baptist Church is located at 760 North Bridge Street. Before the Civil War, both races worshipped together in the Coosa River Baptist Church. After the Civil War, the colored members requested to withdraw to establish their own churches since they had been set free. The request was granted, and a plot of land was donated to Second Missionary Baptist. The first frame sanctuary was erected in 1887. In 1899, the church was destroyed by a violent storm; however, members rebuilt the church that same year. (Kristin Myers.)

In 1947, a number of Episcopalians gathered to form a church. A small concrete-block structure located on Austin Lane was the first church building. In 1968, the congregation explored of expansion. The old Cantelou-Law Cotton Warehouse was purchased by a couple (members of the church) and donated to the congregation. Many accoutrements from both the first building and nearby churches were donated or purchased and incorporated into the new church. A companion structure for classrooms and a parish hall was also built. A consecration service was conducted in 1971. (ECHS.)

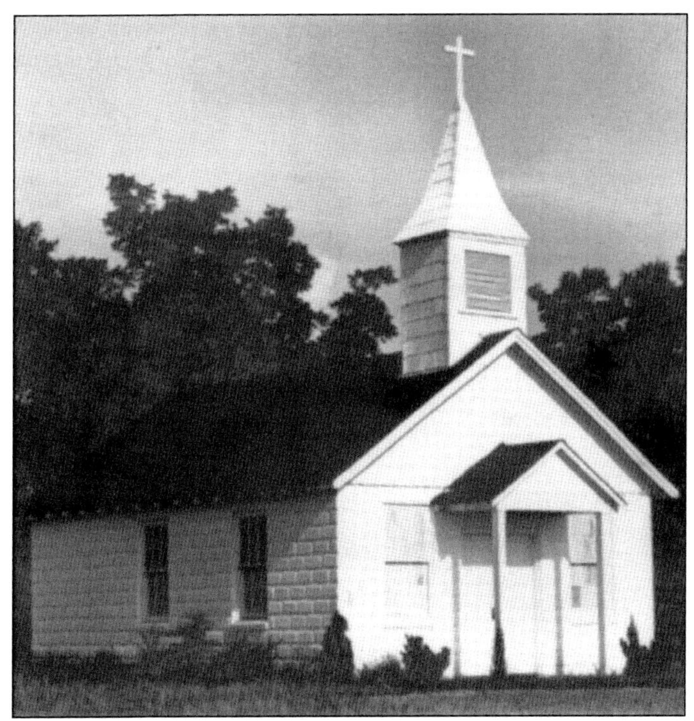

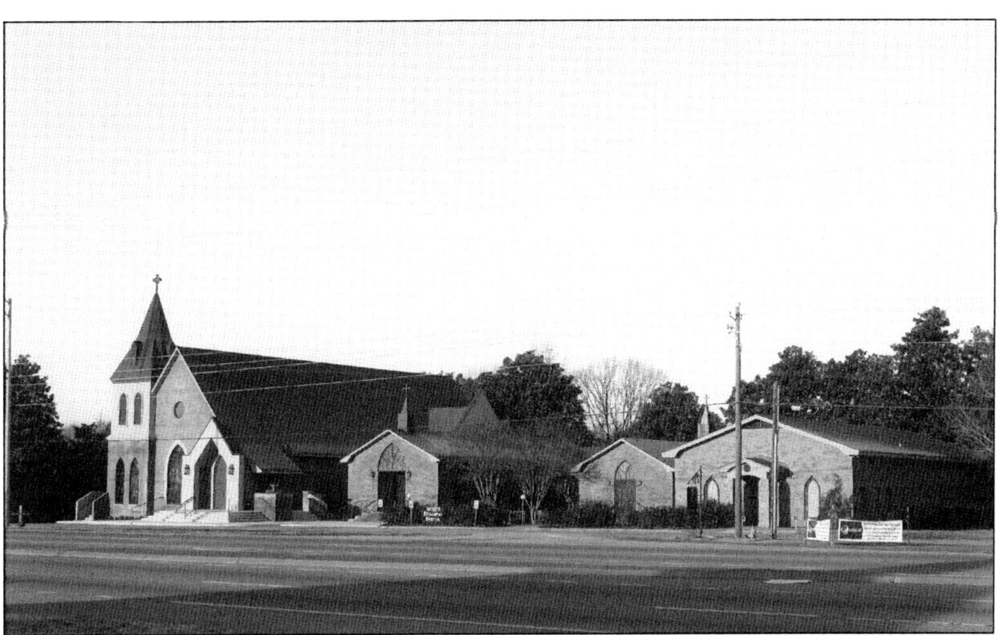

The Episcopal church organized in Wetumpka in 1837 had ceased to exist by the early 1850s. Its demise was caused by political unrest and lack of membership. With its reorganization in 1947 and the construction of its church building, the congregation began to grow. In October 2009, the new sanctuary and present complex were consecrated by its loyal membership. Trinity Episcopal Church is located at 5375 US Highway 231. (Barry Chrietzberg.)

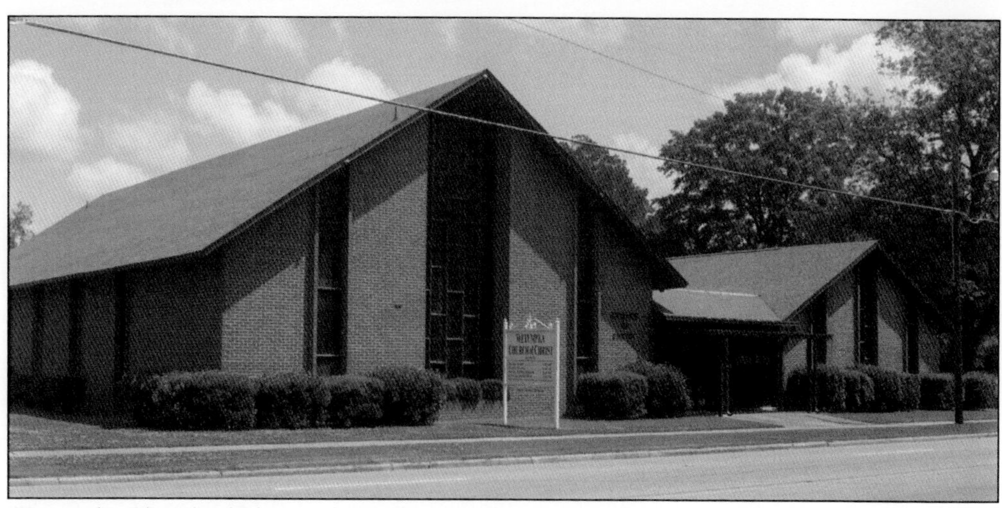

Wetumpka Church of Christ is located at 408 West Bridge Street. In 1919, a group of people who migrated from Pond Creek, Tennessee, met in homes and at the Speigner farm—members were known as the Tennessee Farm Congregation until they moved to town in 1924. In early 1926, they purchased one and, eventually, all the lots in that entire block. In 1958, the group remodeled the building and added brick siding. The church building now includes a 350-seat sanctuary, a well-stocked library, and other rooms to accommodate a growing congregation. (Barry Chrietzberg.)

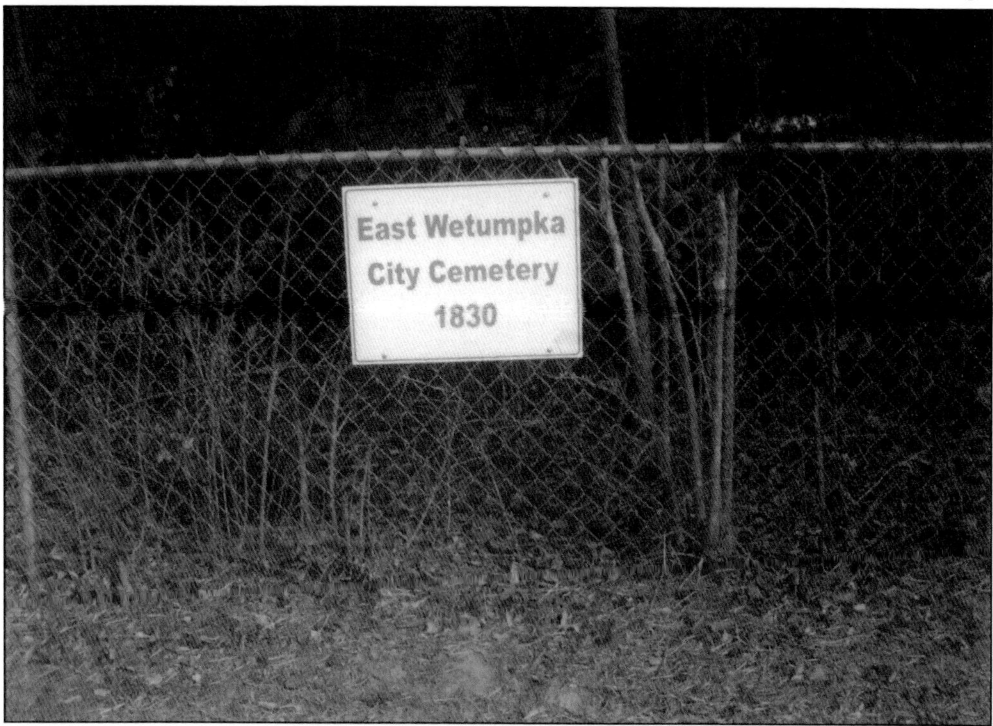


The most recent clearing of debris and undergrowth from the old abandoned East Wetumpka Cemetery was performed by two members of the Elmore County Historical Society. This cemetery, in use from 1830 to 1850, is in a unique location on a ridge between the forks of two creeks and the Coosa River. A survey of the cemetery revealed 16 known graves, some with headstones, and eight more possible graves, dating between 1836 and 1858. (James Hicks.)

The Harrogate Springs Cemetery is located on Harrogate Springs Road, with approximately 50 graves, including those of both whites and blacks. The tombstone of a young slave girl who worked at the hotel is said to have been erected by the young men who were hotel guests. The many names she was given by the gentlemen are inscribed on the tombstone, which reads: "Henry Ritter/Ema Ritter/Dema Ritter/Sweet Potatoe/Creama Tarter/ Caroline Bostic/Daughter of Bob and Suckey Catlen/Born at Social Circle 1843/Died at Wetumpka 1852." The stone is currently located in the Elmore County Museum. (Peggy Blackburn.)

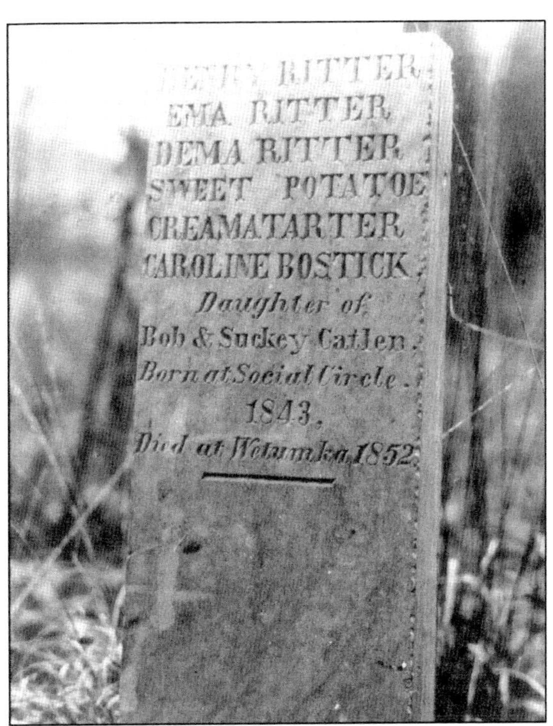


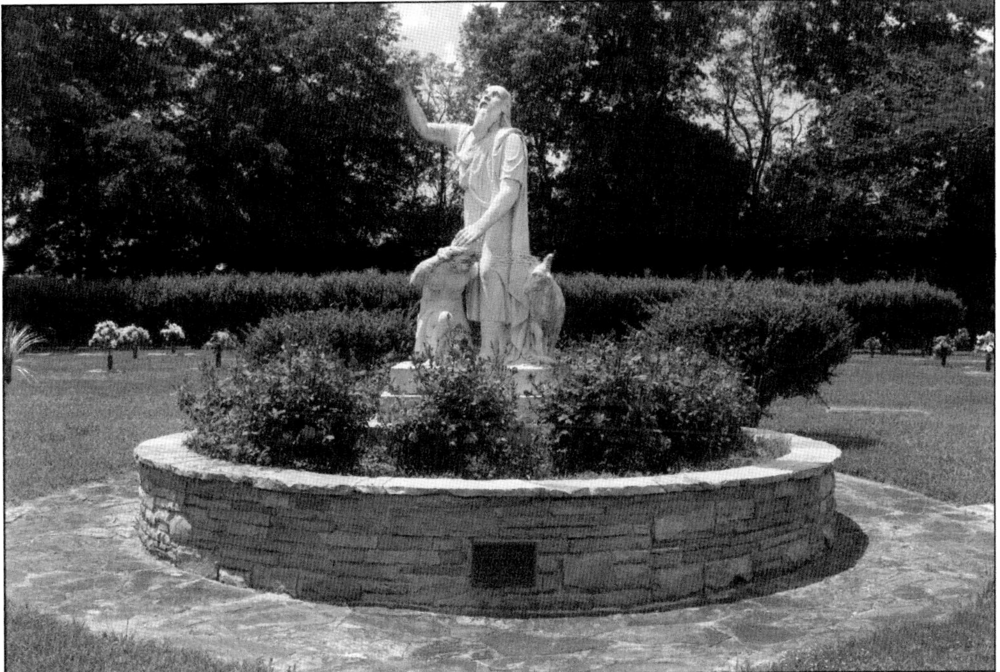

Pine View Memorial Gardens, 2325 Holtville Highway, is a privately owned perpetual care garden, incorporated in 1957. This land was the Fifth District Agricultural School farm acreage. Bettie Welden is the current owner. Eight to nine acres are included in four beautifully developed gardens—Garden of Faith, Garden of Prayer, Garden of Living Waters, and Garden of Valor. The gardens are maintained through purchase of burial plots. (Barry Chrietzberg.)

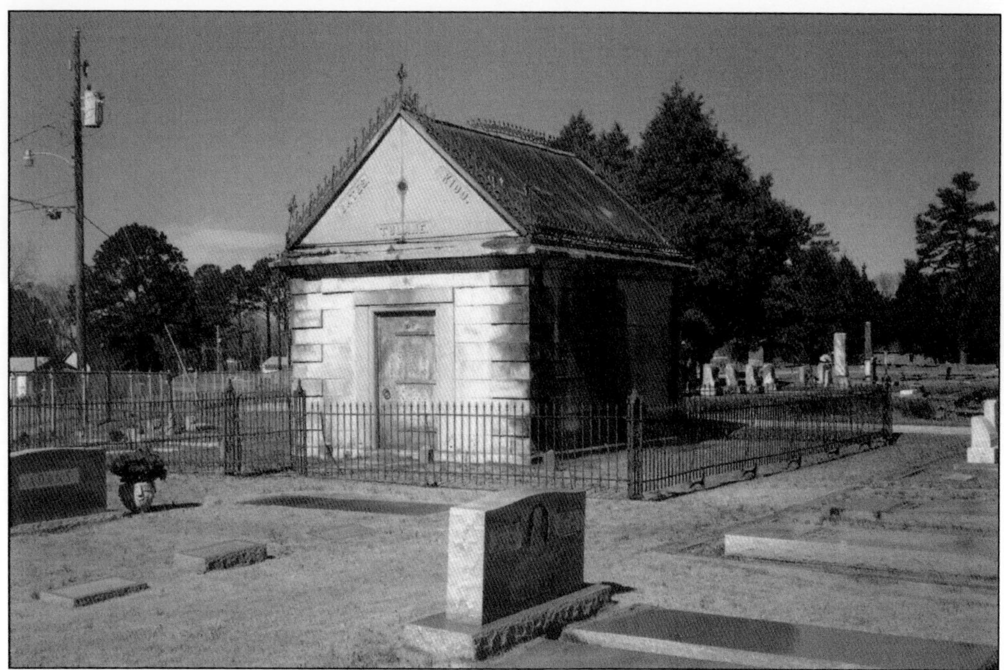

The Tulane-Bates-Kidd burial vault is located on the west side of the cemetery. It contains 15 sealed wall compartments and one burial under the floor. An article in the September 5, 1889, edition of the *Elmore Democrat* reads, "It was built by Messrs. Curbow and Clapp, of Montgomery, Alabama for H.B. Tulane of this place. The vault is of Alabama limestone, eighteen by twenty-five feet and has fifteen compartments. It will be used for the Tulane, Bates and Kidd families." Tulane University is named for this same family. (Kristin Myers.)

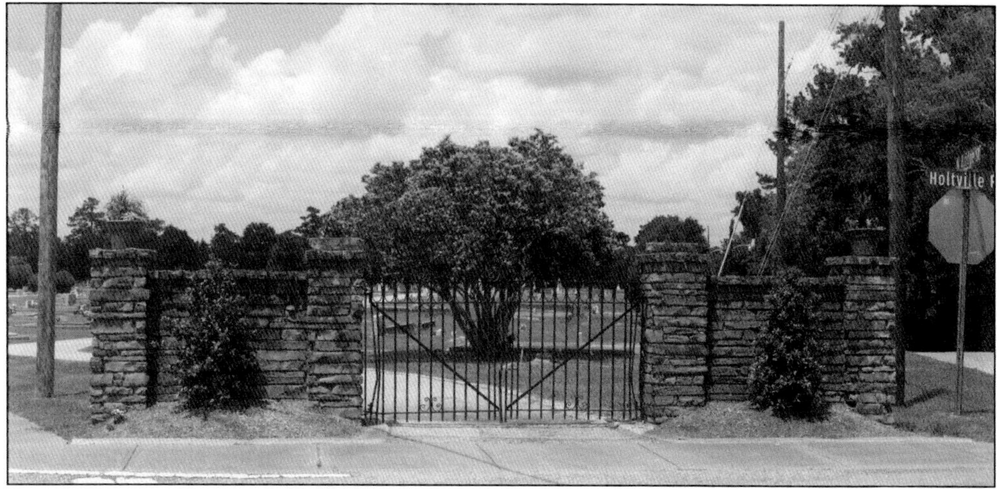


Wetumpka City is a large cemetery located on the west side of the Coosa River at 776 North Bridge Street. It has been in use since the 1830s.The oldest grave is that of Laura A. Merrill, a schoolteacher who died in 1834 at the age of 37. Other burials include "Little Barbery, who departed this life November 12, year unknown; she was two years old." Rev. Robert Holman, pastor of the First Presbyterian Church in Wetumpka, was born in Kentucky in 1801 and died in New Georgia in 1841 and was laid to rest here alongside graves of other interesting people in their final resting places. (Barry Chrietzberg.)

# *Seven*

# Cultural Locations

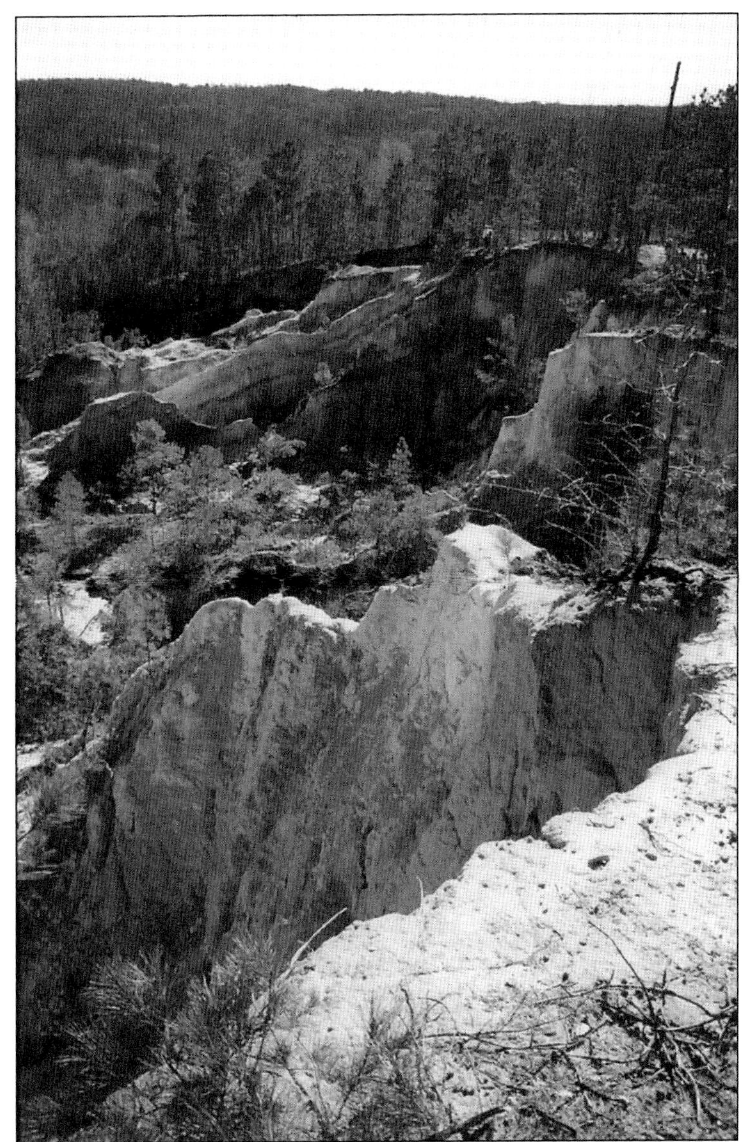

The location of the Wetumpka Impact Crater, or Astrobleme, a "star wound," occurred because of a cosmic event that was only recently confirmed by extensive investigation and deep core drilling conducted on-site. Rock samples revealed the presence of "shocked quartz" in mid-1999. Wetumpka is the site of the only authenticated impact crater in the eastern United States and one of only 200 craters worldwide. Scientists describe it as the best-preserved marine impact crater in the world because the location was covered by a shallow sea at the time of impact. Bald Knob Mountain is the highest point on the crater rim. This photograph shows the area commonly known as "The Cliffs." (Barry Chrietzberg.)

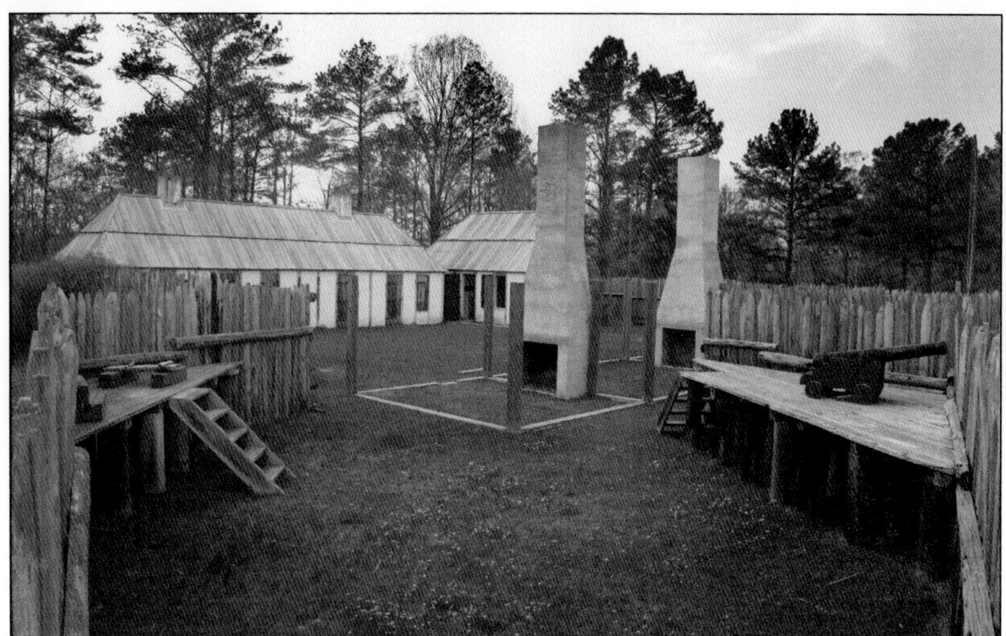

Just south of downtown Wetumpka, at 2521 West Fort Toulouse Road, evidence of over 6,000 years of the area's history is among the 165 acres of Fort Toulouse/Jackson State Historic Site, located where the Coosa and Tallapoosa Rivers meet. Here, visitors can explore both French and American forts, a Mississippian mound site, wildflower fields and forests on the William Bartram Nature Trail, the museum and Graves House filled with archaeological artifacts, and even get a tangible taste of yesterday's traditions at the living history weekends held once a month. (Fort Toulouse/Jackson.)

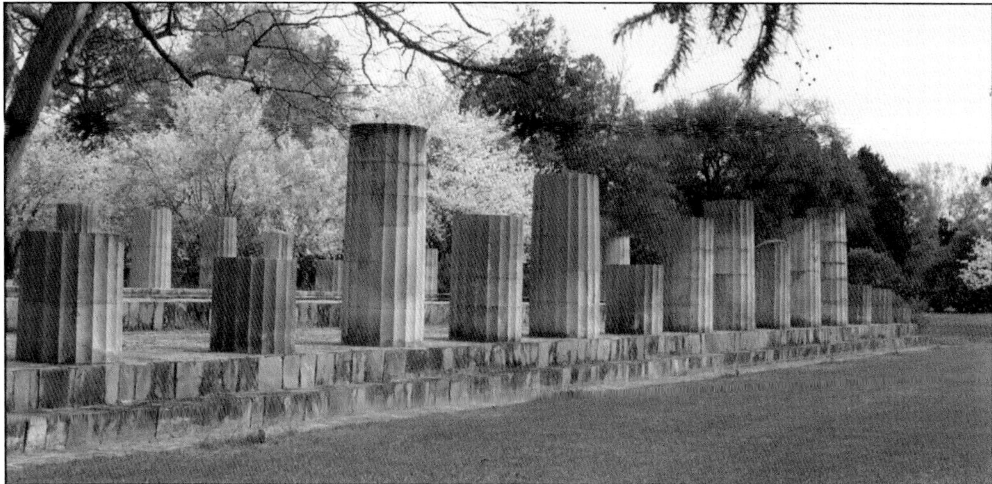

A stroll through the 17 acres of flowering blooms and the impressive collection of statuary awaits visitors to 3001 Jasmine Hill Road. A tour of Jasmine Hill includes a walk through the full-scale replica of the Temple of Hera ruins as found in Olympia, Greece; the scaled replica Olympian Center; and the cottage and many artifacts brought back by owners Ben and Mary Fitzpatrick from their many trips to Greece. The Gardens and Outdoor Museum are an ideal place for weddings, parties, dinners, and receptions, and also a choice spot for meetings, seminars, and photography sessions. (Peggy Blackburn.)

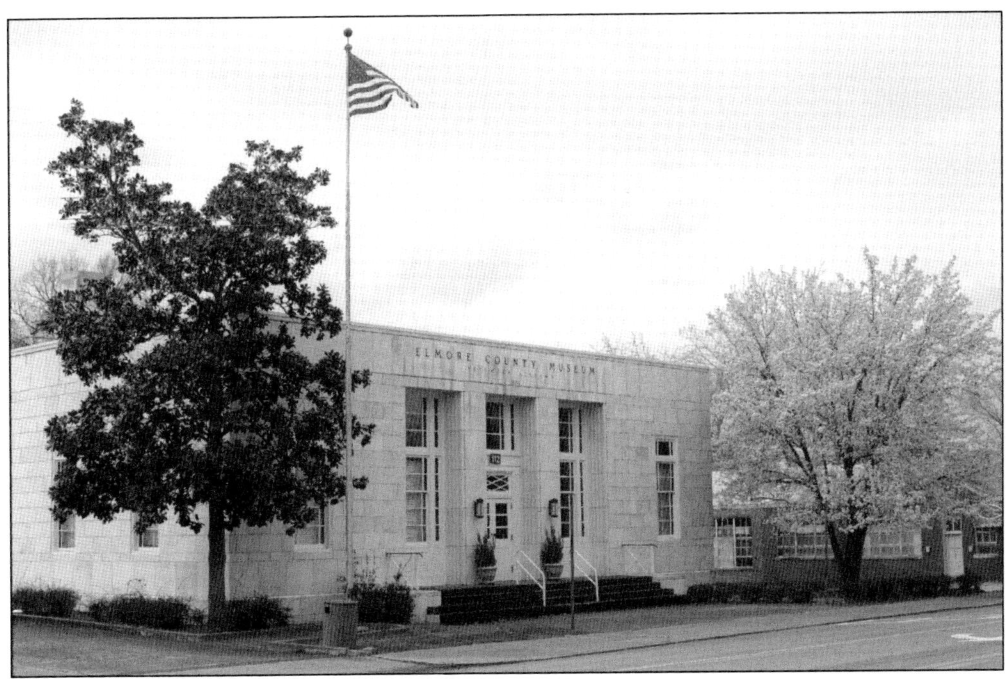


The Elmore County Museum was established in 1984 and had its first space on Company Street; it later moved to the Alliance Warehouse, located at 112 South Main Street, which was constructed in the 1820s as an Indian trading post. The old Wetumpka Post Office was leased to the Elmore County Historical Society on February 15, 2008, for use as a museum. Many artifacts are now preserved in the museum, including items that portray everyday life in early Alabama, like a barn loom, a spinning wheel, bed coverlets, metal farm implements, paintings, photographs, documents, various community records, and family history data sheets. (ECHS.)

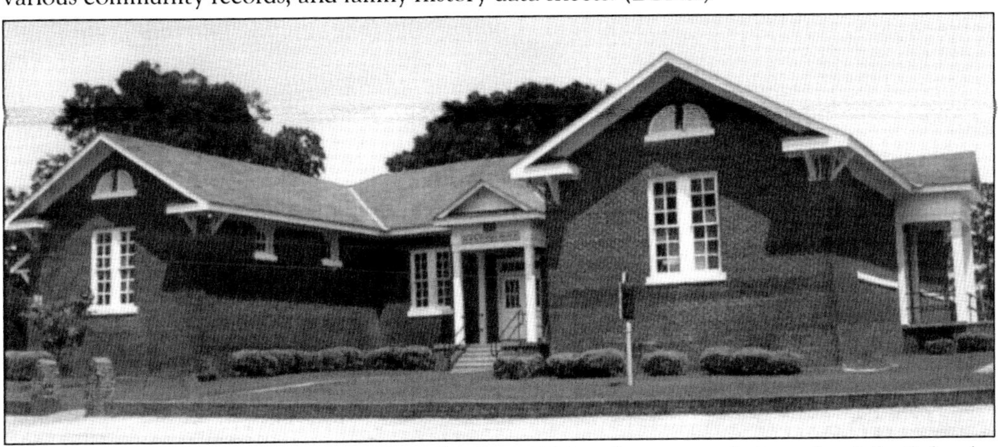

The Elmore County Training School was built in 1924 and was one of nine schools built by the Julius Rosenwald Foundation. This was the first county school for African Americans. Rosenwald, president of Sears, Roebuck and Company, and Booker T. Washington, president of Tuskegee Institute (now Tuskegee University), initiated the building program. In 1986, former mayor Jeanette Barrett felt the landmark could be an asset to the community. She recruited individuals to help save the structure, and they created the Elmore County Black History Museum. This museum, located at 202 Lancaster Street, opened in 1986 and houses history from the black communities in Elmore County. (ECHS.)

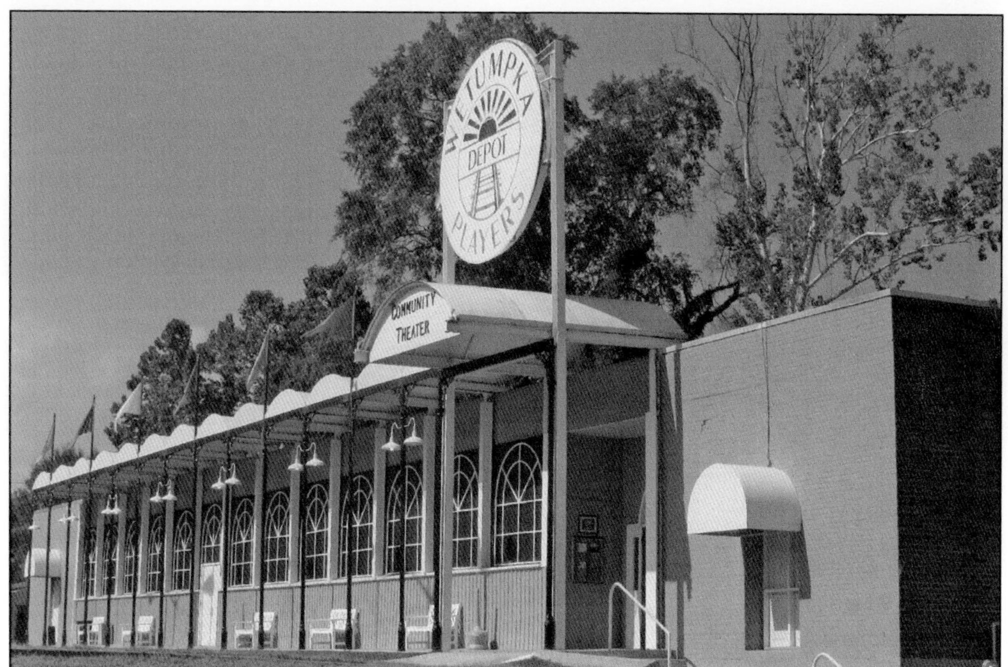


Founded in 1980 by a small but dedicated group of theater enthusiasts, the award-winning Wetumpka Depot Players are now the region's oldest community theater. The Players fulfill their mission of entertaining, educating, and reaching out by producing five–seven productions a year, and by hosting theater arts workshops. The troupe originated in the historic L&N train shed behind the First United Methodist Church. Local citizens as well as visitors from across the state make up the sold-out audiences. The troupe was recognized by the Southeastern Theater Conference–Best Production and represented the Southeast at the American Association of Community Theater festival in Rochester, New York, in 2011. It is located at 300 South Main Street. (Barry Chrietzberg.)

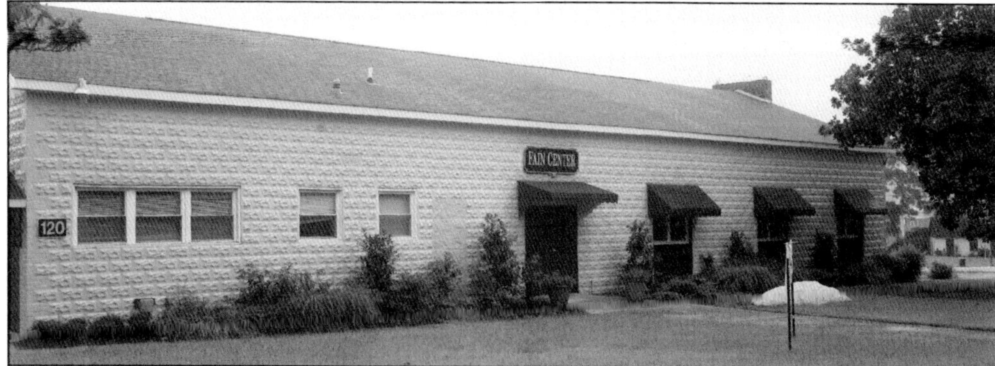


In 1947, plans for a community park were formulated and funds were raised by a group of Wetumpka citizens. The plans called for a community house and a swimming pool. The community house was completed in October 1947. The following year, a swimming pool and bathhouse were opened. The park area was further developed by the addition of a barbecue pit, two tennis courts, a sheltered eating area, and a hut for the Boy Scouts and Girl Scouts. The community house was named the Fain Center in honor of Edward C. Fain, one of the early organizers of the park. The Fain Center is located at 120 Cotton Street and is currently being used as a senior center operated by the City of Wetumpka. (Barry Chrietzberg.)

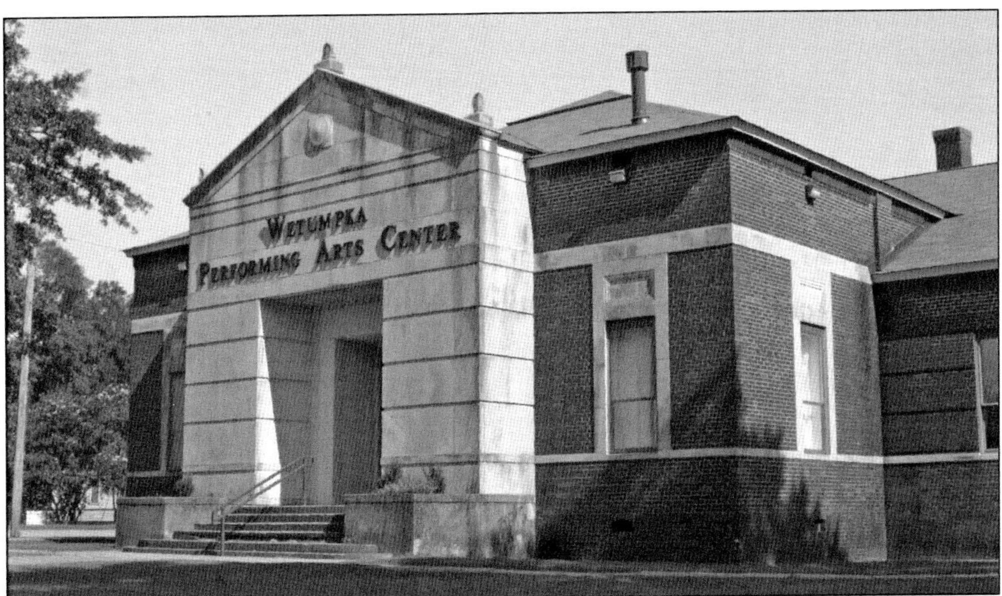


The Wetumpka Performing Arts Center, along with the Alabama River Region Arts Center, occupies the original Wetumpka High School constructed in 1939 at 300 Tallassee Street. The school's auditorium constitutes a performance center with more than 500 seats and a stage large enough to accommodate concerts, theatrical performances, and pageant contests. The arts center, located in the same building, is a volunteer-based, community-supported nonprofit organization that derives funding from public and private donations, contributions, artist space rental, gallery art sales, and special events. The center's mission is to enhance community life through an environment where all can "study, create, and present art." (Kristin Myers.)

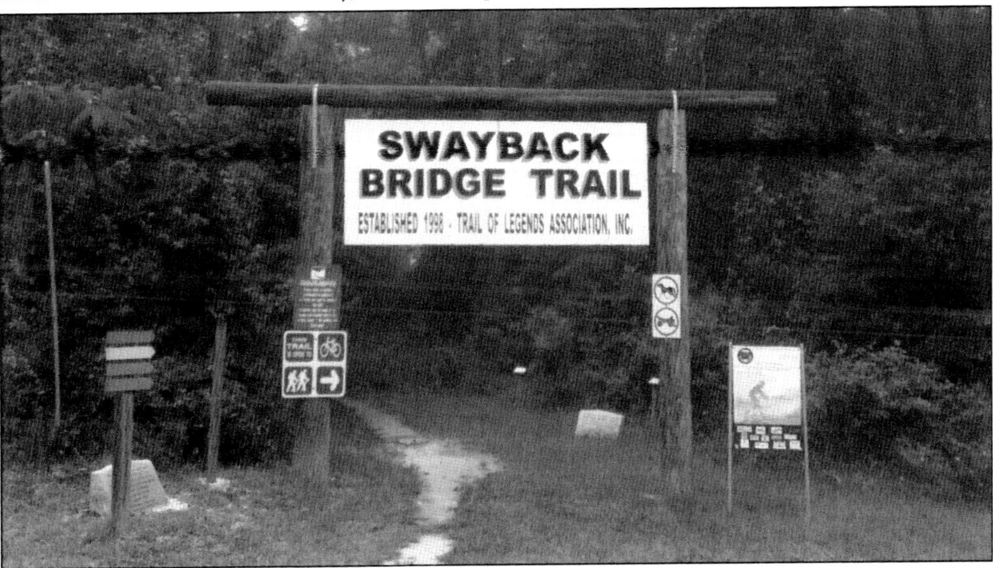


Swayback Bridge Trail was established in 1998 by the Trail of Legends Association. The trail is a rugged 12-mile path located near Lake Jordan. Markers along the way guide those competing in sanctioned competitions. It is almost completely single-track, with some tight technical sections and steep climbs. The trail site is off Old US Highway 231 near Camp Chandler, north of Wetumpka. The "Attack on Swayback" bike competition began in 2003. (ECHS.)

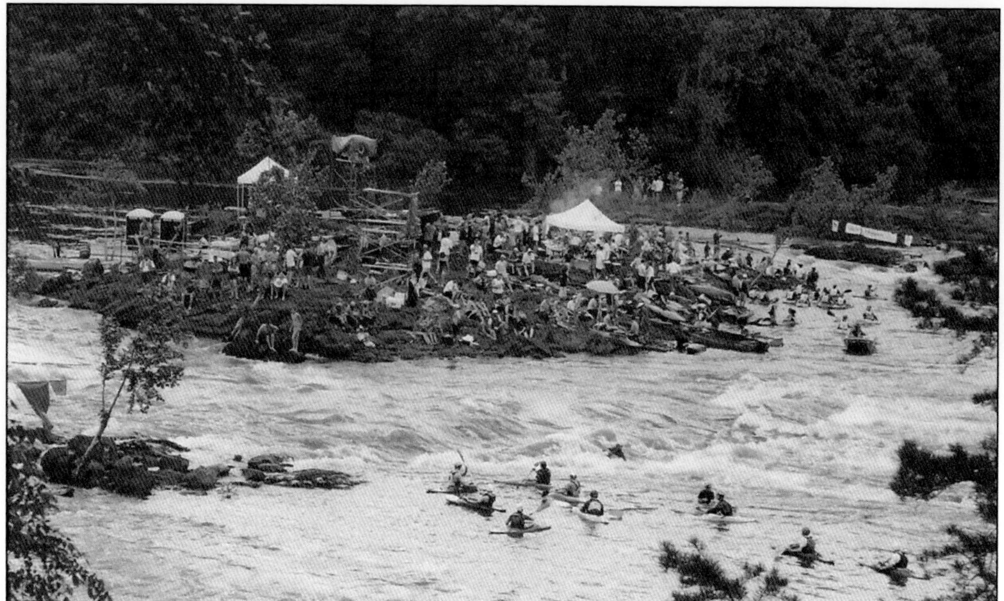

Riverfest, sponsored by the Wetumpka Area Chamber of Commerce, began in 2001 with two professional musical acts and in later years featured local entertainers. This festival evolved into Craterfest in 2013; Chamber's Brown Bag Concerts began in 2002; Coosa River Challenge Adventure Race began in 2002; and Christmas on the Coosa began in 1972. Many choose to fish or boat, but for the more adventurous, areas for canoeing and kayaking are plentiful. Moccasin Gap features the only whitewater south of the Ocoee suitable for surfing (riding a kayak on top of the water) and ender (flipping a kayak end over end) as a part of sanctioned competitive judging. (Barry Chrietzberg.)

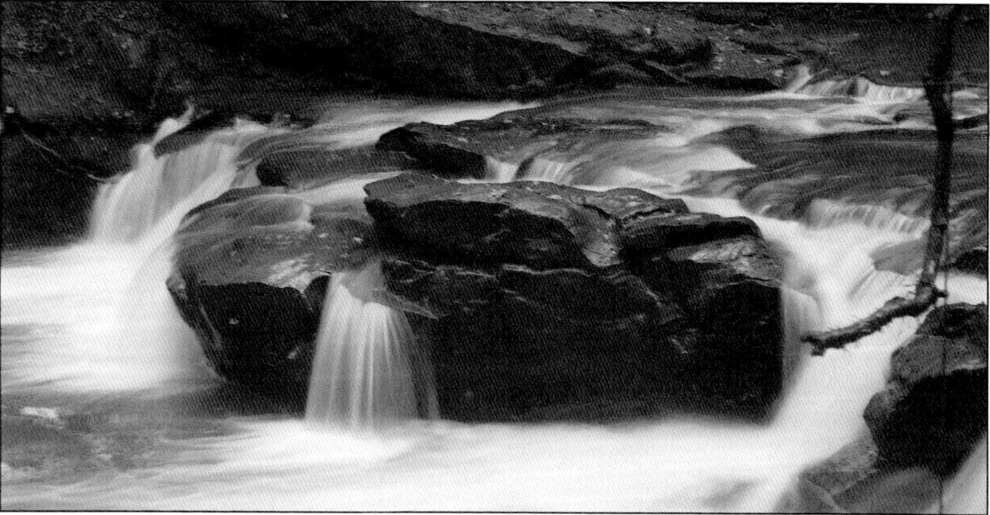

The Corn Creek Park is located near the Coosa River, behind the Elmore County Judicial Complex and Elmore County Jail. It was created by active members of the Coosa River Paddling Club in July 1999 under the leadership of the club and the Elmore County Commission. It affords opportunities for kayakers and paddlers to enter the water, fish, or picnic. Eagle Scouts have identified and marked trees and other vegetation, as well as constructed picnic tables and other public usage areas. (Barry Chrietzberg.)

Gold Star Park borders the Coosa River, which separates the east and west—or business and residential—sides of Wetumpka. The expansive multi-acre park accommodates facilities such as a playground, a walking trail, benches, an outdoor covered stage and limited bleacher seating, picnic tables, a gazebo, restrooms, a boardwalk, a boat launch, and a parking area. (Barry Chrietzberg.)

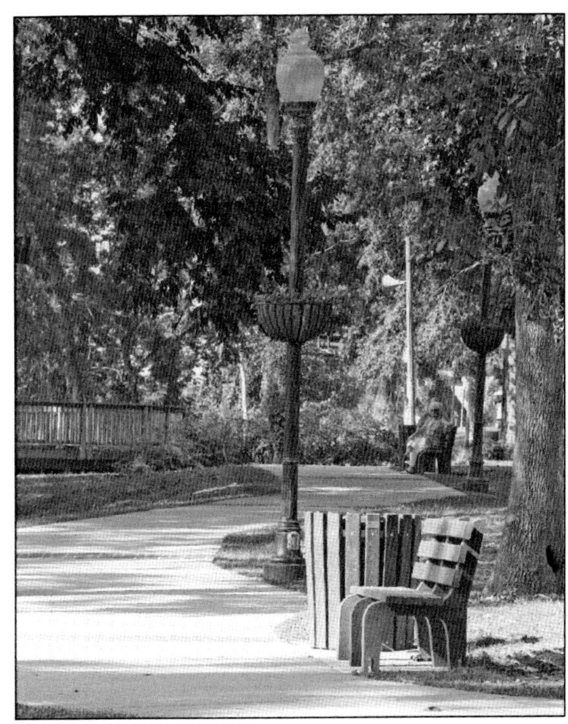

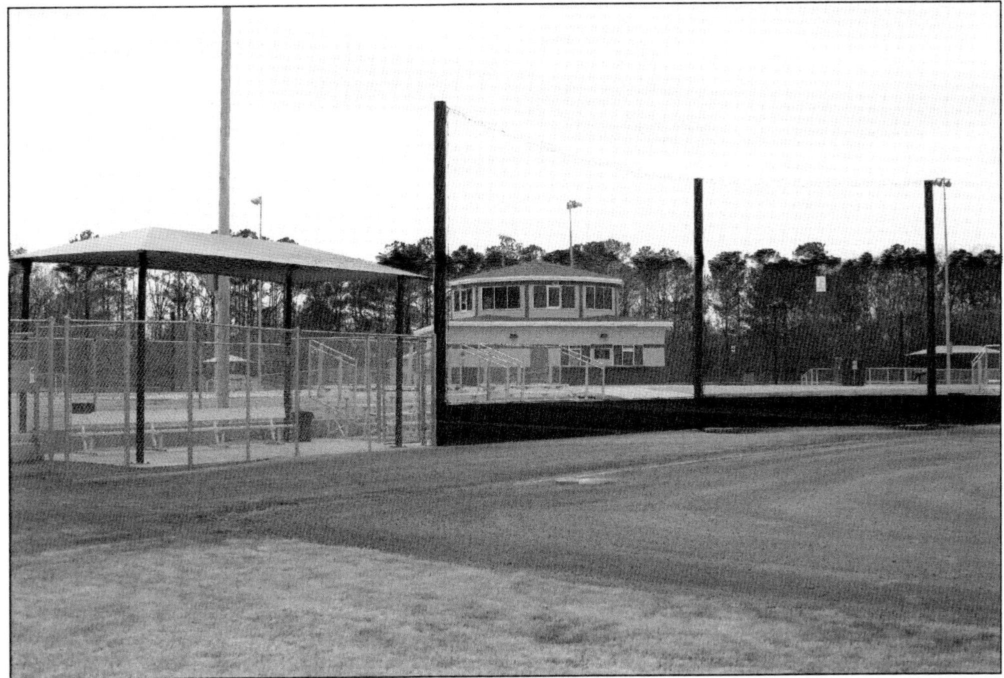

The Wetumpka Sports Complex consists of five fields in a hub setting with a centrally located press box and concession stand. Eight-foot fences stand around the permanent outfield, which measures 200 feet from home plate to the outfield. The spacious dugouts are connected to bullpens on each side of the field. There is ample parking, ten batting cages, and three warm-up areas. The location accommodates many softball tournaments each year. (Barry Chrietzberg.)

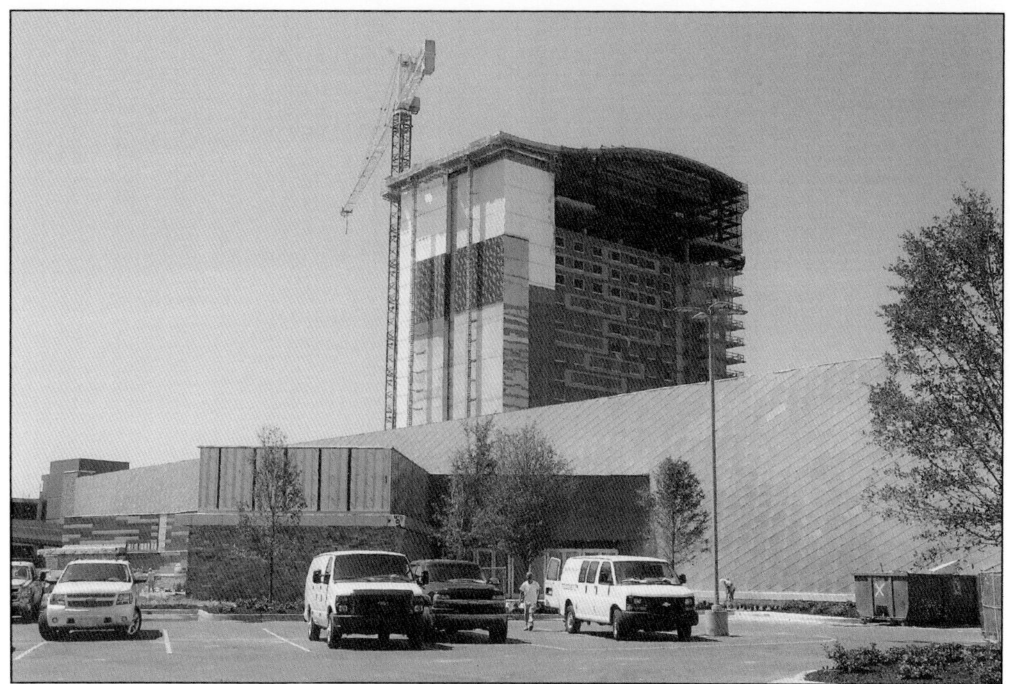

Creek Casino Wetumpka at 100 River Oaks Drive overlooks Wetumpka's Coosa River. Although located within city limits, these are tribal lands that include the sacred Hickory Ground and belong to the Poarch Band of Creek Indians. The tribe has invested $246 million to build a new deluxe casino resort on its property. The gaming floor will be 90,000 square feet and will feature more than 2,500 electronic gambling machines. The hotel will include 285 rooms and suites with ample parking. New dining options will include a fine dining restaurant, a grill, a coffee shop, a snack bar, and a buffet overlooking the river. The grand reopening is scheduled for early 2014. (Photograph by Kevin Taylor for the *Wetumpka Herald*; Peggy Blackburn.)

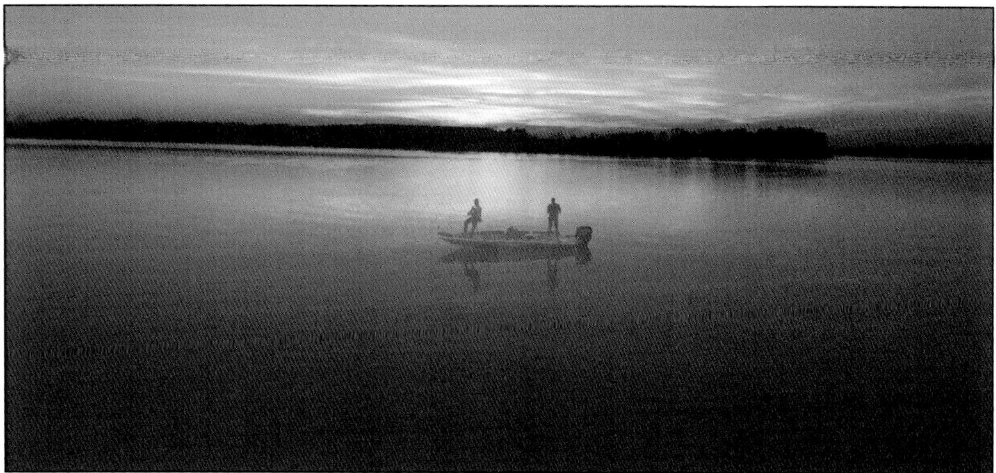

With its many lakes, rivers, and streams, water-related activities are at the top of Wetumpka's recreation list. Lakes Martin and Jordan are standouts for boaters, skiers, fishermen, and swimmers. The Coosa River attracts kayakers and canoeing enthusiasts seeking to participate in sanctioned surfing and ender competition. Public pools provide opportunities to swim in calmer waters. (Barry Chrietzberg.)

# *Eight*

# Wetumpka Gatherings

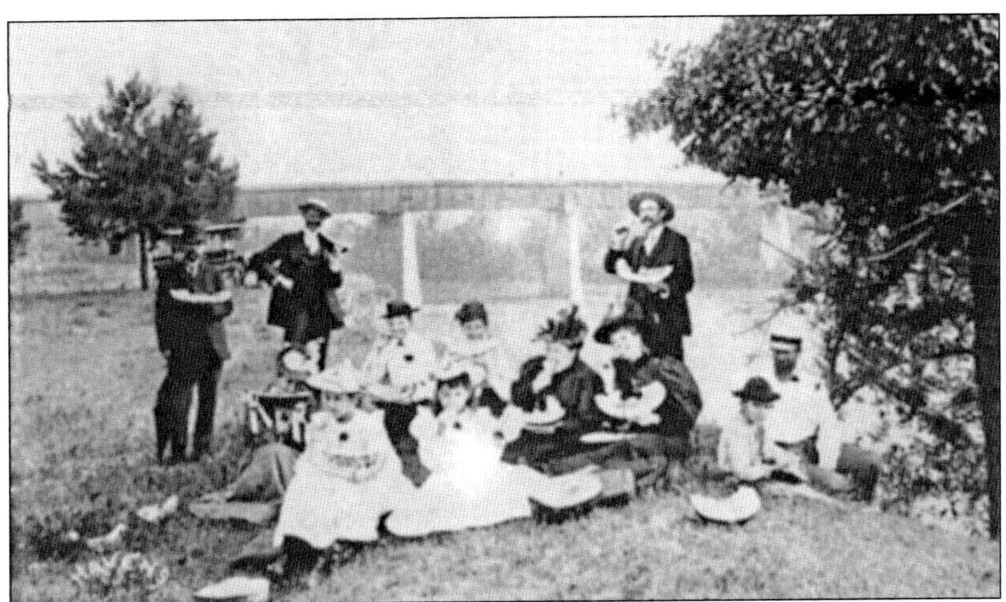

A picnic and watermelon-cutting are being enjoyed by a group on the Coosa River in the early 1880s. Note the Covered Bridge in the background. (ECHS.)

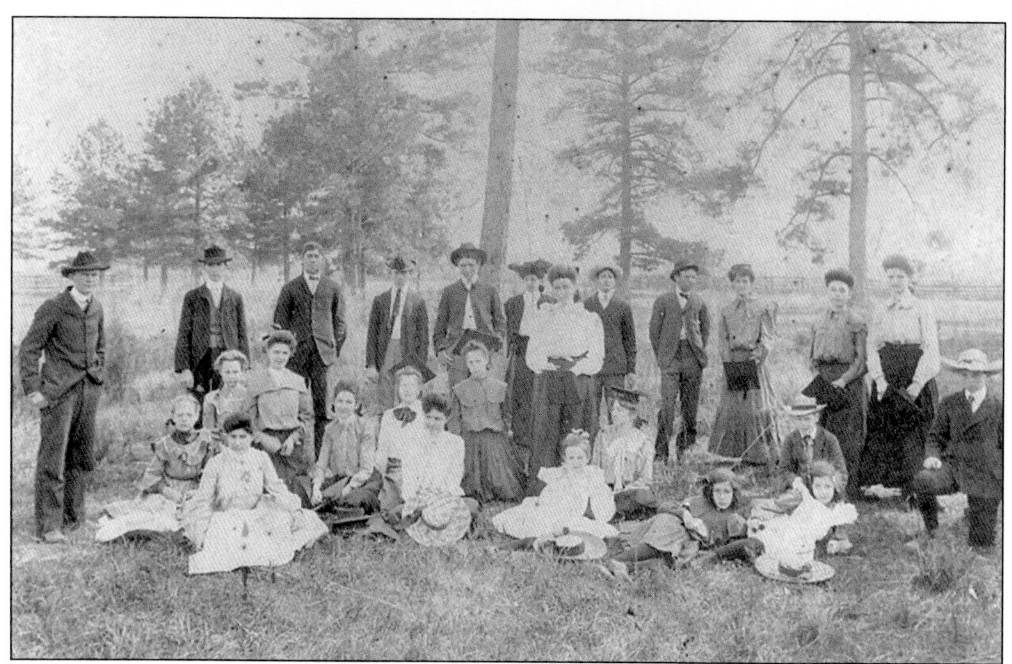

A c. 1900 school or graduation gathering includes ladies wearing mortar boards. (ECHS.)

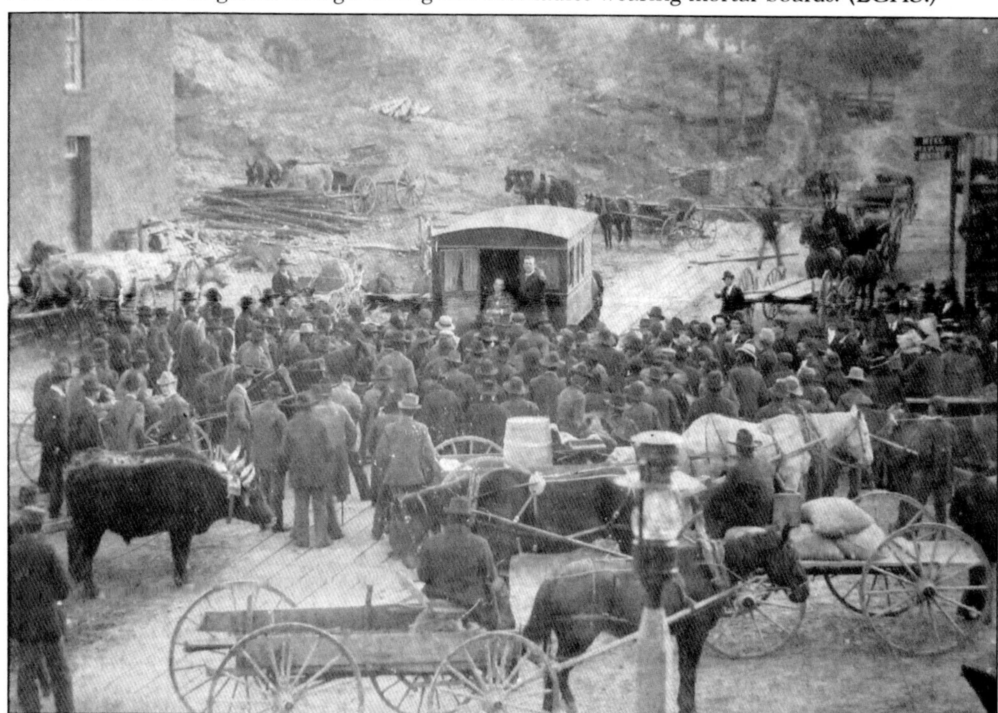

In 1831, William Suttle, George Johnson, and William Howard settled on the east side of the Coosa River. Johnson, a carpenter, built the first storehouse. In 1833, a Mr. Horton built saw- and gristmills on the river; he also owned the first boardinghouse (a two-room log house near a blacksmith just above Chicken Row). This gathering is possibly a political rally in 1892 at the present-day intersection of Hill and Company Streets. (ECHS.)

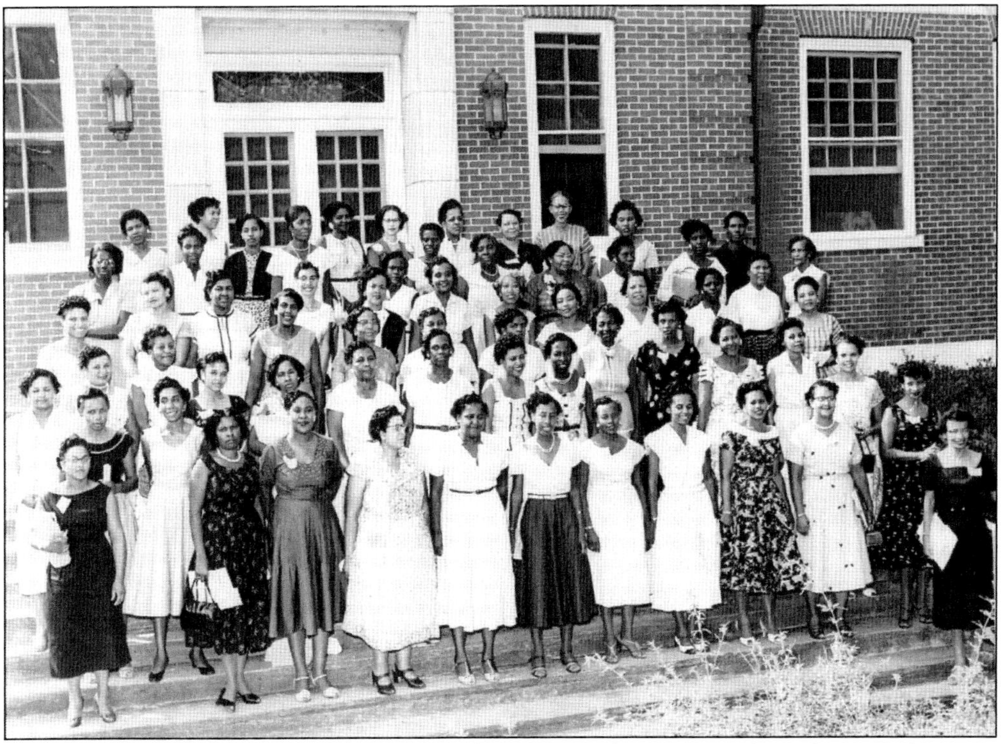

This is apparently a gathering of teachers and home agents from Wetumpka and surrounding area attending a c. 1950 meeting at Tuskegee Institute. (Elmore County Black History Museum.)

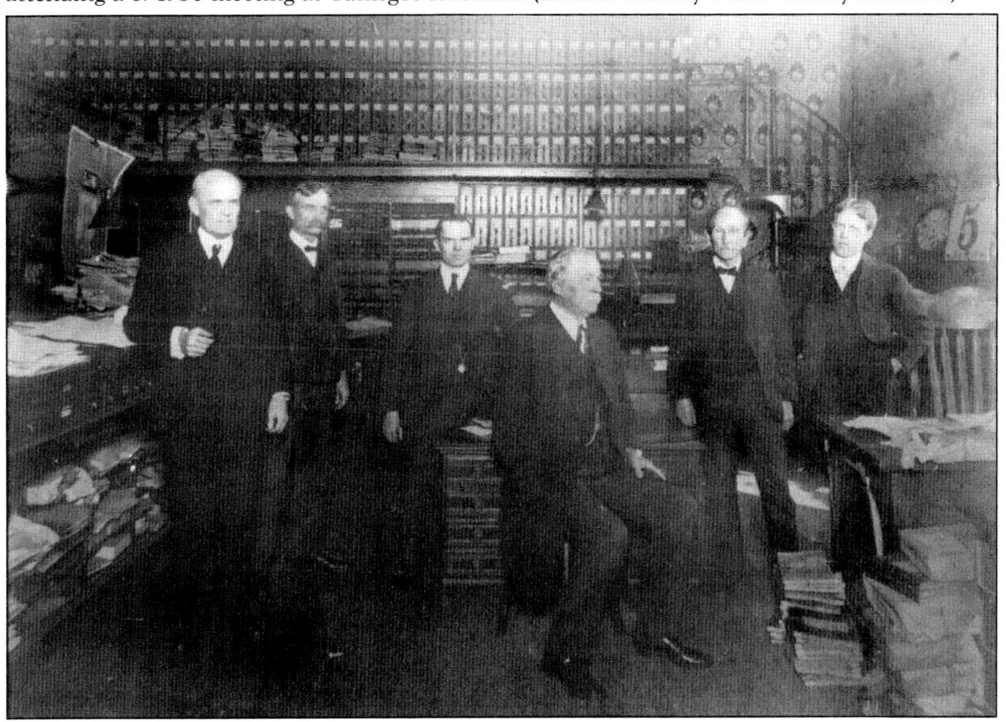

Court officials are in a second-floor office of the 1884 courthouse around 1890. (ECHS.)

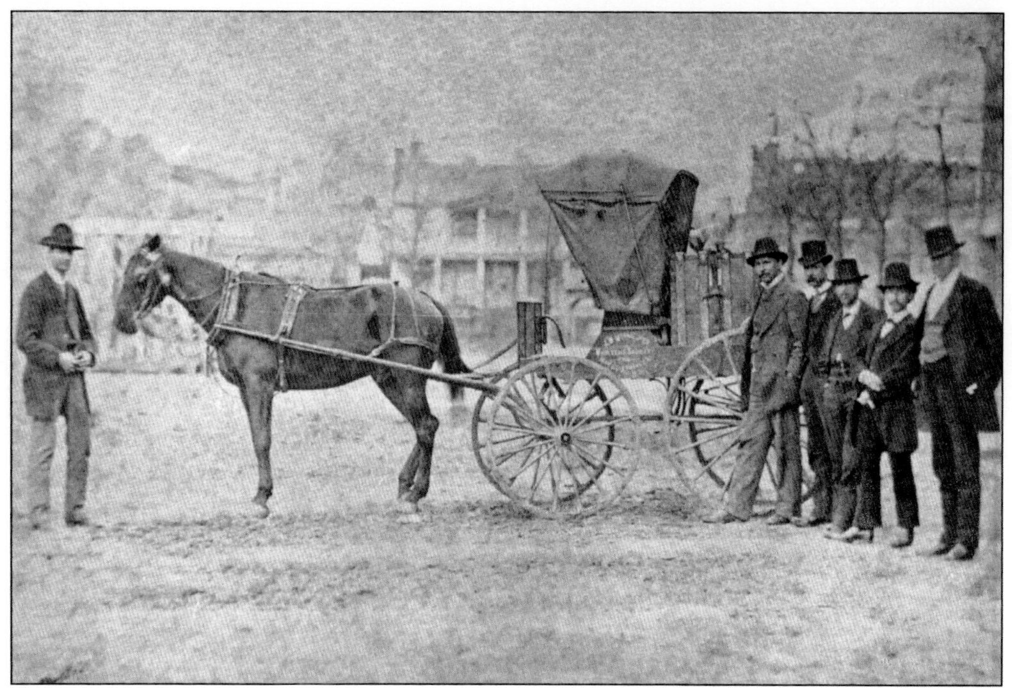

Only two of these distinguished businessmen with this horse and buggy are identified. The tall man on the far right is Rufus L. Logan. He was associated with Charles K. McMorris, his brother-in-law, in the mercantile business. The shorter man next to him is Preston Crocheran, and the unidentified men are leaders in the community. This photograph is dated 1879–1880. (ECHS.)

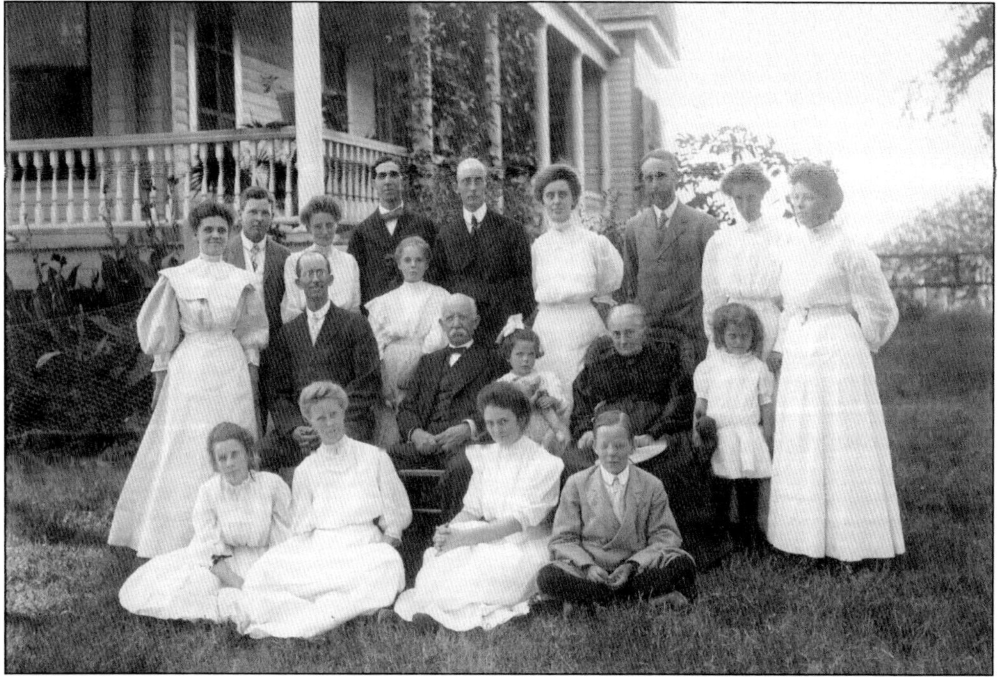

This early-1900s image is of the family of probate judge Cabot Lull and his wife, Sarah Foster Lull. (ECHS.)

King's Barber Shop was located in the Bank of Wetumpka basement around 1915. Identified in this photograph are, from left to right, Owen Laney, Josephus Jowers, Lacy Martin, Barney Britt, either "Peanuts" Saxon or Willie Westbrooks, Adie Ruffin, Talmadge Sanford Sr., Judge George Smoot, Joe Clifton, and unidentified. (ECHS.)

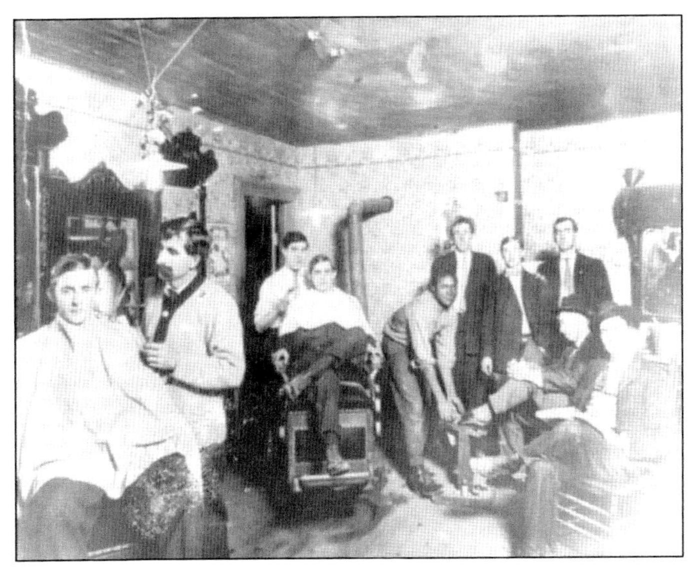

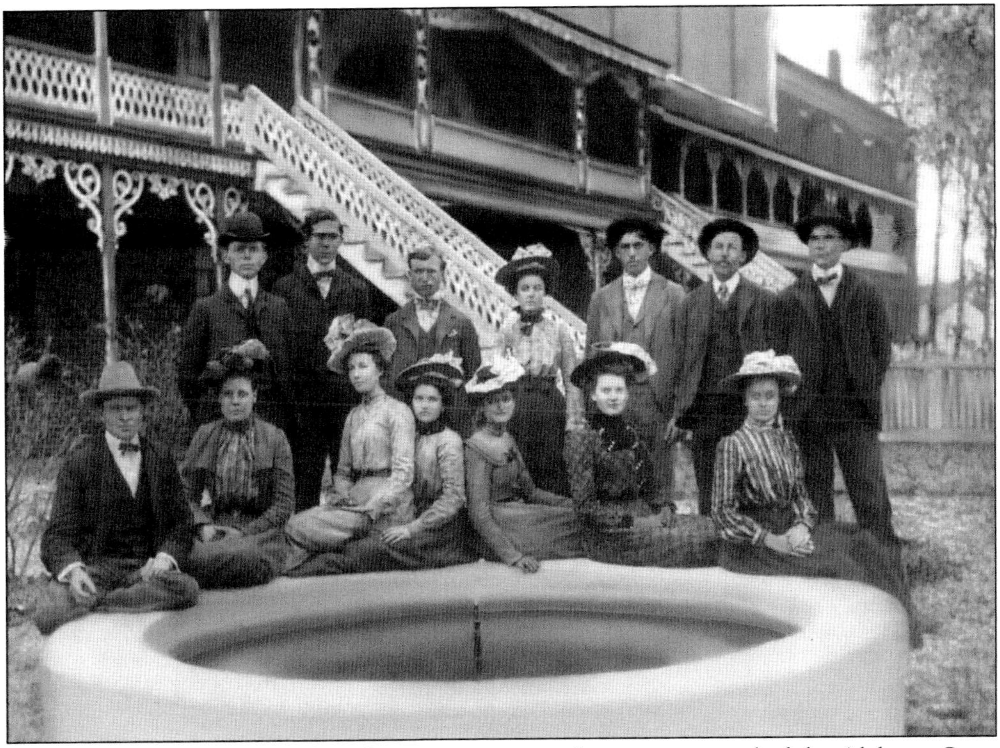

Young couples are on a Sunday-afternoon outing at the entrance pool of the Alabama State Penitentiary. This photograph was made around 1903. (ECHS.)

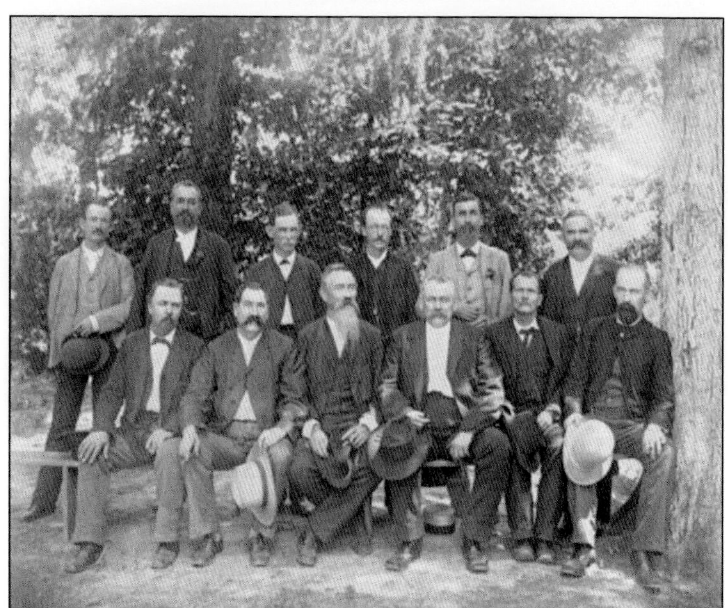

This is a reunion of the 6th Alabama Infantry Confederate Troops at Jackson's Lake in the early 1900s. (Velma Nix Gober and Peggy Blackburn.)

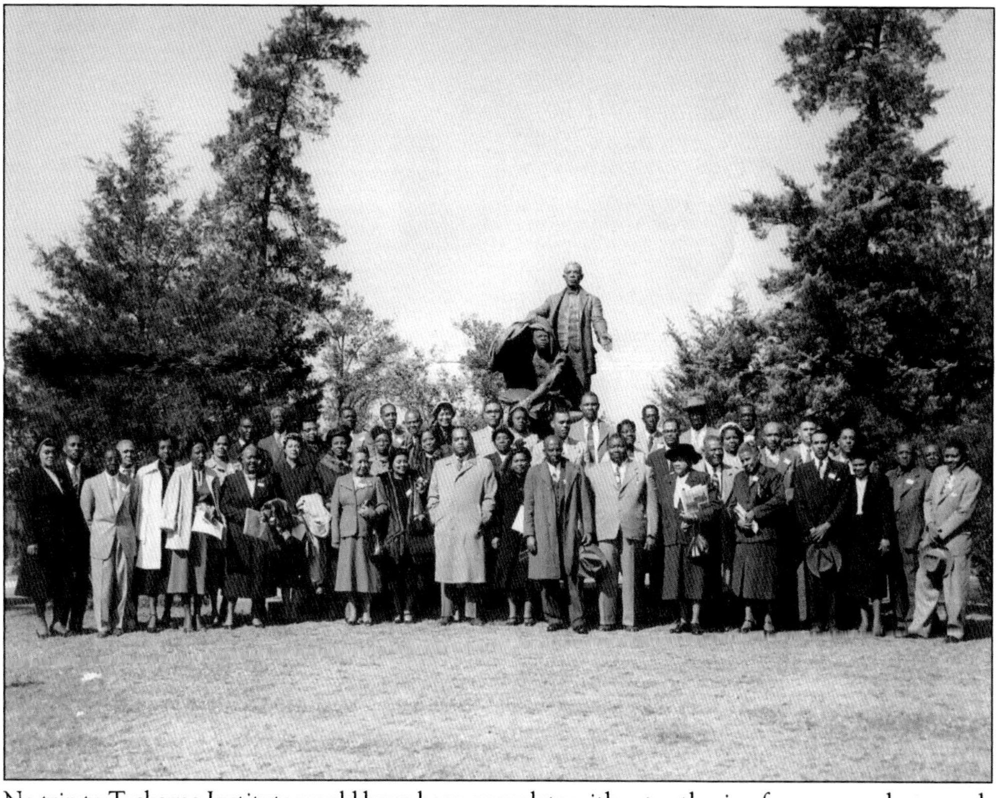

No trip to Tuskegee Institute would have been complete without gathering for a group photograph at the *Lifting the Veil of Ignorance* statue. Dr. Booker T. Washington, founder of Tuskegee Institute, hired Dr. George Washington Carver to spearhead the scientific research on agricultural matters. This research led to many and varied uses of the common peanut. This image was made around 1955. (Elmore County Black History Museum.)

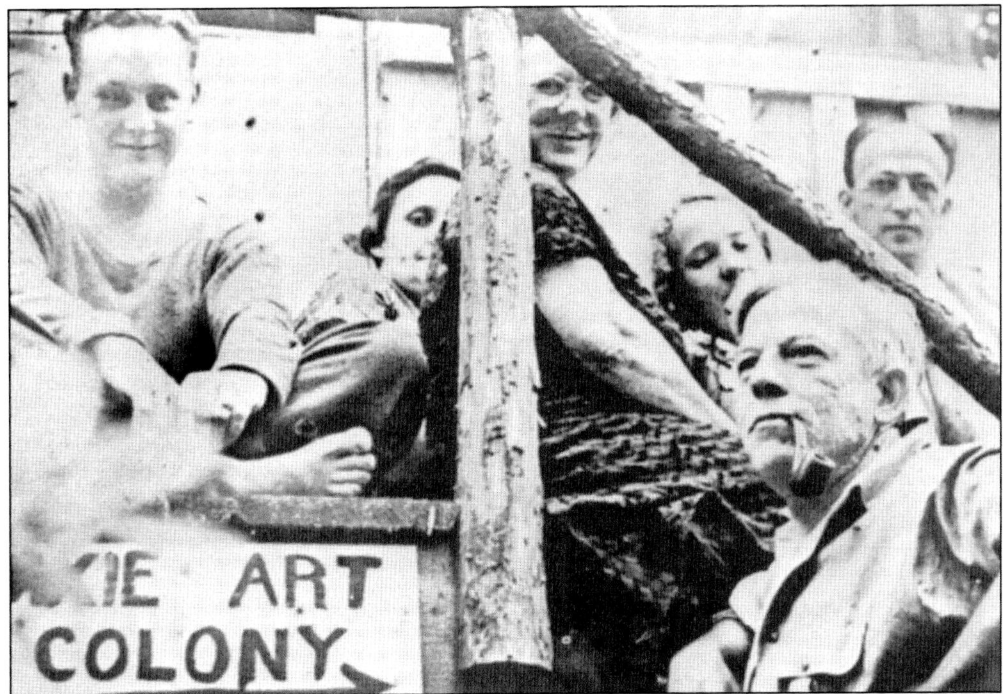


This c. 1940 image shows a casual gathering of the members of the Dixie Art Colony with organizer Kelly Fitzpatrick at bottom right, smoking his pipe. (Peggy Blackburn.)

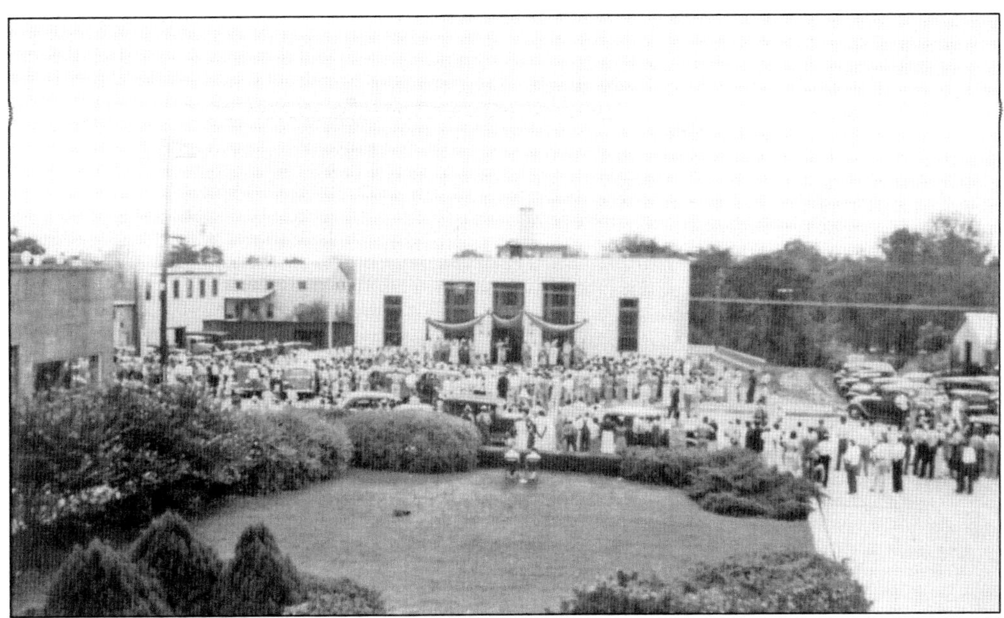

Locals have gathered on September 9, 1937, to dedicate the new US post office on South Main Street. Joe Allen Turner was almost six years old and in the crowd that day. (ECHS.)

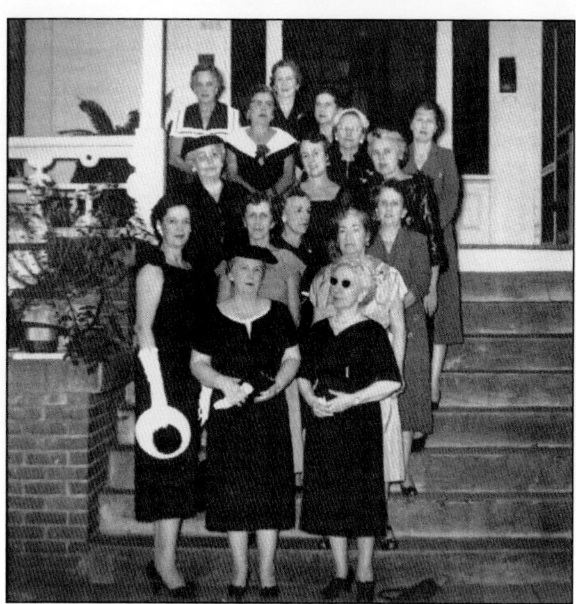

In September 1956, in the early days of the formation of Wetumpka Fine Arts Club, these influential women of Wetumpka were all members. They are, from ground level at the front point, Thelma Holley Milner, Florence Golson Bateman, Elizabeth Tacker Edwards, Dora Ashurst Melton, Bessie Lola Gamble Reneau, Frances McKnight Robison, Mary Johnson Thomas, Fredna Peckingpaugh Cotlin, Medora Lancaster Smith, Mary Ellen "Baby" Bower Dudley, Pauline Roy Huddleston, Bernadine Williams Pennington, Agnes Stewart Gantt, Janie Lou Holley Martin, Harriett Tutwiler Nolen, and Lucile Easterling Sedberry. (ECHS.)

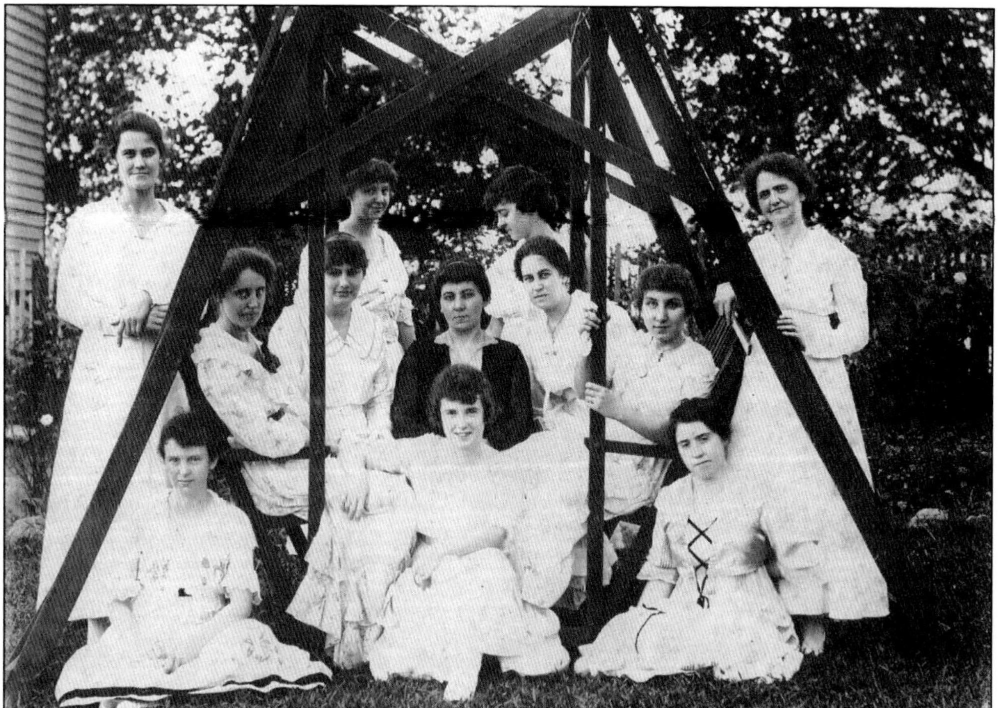

These young ladies are members of the Sunday school class of First Baptist Church around 1910. (ECHS.)

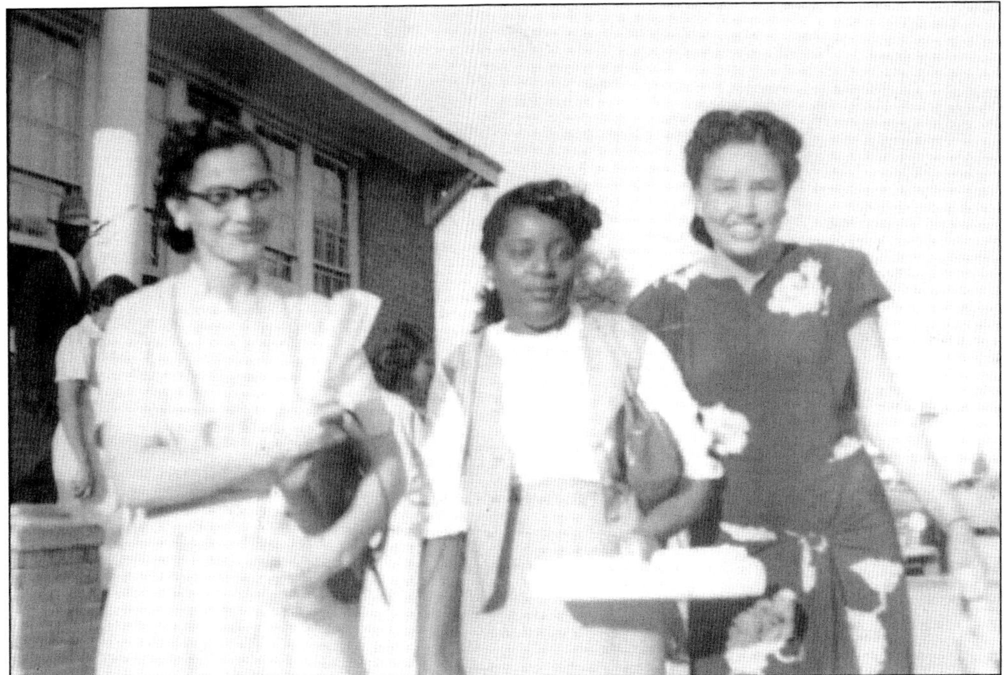

Pictured in this 1940s-era photograph, these ladies were community leaders and advocates for education in the Wetumpka area. They are, from left to right, Thelma Bradford, Aurelia Crenshaw Berry, and Maude Williams Doby—all active members of educational organizations and forward-thinking leaders of the times. (Elmore County Black History Museum.)

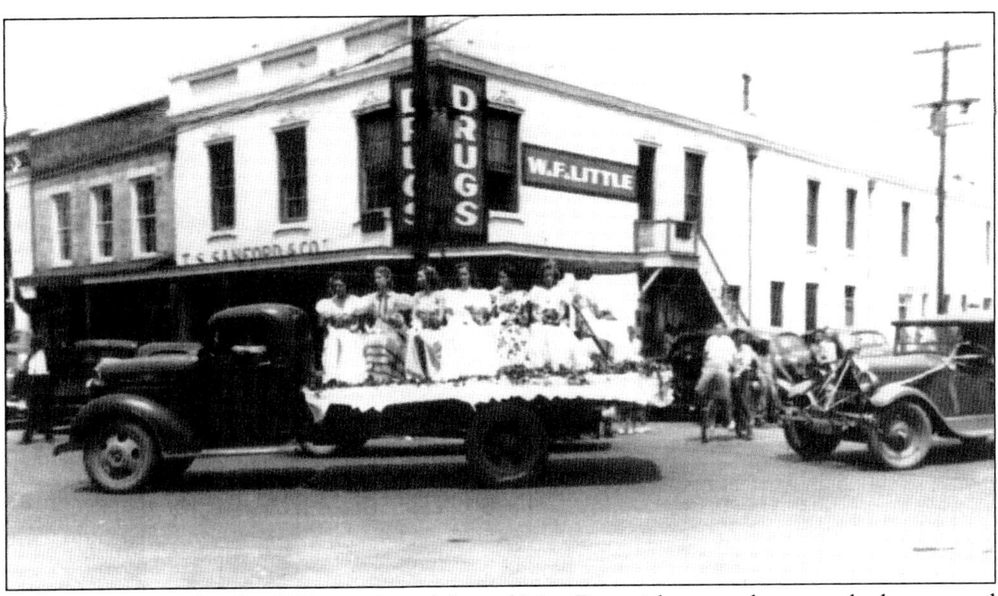


For many years, schools of Wetumpka celebrated May Day with a parade, maypole dances, and crowning of the May Day queen. Pictured is one such day in 1941. The location is downtown by Little Drug Company and Sanford's Men's Store. (ECHS.)

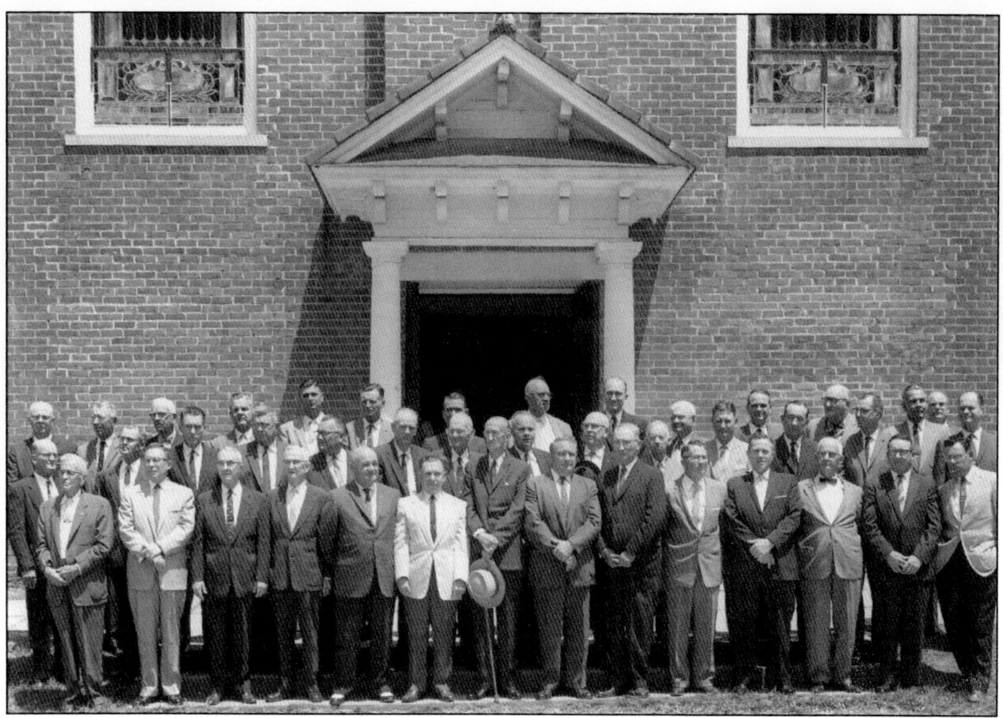

Above are members of the First Methodist Church Sunday school class for men around the 1950s. Below are members of the First Methodist Church Sunday school class for women at the same time. (Both, ECHS.)

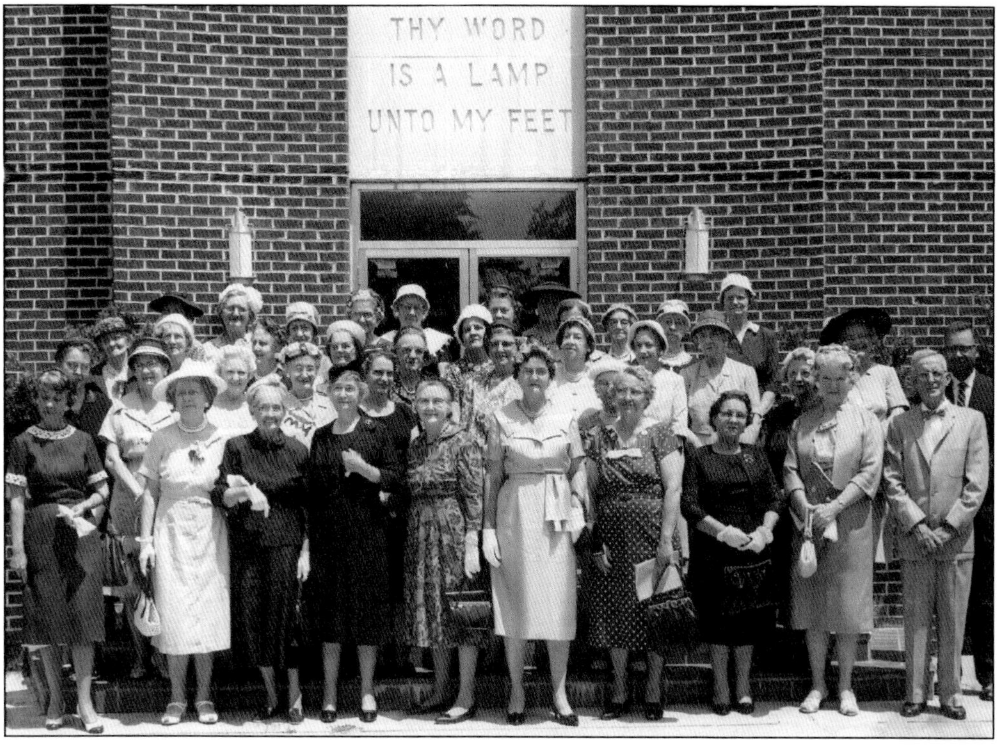

# *Nine*

# Wetumpka's Sons and Daughters

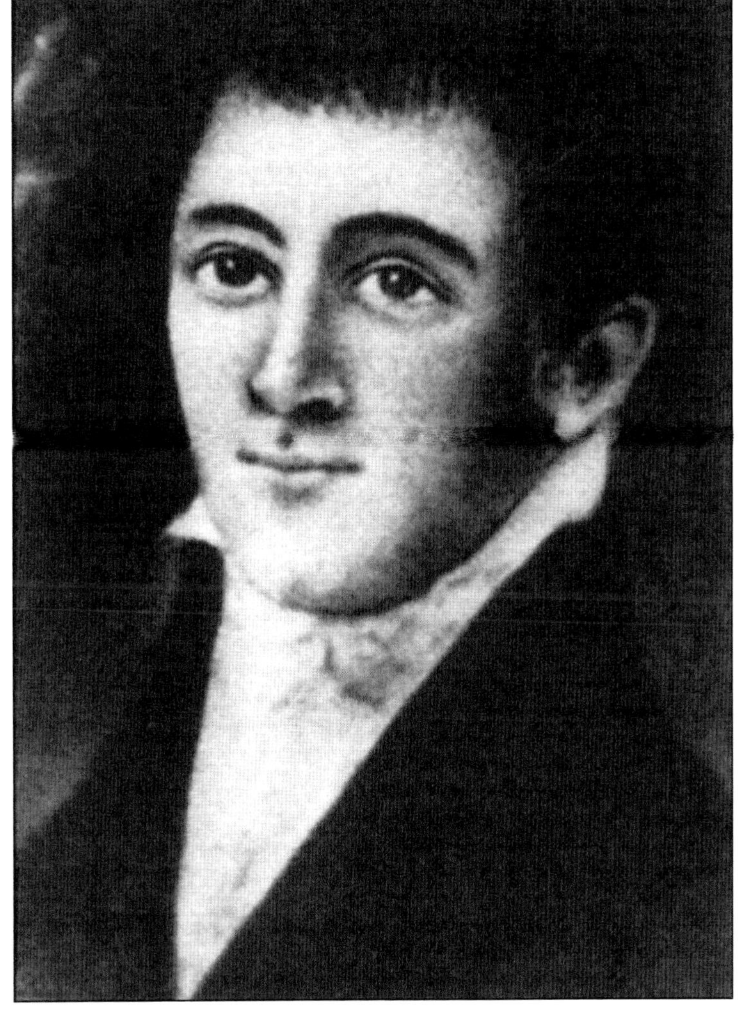

Gen. John Archer Elmore (1762–1834) was a military officer and politician. Born in Virginia, Elmore joined the Continental Army during the Revolutionary War. In 1819, he moved to Autauga, Alabama, where he was elected as a state legislator and served until his death in 1834. He was married twice and fathered 19 children. Autauga was renamed Elmore County in his honor. (Alabama Department of Archives and History.)

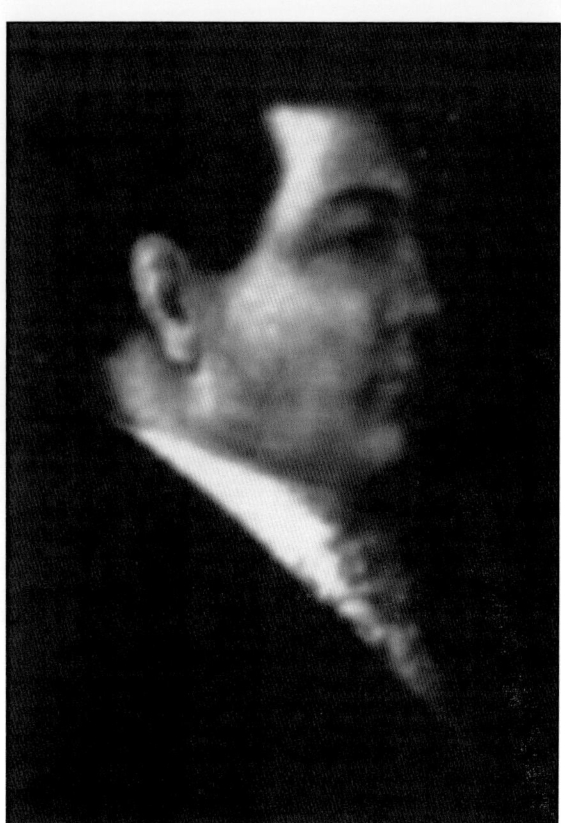

Gov. William Wyatt Bibb (1781–1820) was a United States Senator from Georgia. He was governor of the Alabama Territory from 1817 to 1819, and the first governor of Alabama after it became a state in 1819. Bibb was a member of the Democratic-Republican Party when he actively engaged in politics. In 1820, Bibb suffered a fall from his horse and died of internal injuries. (Alabama Department of Archives and History.)

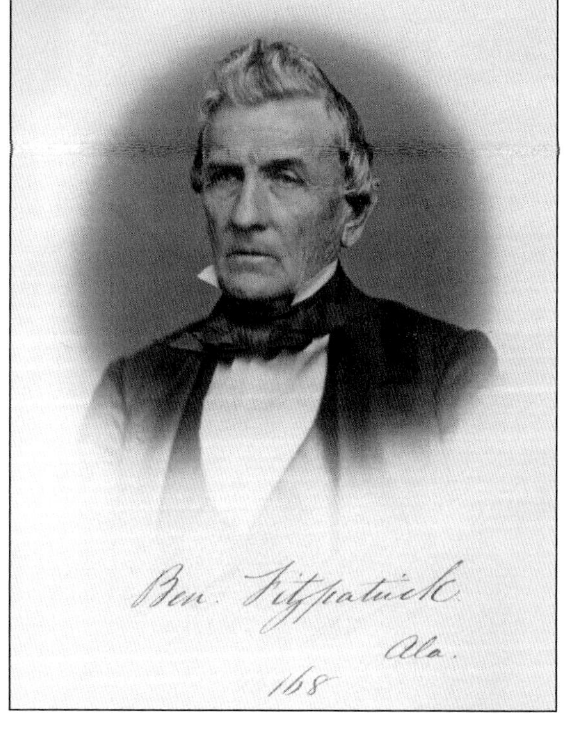


Gov. Benjamin Fitzpatrick (1802–1869) was an American politician who served as the 11th governor of Alabama and as a US senator representing Alabama. Fitzpatrick served as solicitor of his judicial circuit from 1822 to 1823. He was governor from 1841–1845 and was later appointed to the Senate. He withdrew from the Senate following the secession of his home state. (Alabama Department of Archives and History.)

Thomas Williams (1825–1903) came to Wetumpka in 1834. He was the eldest of six children and had a limited education. With great determination, he attended East Tennessee University. He read law, was admitted to the bar, and practiced for 22 years in Wetumpka. Willams married Rebecca E. Judkins and became the father of six children. He farmed about 12,000 acres of fine Elmore County land. He was elected to the Alabama Legislature in 1878, and shortly thereafter he was elected to Congress, where he served with ability and distinction. (ECHS.)

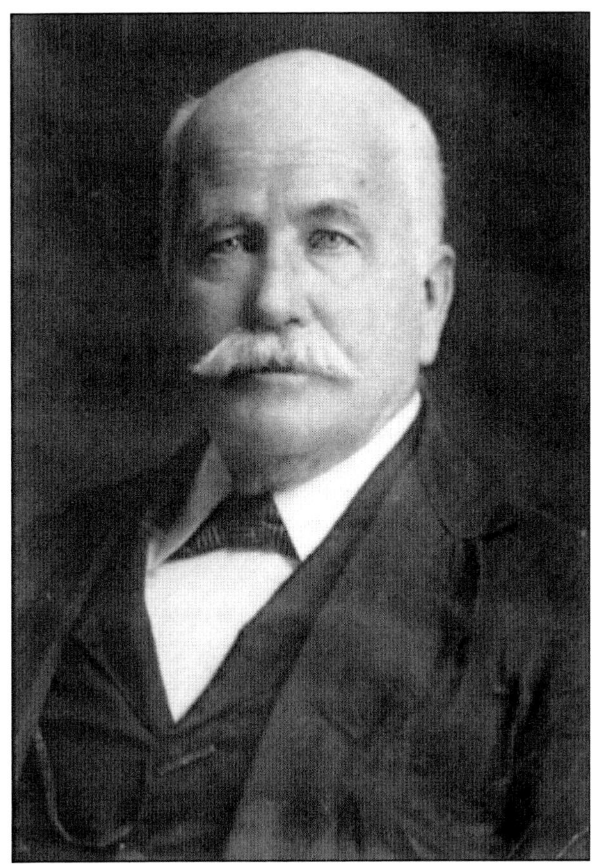

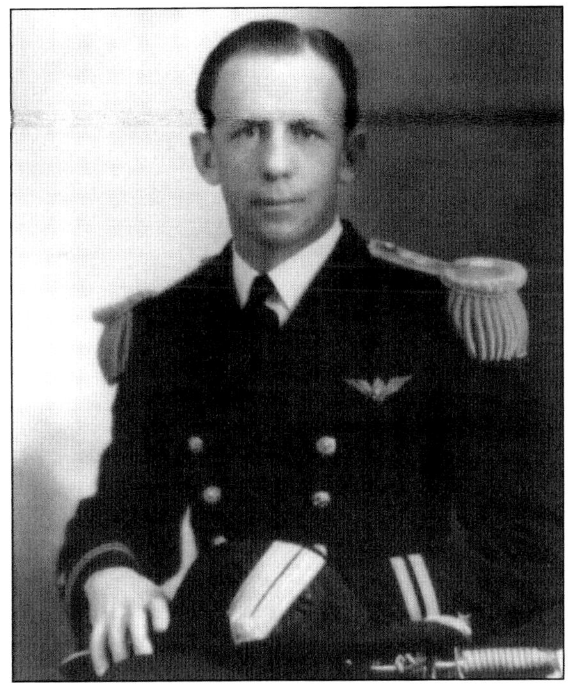

Capt. John Geraerdt Crommelin (1902–1996), eldest of the five Crommelin brothers, saw his first airplane at age nine in 1911 in Montgomery, where the Wright brothers had opened a small flying school. Crommelin passed the tests for Annapolis and joined the Navy in 1919. He was the first of the brothers to graduate. Although he was a midshipman, he yearned to be a flyer. His reputation as a stunt pilot landed him in the organized Navy flight team. His ship was hit in 1943, but he survived and was picked up at sea. After 27 years, he retired as a captain in 1950. (ECHS.)

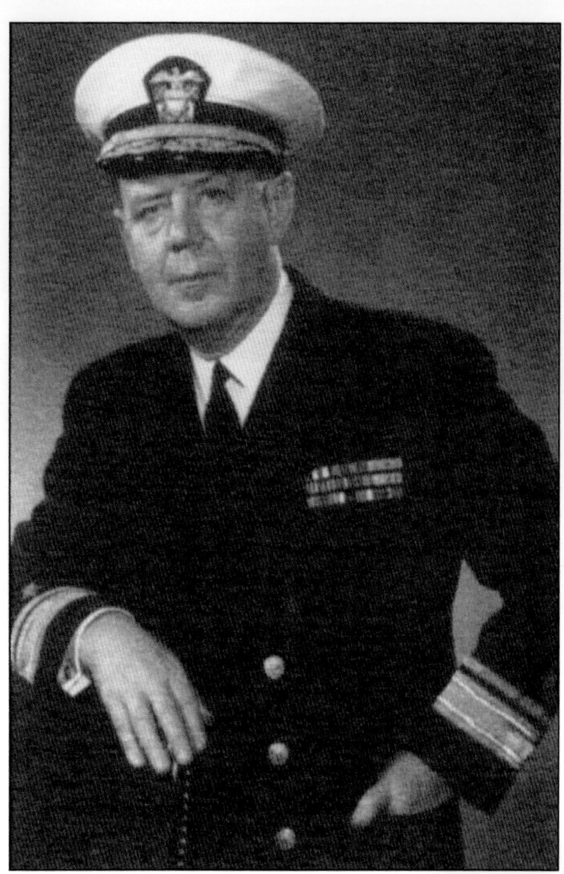

Adm. Henry Crommelin (1904–1971) was the second of the five Crommelin brothers. He was educated in Montgomery, and his appointment to the US Naval Academy came in 1921. As a midshipman, he played football and boxed. Because of his eyesight, he was the only one of the brothers prevented from flying. He made his mark aboard destroyers and attained a higher rank than any of his four ambitious aviator siblings. His service earned him the Silver Star and the Bronze Star. He returned to Alabama and bought Sugarberry Hill, where he lived until his death in 1971. (ECHS.)

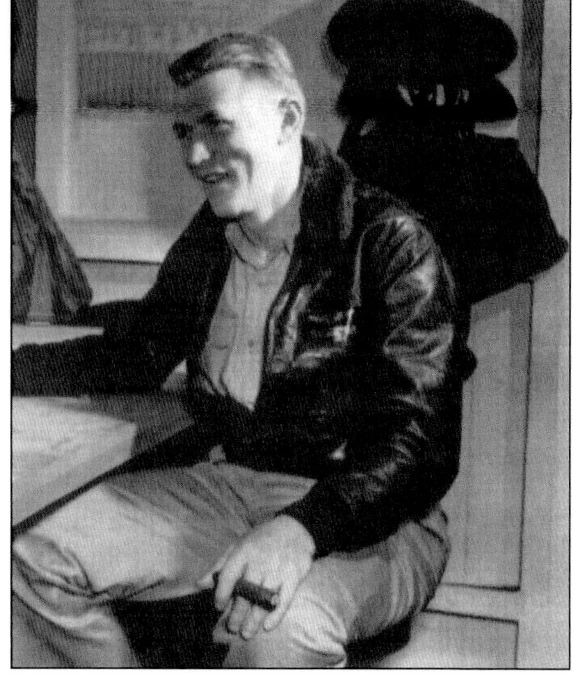

Charles L. Crommelin (1909–1945) graduated from the US Naval Academy in 1931. His exceptional flying skill became apparent, and he joined the elite group of Navy test pilots and took up an experimental SOC fighter that had crashed twice. Though seriously injured, he was determined to continue flying. After extensive rehabilitation, he returned to flight in 1943. During a low-level strafing attack, his plane was hit with a blast that exploded in the cockpit. His injury and determination to walk away was filmed in the combat film *The Fighting Lady*, which won an Academy Award for best documentary in 1945. His continuing attacks on the enemy resulted in his death in 1945. (ECHS.)

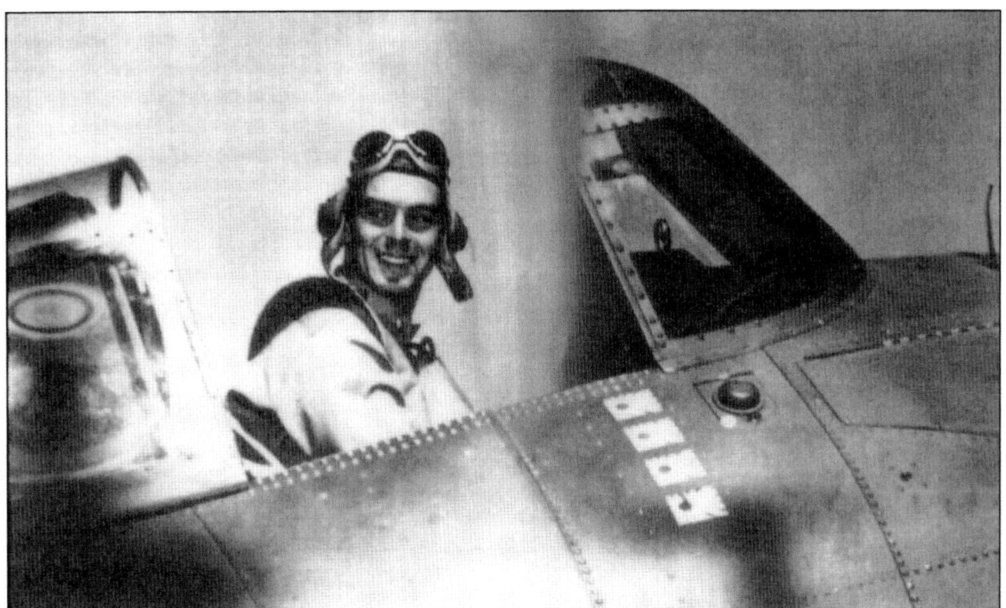

Richard Gunter Crommelin (1917–1945) was the fourth and most decorated of the famous Crommelin brothers. As an academy graduate in 1938, his first duty was aboard the battleship *Pennsylvania*. He joined John and Charles in wearing naval aviator wings by December 1940. Richard was the first of the brothers to see combat. In July 1945, Richard was leading a strike when one of his own planes collided with and destroyed his plane's tail. The tragedy was similar to that of his brother Charles. A *New York Times* report published in August 1945 states both these deaths broke up "the fleet's most famous flying family." (ECHS.)

Quentin Crommelin Sr. (1918–1997), the fifth of the sons, attended the academy in 1937, where he became the fourth Crommelin to earn his Navy wings. He followed the war to the Japanese home islands with massive raids on factories and military installations. He served in virtually every aspect of the Navy, as a commander of fighter squadrons. He retired in 1973 with the rank of captain, after a 34-year career spent principally in command at sea. A 32-foot-tall granite obelisk located near Crommelin's Landing in Gold Star Park commemorates Captain Crommelin and his four naval hero brothers. (ECHS.)

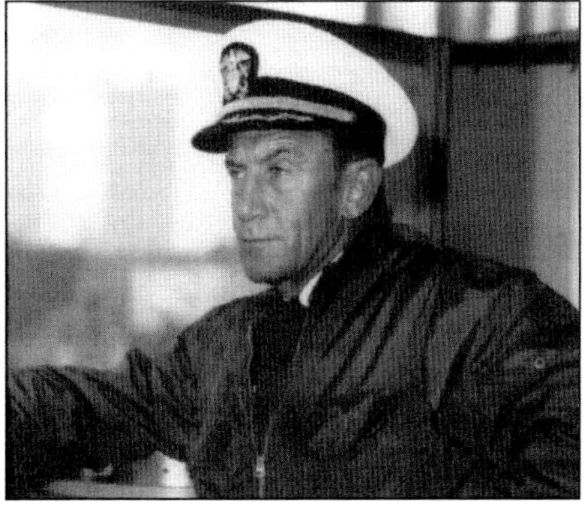

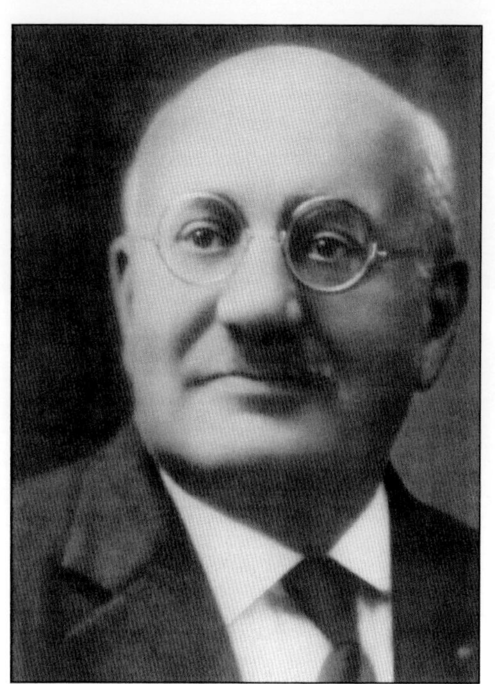

The Hohenberg brothers, Morris (pictured) and Adolphe, will be remembered as philanthropists instrumental in the development of Wetumpka. They were leaders in business and civic affairs and quick to come to the aid of those in need. Morris, the elder, was born in 1857 in Germany. Adolphe was born in 1864 and followed his brother to America in the late 1870s. Together, they formed the firm M. Hohenberg & Co., which became one of the biggest and oldest in Alabama including banking, cotton, and general merchandise. Their business extended beyond Alabama to London and Paris. (ECHS.)

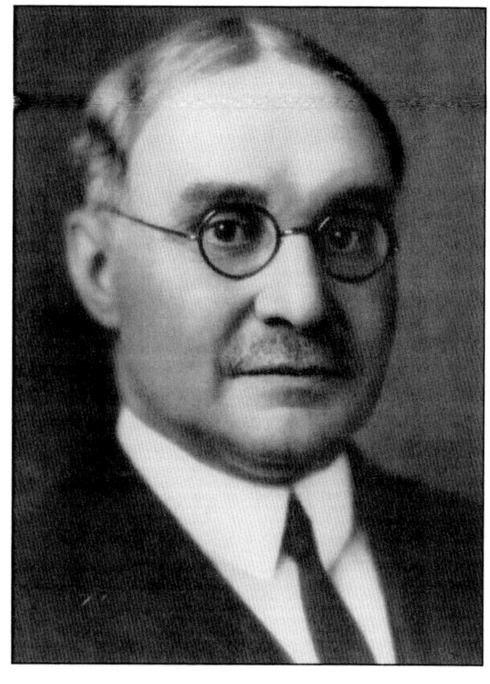

In 1905, the brothers organized First National Bank of Wetumpka, where Morris served as president and Adolphe (pictured) was vice president. While they worked in the banking industry, they maintained their interests in the large grocery and dry goods firm that operated as Hohenberg, Lacy, and Farrow Mercantile Company. They had extensive interests in real estate, farming, and timberlands as well as the cotton market in the county. Adolphe served on the board of the State Secondary Agriculture School in Wetumpka and gave $25,000 for the erection of an elementary school building in Wetumpka. (ECHS.)

Pictured in 1949, John Kelly Fitzpatrick (left), Florence Golson Bateman (center), and Marie Bankhead Owen are viewing a life-sized oil portrait of Bateman, painted by Fitzpatrick, a Wetumpka artist and her longtime friend. Bateman was honored by having the portrait placed in the Music Room of the Alabama Department of Archives and History in Montgomery. An accomplished musician, composer, and teacher, she was the first to be chosen to receive such an honor. Looking on is Marie Bankhead Owen, director of the State Archives. Fitzpatrick was an artist of national note. (Peggy Blackburn.)

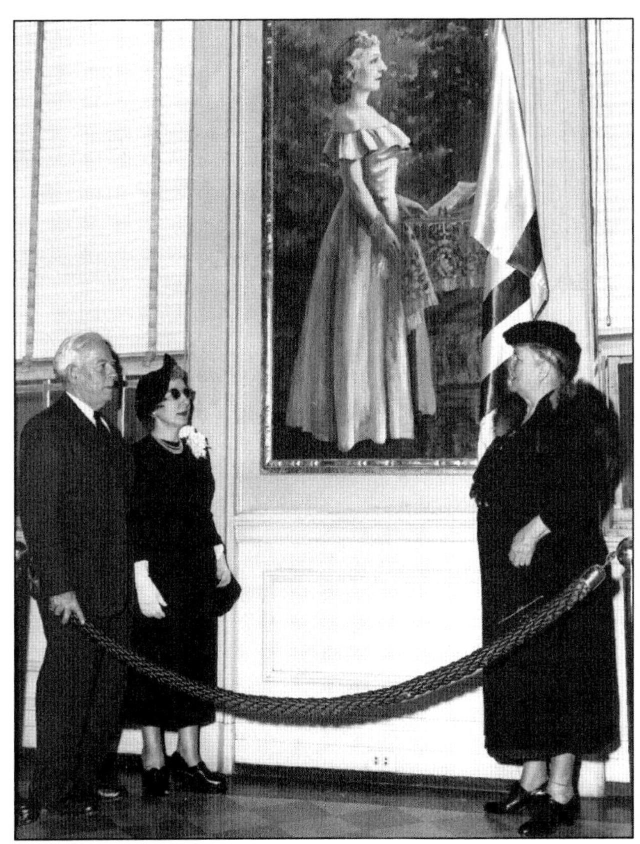

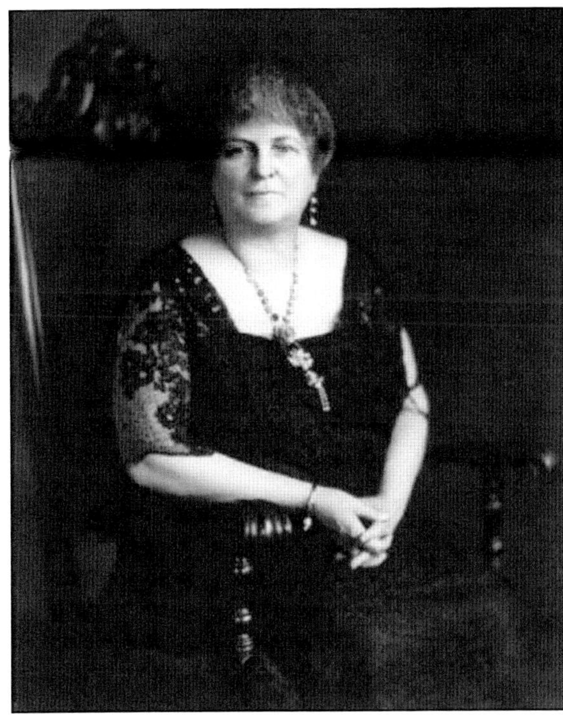

Marie Bankhead Owen (1869–1958) was the daughter of John H. Bankhead and Tallulah J. Brockman Bankhead. Her father served in the United States Senate and two brothers served in the United States House of Representatives. Her husband, Thomas M. Owen, was director of the Alabama Department of Archives and History, the first of its kind in the nation. At his death in 1920, she became director and served for 35 years. She was only the second woman to head a state agency in Alabama. (Alabama Department of Archives and History.)

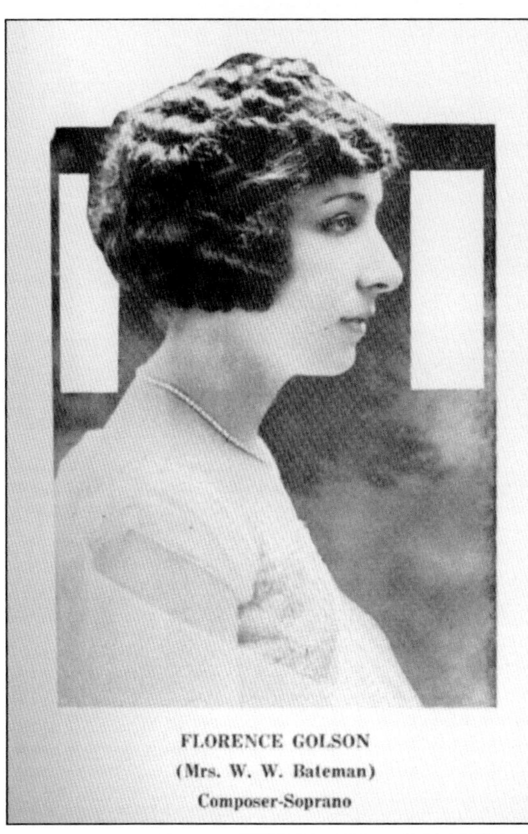
FLORENCE GOLSON
(Mrs. W. W. Bateman)
Composer-Soprano

Florence Golson Bateman (1891–1958) was a concert artist, voice teacher, and composer. Her lyric soprano voice has been described as being high and light like a bird's. Her musical talents and many achievements are the pride of Alabama. In 2000, she was inducted into the Alabama Women's Hall of Fame. The portrait of Bateman shown on page 115 has recently been completely restored and moved to the Elmore County Museum for display. (ECHS.)

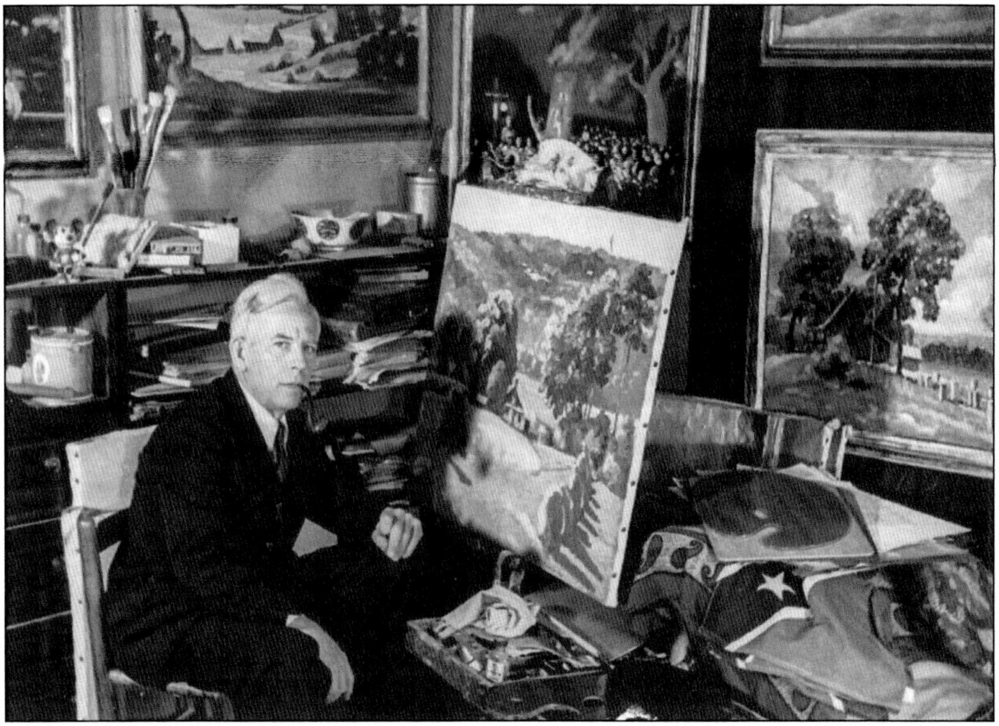

John Kelly Fitzpatrick, pictured here in his studio, became the director and central figure of the Dixie Art Colony when it was established in 1933. In its first few years, the colony traveled to several sites to paint. It received a permanent home from Mrs. Michael Carmichael on the banks of Lake Jordan. She had several cabins constructed on the site for the use of the painters during their summer and fall sessions. (ECHS.)

Artist John Kelly Fitzpatrick (1888–1953) was regarded by many to be the finest interpreter of the Southern scene. He painted in vivid colors, which prompted a friend to say "that he painted so much sunshine because he knew that many times life was without this to so many people." He was an organizer of the Montgomery Museum of Fine Arts and the Dixie Art Colony as well as a beloved teacher to many enthusiastic art students. His works have become highly collectable. (ECHS.)

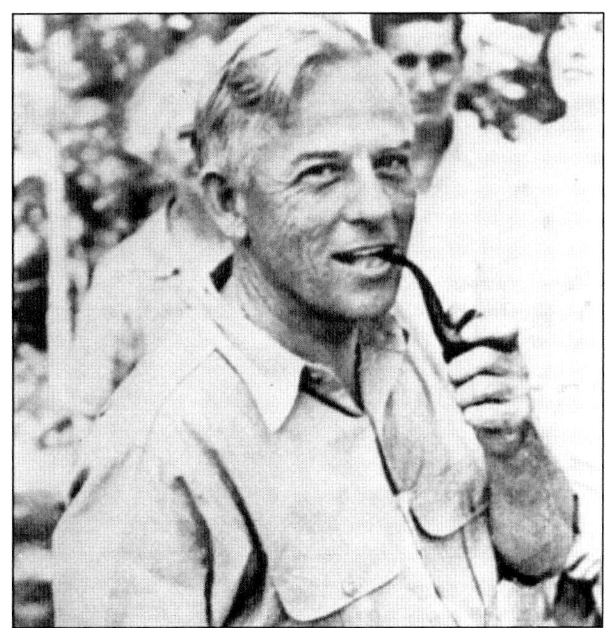

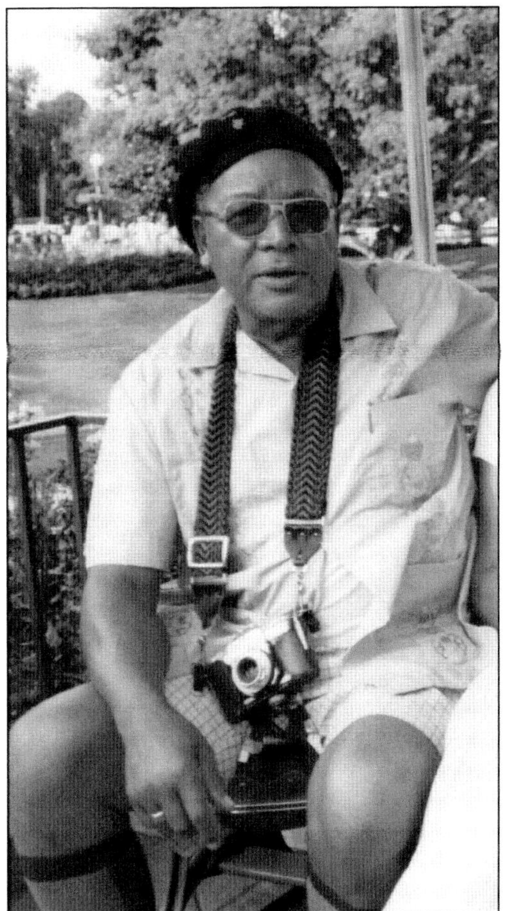

Dr. Joseph Bradford was born in Noxubee County, Mississippi. He worked the family farm before completing his bachelor's degree in agriculture education at Tuskegee Institute. After serving several years as county extension agent, Bradford earned his PhD at the University of Wisconsin. Active in public affairs, he served in the civic league and United Development Association in Elmore County. He was also a member of the NAACP and a cofounder of the Elmore County Land Association. (Elmore County Black History Museum.)

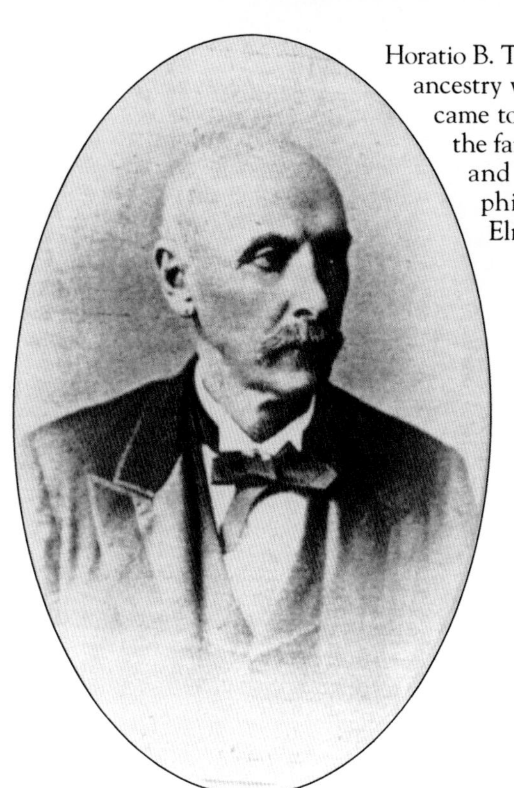

Horatio B. Tulane (1835–1897) was a merchant with French ancestry who was born in Bay St. Louis, Mississippi. He came to Wetumpka with his father, Louis Tulane, and the family in 1848. He became a successful merchant and landowner. He will be remembered for his philanthropic contributions to Wetumpka and Elmore County. He never married. (ECHS.)

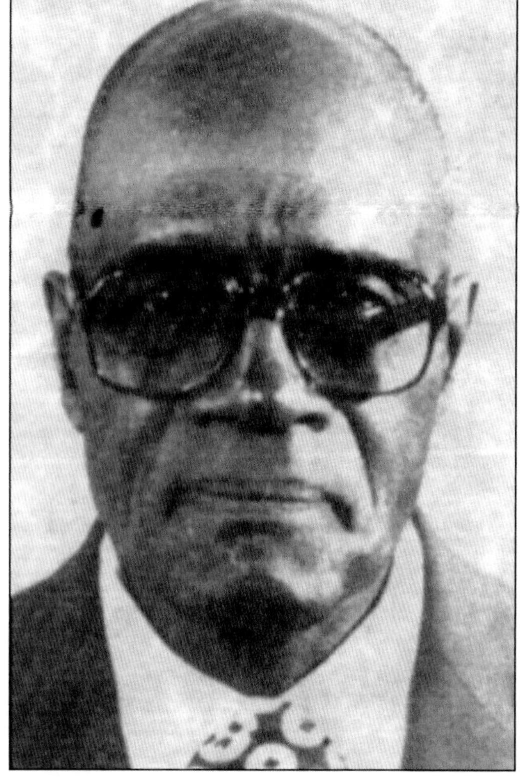

Rev. J.L. Jones (1907–1991) was the son of Georgia and Squire Jones. Jones graduated from Elmore County Training School and attended Selma University, after which he was ordained as a minister. He served as pastor at several Alabama churches, including Cathmagby Baptist Church, for some 30 years. He was also active in the NAACP, the Elmore County Coordinated Organization, and was the co-owner of the Jones-Goodman Funeral Home. (Elmore County Black History Museum.)

Margaret Macon Humphries Ruffin (1886–1952), known to many as "Miss Margaret," was born in Elmore County. She received a degree in music from Judson College and continued her studies at the American Conservatory in Chicago. In 1914, she married Wilbur G. Humphries and moved to Chicago, where he was employed. After his death in 1917, Margaret returned to Wetumpka and began her career as a piano teacher. In the mid-1920s, she became the organist at the First Baptist Church of Wetumpka, where she had played since childhood. She served as organist there until 1951. (ECHS.)

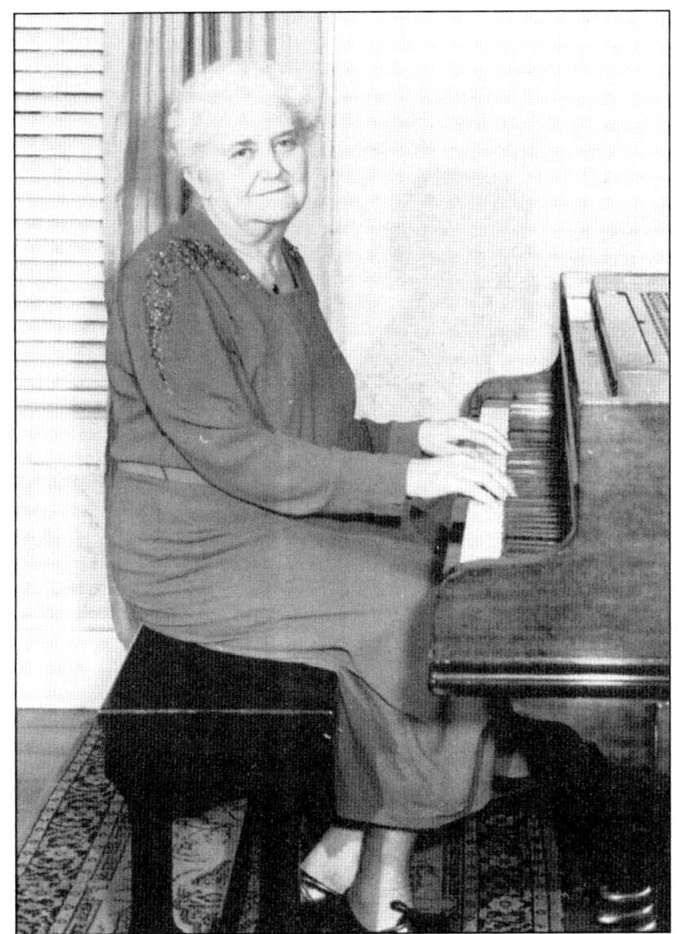

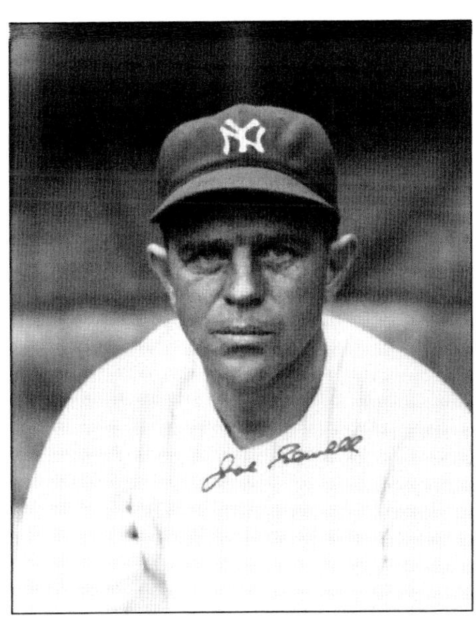


Joe Sewell (1898–1990) played baseball at the University of Alabama in 1920, for the Cleveland Indians from 1920–1930, and for the New York Yankees from 1931–1933. He batted just ahead of Babe Ruth. Sewell posted a lifetime batting average of .312, topping .300 in 10 of his 14 years. According to his biography at the National Baseball Hall of Fame, he has been deemed the most difficult man to strike out in the history of the game. He held the record for most consecutive games played—1,103, until bested by Lou Gehrig. Sewell was elected to the Hall of Fame in Cooperstown, New York, in 1977. (Peggy Blackburn.)

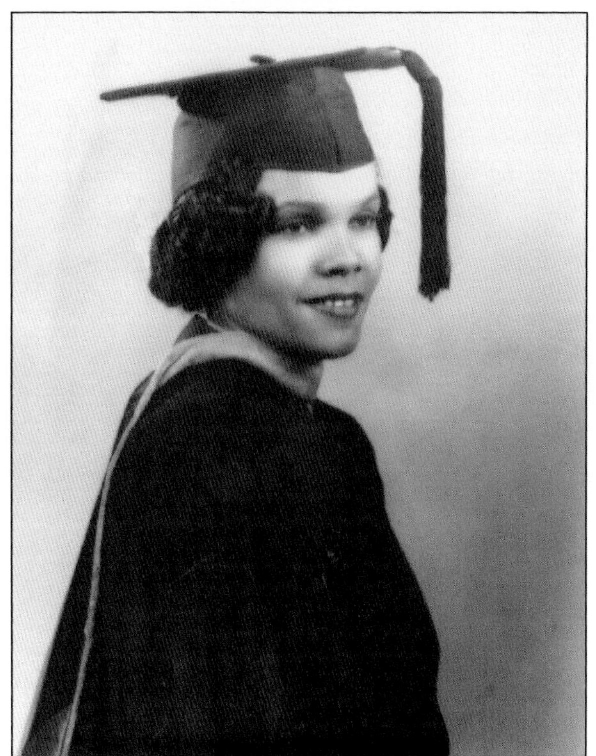

Eloyse Jones (1911–2005) was the daughter of Mr. and Mrs. Authur Jones. She taught home economics at the Elmore County Training School for more than 30 years and substituted later on at Wetumpka High School. Her advanced education came from Alabama State University and Tuskegee Institute. She believed that ladies should be "prim and proper" and dressed in their hats and gloves. She participated in teachers' associations and sororities and inspired many of today's black adults. (Elmore County Black History Museum.)

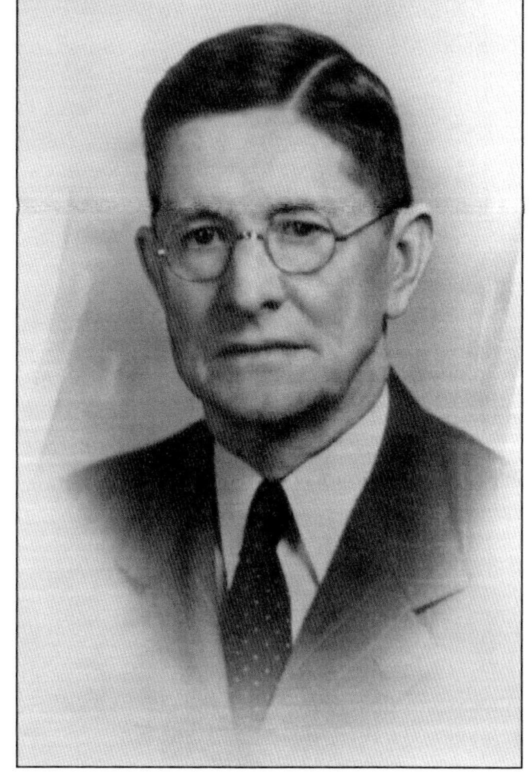

Probate judge George Houston Howard (1879–1971) attended what is now Troy State University and was an Elmore County schoolteacher early in his career before serving 14 years as the Elmore County Superintendent of Education. Judge Howard had a lengthy record of public service, devoting 45 years to acting as superintendent of education and as a probate judge. Among many other accomplishments, he had the distinction of overseeing the planning and construction of the Elmore County Courthouse and the Bibb Graves Bridge during his 30 years as probate judge. (Elmore County Probate Office.)

Roscoe Lee (1909–1989) was born in Choctaw County, Alabama, to Mr. and Mrs. Major A. Lee. Roscoe Lee devoted his life to serving the farmers of Alabama. He held advanced degrees from Tuskegee Institute and worked for decades as the county extension agent and representative of Farmers Home Administration. He assisted many black residents with obtaining funding for their farms and educated farmers about how to maximize their crops. (Elmore County Black History Museum.)

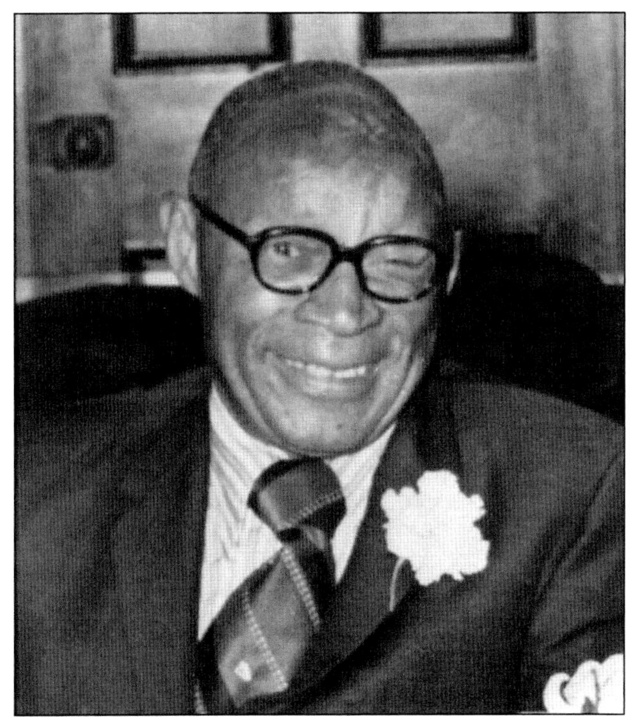

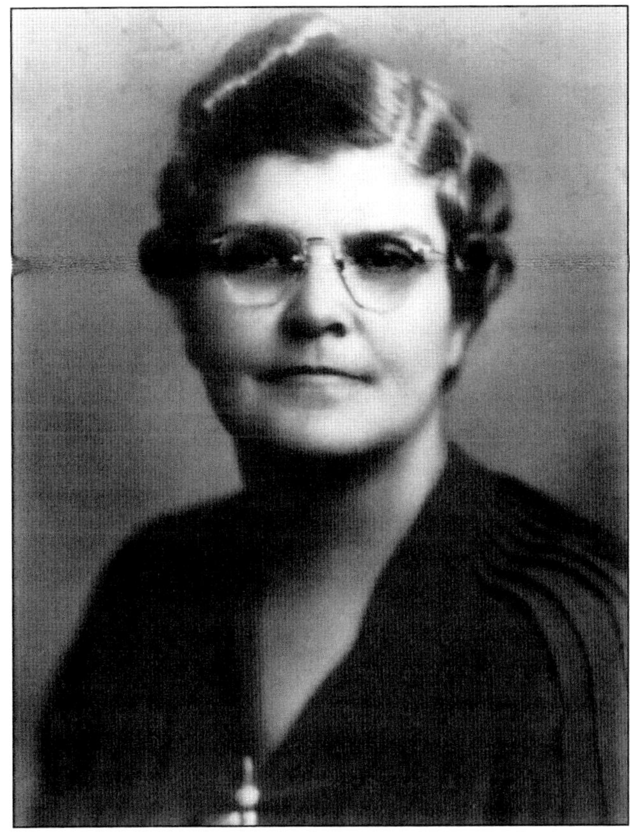

Sheriff Jessie Welch Austin (1884–1987), who served as her husband's chief clerk, ran in 1939 because her husband could not, by law, succeed himself. She made history as the first woman elected sheriff in any county in Alabama. She served a four-year term. Several years later, she was named superintendent of Julia Tutwiler Prison for Women. This trailblazer lived to the ripe old age of 103 and is buried in the Wetumpka City Cemetery. (Jacqueline E. Austin.)

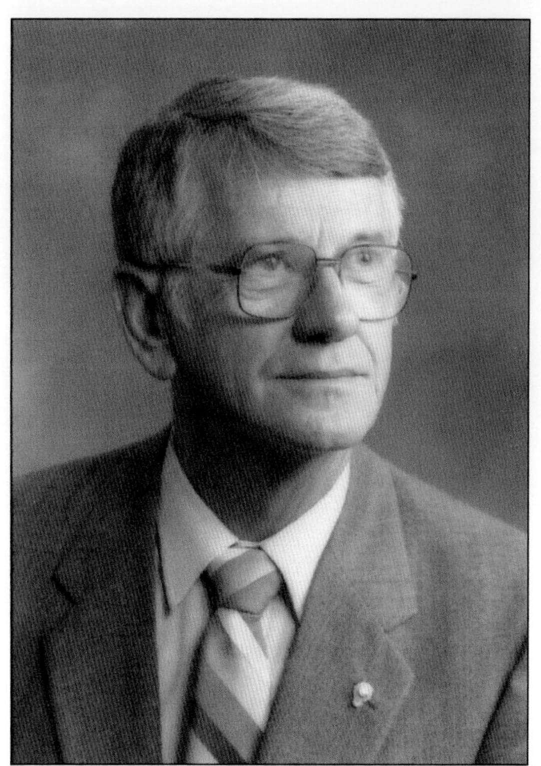

Probate judge Edward E. Enslen (1927–2009) served the people of Elmore County beginning in 1958 as the 18th tax assessor. In 1970, he was elected the 13th probate judge and served for 24 years until his retirement in 1994. He compiled an impressive list of services throughout his career. While the county experienced unprecedented population growth, he led an expansion of many departments and initiatives, including the purchase of land for the construction of a judicial building and jail. Enslen served in leadership positions in many civic organizations and was awarded the 2001 Community Involvement Citation given by the Wetumpka Area Chamber of Commerce. (John E. Enslen.)

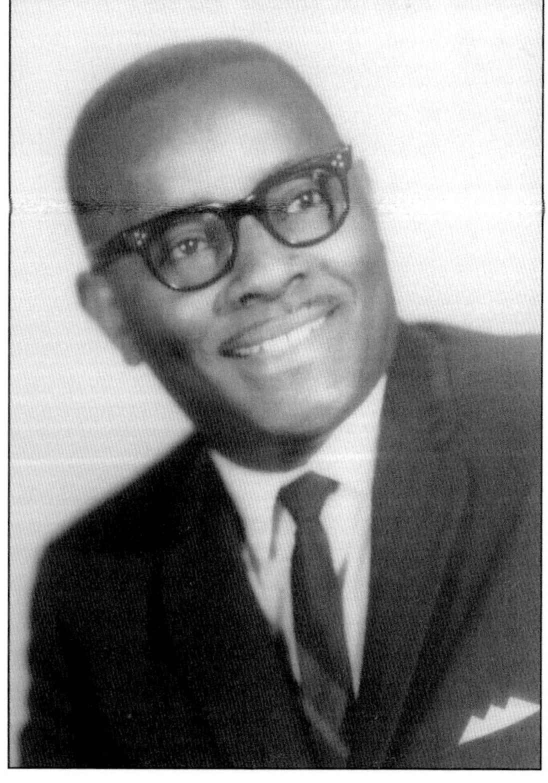

Courtney Bernard Crenshaw (1926–2005) was the son of Alonza and Alice Crenshaw. He received his education in Elmore County and then entered the United States Army. After his discharge, he earned advanced degrees in agricultural education from Tuskegee Institute. Teacher, coach, and administrator, he has the distinction of initiating the first Head Start program in Elmore County. Very active in the community, he was deeply involved in youth activities and officiated at high school and college games in all sports. (Elmore County Black History Museum.)

Mayor Jeanette Edwards Barrett (1922–1988) had the distinction in July 1984 of being elected the first woman mayor of Wetumpka and had begun her second term at the time of her death. Barrett served in many leadership capacities including president of the Elmore County Historical Society as well as other business and professional organizations. She received accolades from various local associations. The Jeanette Barrett Civic Room located in downtown Wetumpka was dedicated in her memory. (Clinton Barrett family.)

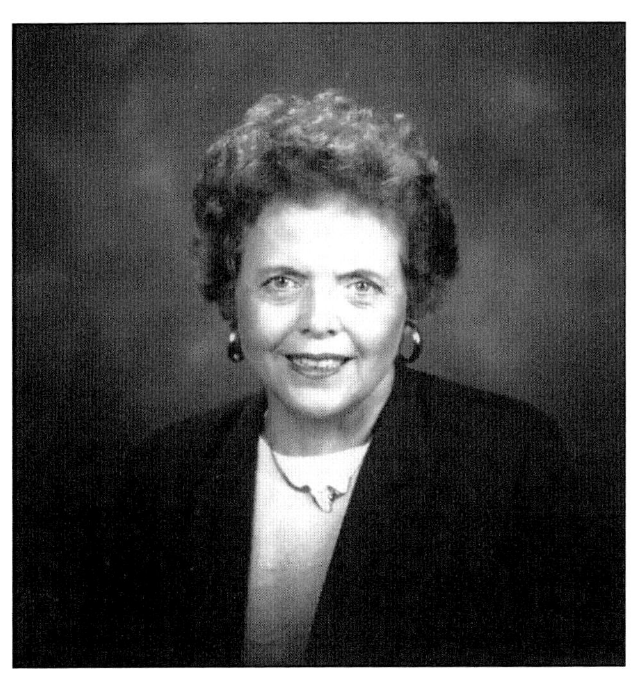

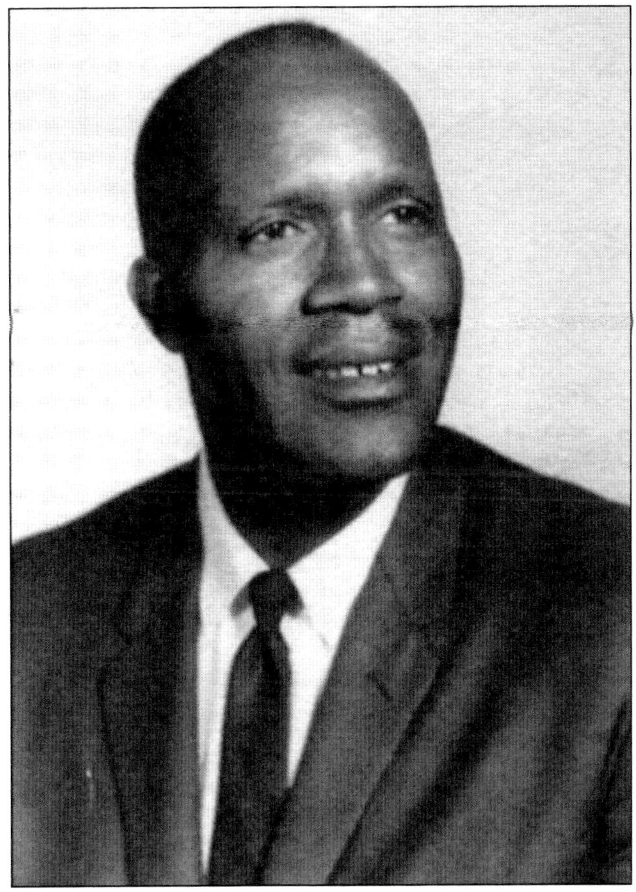

John Lee Jones was born in 1910 and attended Mount Canaan Elementary School and Elmore County Training School. He received his bachelor's degree in 1938 and his master's in 1957. Sandtown School in Millbrook, established in 1919, was expanded under his leadership as professor and principal. His tenure began in 1942 and extended through 1969. Jones was instrumental in developing many black community organizations in the city and county. (ECHS.)

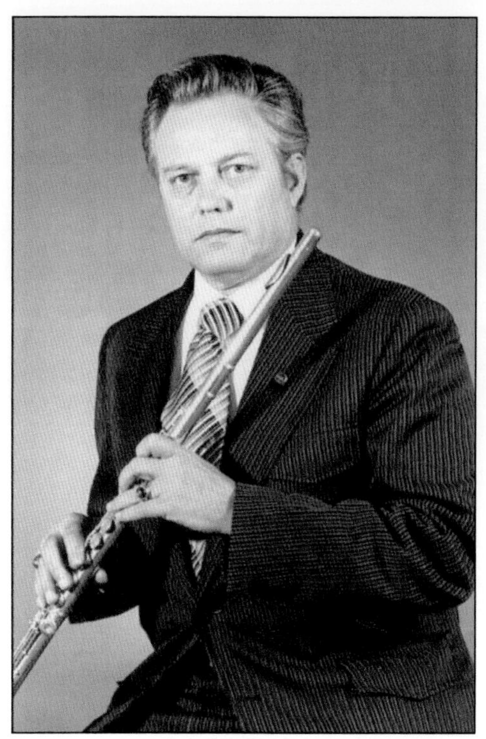

George Truman Welch (left) was born in Claud and spent some years in Birmingham, where he played his first job as a professional musician at the age of 11. He received training at the DeVilla School of Music and the Army Music School during World War II. While there, he was director of the 13th Air Force Show Band. Welch directed the Elmore County Band for 26 years. He formed this band with students from Wetumpka High School and Elmore County High School. During those years, he led the Elmore County Band to many honors, including first-place honors at the Virginia Beach Music Festival in 1963 and the Mid-West National Band Clinic in 1965 (below). In later years, he became a woodwind instructor at Troy State University from 1972 to 1978 while still playing with local dance and jazz bands. He served one term as mayor of Wetumpka from 1980 to 1984. In 1991, he was awarded as a Montgomery Area Council on Aging "Seniors of Achievement." (Both, Truman Welch.)

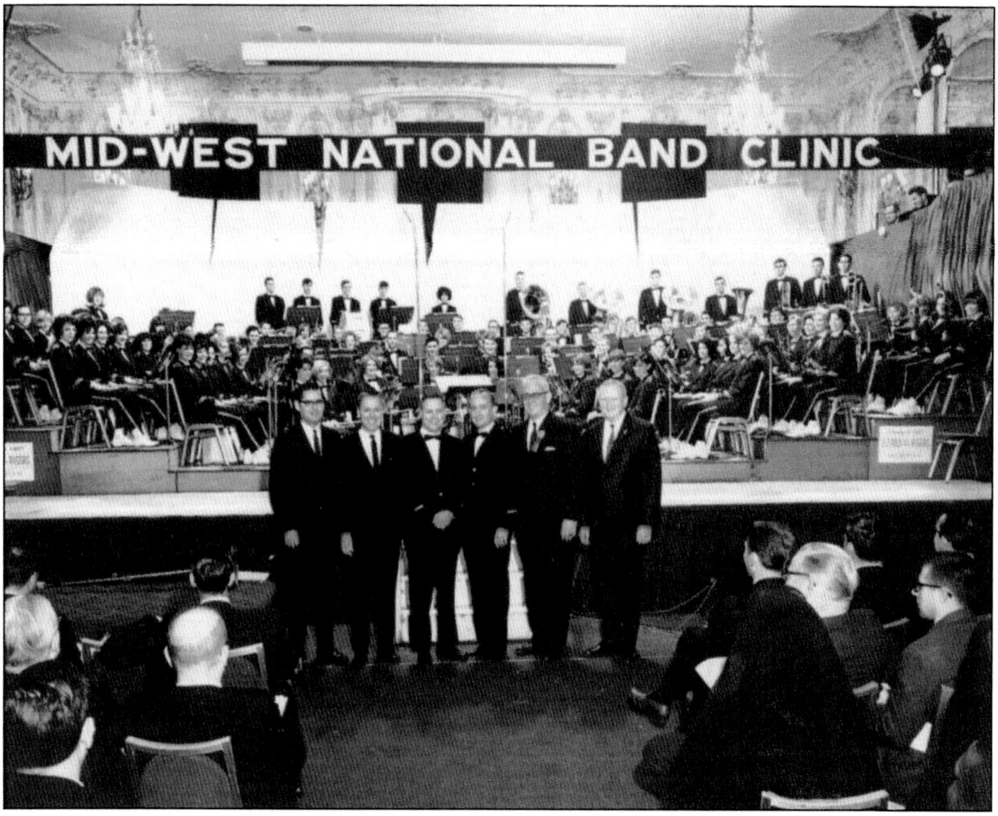

Willie Glenn Westbrooks (1899–1991) was born in Wetumpka and graduated from State Normal High School. Westbrooks worked as a cobbler in Wetumpka for many years. He later received his certificate from Atlanta School of Mortuary Science before establishing Westbrooks and Jones Mortuary. Westbrooks later moved to Los Angeles, California, where he worked for the city until his retirement. (Elmore County Black History Museum.)

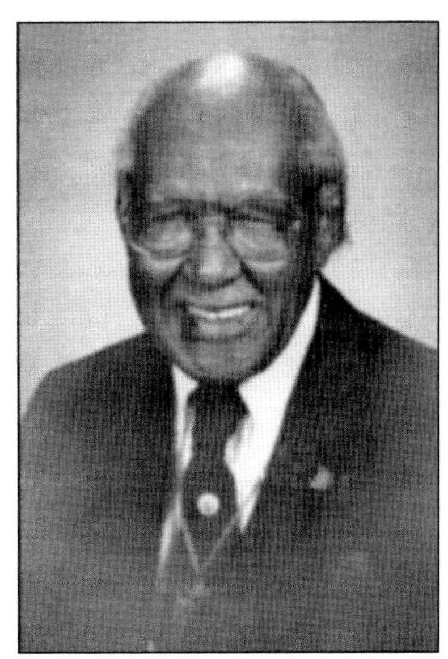

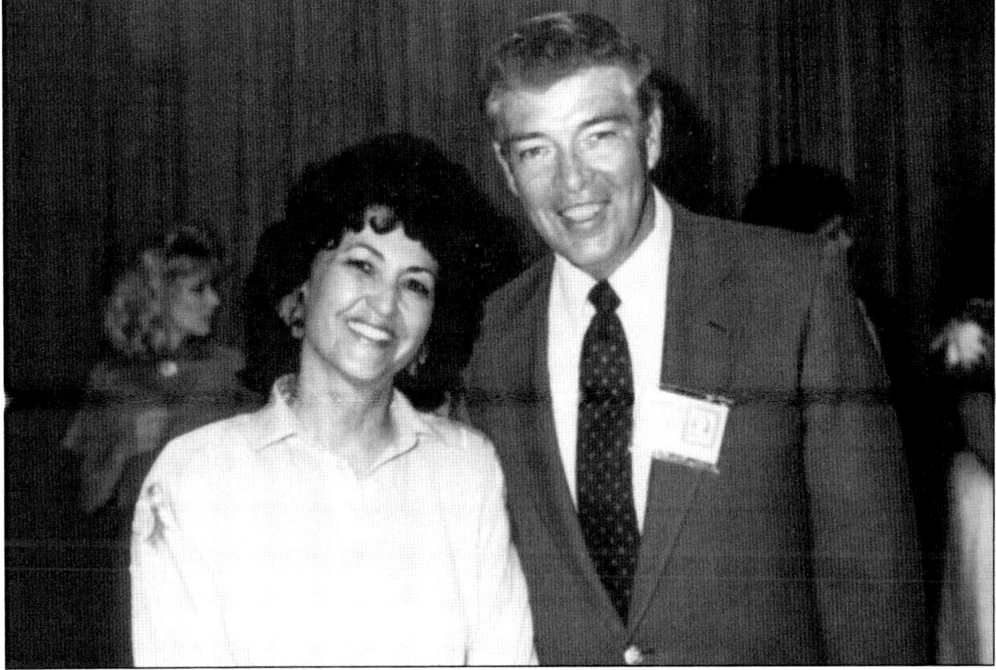

Shirley Ross DeVenney, a native Wetumpkian, has had an outstanding career—from grade school mascot to recognized international performer and instructor. Shirley is noted for outstanding dance line and twirl routines. Her students have won every major title in twirling. She was drum major, feature twirler, and choreographer for the Ole Miss Rebelettes. Shirley's husband, Jack DeVenney, of Ohio, was a champion drum major and contest champion. He pioneered the art of twirling and tossing silks, double flags, capes, knives, rifles, devil sticks, and other novelties. Jack's career included drum and bugle corps, nightclub, stage, and television. Jack and Shirley are internationally respected and have taught and judged in venues across the world. Jack started many special activities in Wetumpka. He was 1994 Chamber Community Involvement Citation Recipient. Jack died in 2013. (Jack and Shirley DeVenney.)

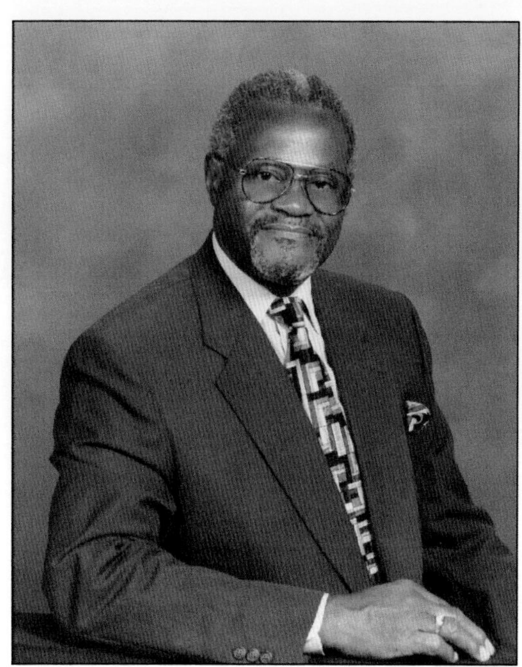

Councilman/mayor Lewis Edward Washington Sr. is a lifelong resident of Wetumpka and a graduate of Elmore County Training School. Washington holds the distinction of being the first African American elected to the Wetumpka City Council after Reconstruction. He served several consecutive terms, also serving as mayor for two months in 1996 after the death of Mayor William Sahlie. His championing of the "common folk" earned him another term on the city council for a total of 24 years of service to the city. (Elmore County Black History Museum.)

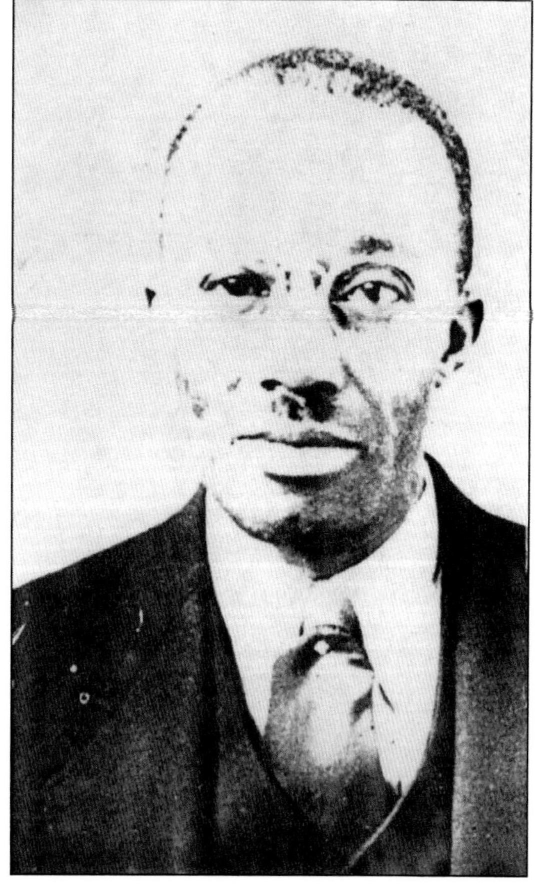

Prof. Weldon Blanton Doby was a native of Magnolia, Alabama. Intensely interested in books and learning from an early age, Doby studied at Wilberforce University and the University of Cincinnati to earn his bachelor's and master's degrees. After serving as dean at Payne University, Doby came to Elmore County in 1930 and became principal of the Elmore County Training School. During his 27 years of service, he worked with his teachers to guide the school toward accreditation. (Elmore County Black History Museum.)

# About the Elmore County Historical Society and Museum

In 1970, the Alabama Historical Commission, in an effort to encourage smaller communities throughout the state to collect, record, and preserve their local histories, instituted statewide organizational meetings of interested citizens. One such meeting was held in Wetumpka and led by the late Jeanette E. Barrett. This organizational meeting was attended by six or eight people who thought it was important to organize a local historical society. The Elmore County Historical Society was formed as a result of this meeting. In May 1971, the charter for the organization was signed by about 100 Elmore County residents.

The society's meetings were held monthly at various locations within the county in an effort to involve more people. Ultimately, it was decided that one central meeting place would be best for the organization. Since Wetumpka was the county seat of Elmore County, it was agreed that the meetings would be held there. The society currently meets in the Elmore County Museum at 2:30 p.m. on the second Sunday of each month from September through May.

In 1996, the society merged with the Elmore County Museum, which was organized in 1984. Its location was in a second-floor room of a county-owned building in downtown Wetumpka. After four years in this location, it had outgrown its space and moved to a city-owned structure—the old Alliance Warehouse building—erected in the 1820s as an Indian trading post. The museum remained in this location until 2009, when it needed more space and a better building. On February 15, 2008, the old Wetumpka Post Office, owned by the city, was leased to the Elmore County Historical Society for the purpose of establishing a permanent home for the museum. The grand opening in this location was held on May 17, 2009.

Through the years, the Elmore County Historical Society, in conjunction with the Elmore County Museum, has sponsored various activities such as walking tours, programs about arts of the past and present, cemetery tours, and special exhibits at the museum to promote and preserve local heritage. The museum has built a varied collection of items of interest to history enthusiasts. The museum is open on Fridays and Saturdays from 10:00 a.m. to 3:00 p.m. and by appointment.